# BLOW BY BLOW

# BLOW BY BLOW

## THE STORY OF ISABELLA BLOW DETMAR BLOW WITH TOM SYKES

**itbooks**

AN IMPRINT OF HARPERCOLLINS PUBLISHERS

BLOW BY BLOW. Copyright © 2010 by Detmar Blow and Tom Sykes. All rights reserved. Printed in the United States of America. No part of this book may be used or reproduced in any manner whatsoever without written permission except in the case of brief quotations embodied in critical articles and reviews. For information address HarperCollins Publishers, 10 East 53rd Street, New York, NY 10022.

HarperCollins books may be purchased for educational, business, or sales promotional use. For information please write: Special Markets Department, HarperCollins Publishers, 10 East 53rd Street, New York, NY 10022.

FIRST U.S. EDITION

Library of Congress Cataloging-in-Publication Data has been applied for.

ISBN 978-0-06-202087-1

10  11  12  13  14  RRD  10  9  8  7  6  5  4  3  2  1

*Blow by Blow* is dedicated
to Isabella's memory

# Contents

# CHAPTER ONE

## *The Call*

I was at our flat in Eaton Square in London when I got the call. It was Issie's devoted younger sister, Lavinia.

'Detmar, I have just come home from shopping,' Lavinia said frantically, 'Issie has swallowed some poison. She says not to worry, as she has sicked most of it up. She seems ok. What shall I do?'

It was my wife Isabella's seventh suicide attempt in fourteen months, and I felt a surge of anxious nausea as I tried to process Lavinia's words.

*Maybe this was it. Maybe this time she'll succeed.*

But poison? Where the hell had she found that? Was it weedkiller, like my father had used? And if it was, then how could she possibly still be alive? Issie was only 5'2½" and weighed 7 stone. My father – 6'1" and 18 stone – had drunk a bottle of paraquat in 1977 and it killed him in half an hour as the liquid burned out his insides. Amaury, my curly-haired 12-year-old brother, was there. He said Dadda never cried out, but that his fists were clenched in pain.

The only thing I knew was that if I was to be of any use to Issie at all, I had to remain calm and non-hysterical. 'Take her to hospital,' I told Lavinia. 'I'll be down as soon as possible.'

In a trance I called the milliner Philip Treacy, Issie's best friend, who was meant to be picking me up later, because we had already planned

1

to go down to Hilles, our house in the country, that weekend. I told him what had happened and he came round with his boyfriend Stefan and picked me up and we set off in his car for Gloucester Royal Hospital.

How could she still be alive? Maybe, I found myself hoping, as we crawled at an agonizingly slow pace through west London towards the M4, it wasn't weedkiller. But I had a dreadful hunch that it was, because just a couple of months beforehand I had taken delivery of a bottle of paraquat at Hilles, ordered by Isabella.

I had been horrified, furious, and had asked Isabella, 'What the hell is this? What are you doing?' She had just remained silent.

I took it back to the farm shop in Gloucester where she had ordered it and told them, 'The person who ordered this is trying to kill herself. Never send it again.' The poor lady I spoke to was very upset.

I stared out of the car window in a daze as we hit the motorway and finally started picking up some speed. Surely the same farm shop wouldn't have sold her paraquat? Could it be something she had found in the garage from my father's stack of poison, left there since the seventies, which would be 30 years out of date?

When we finally arrived in Gloucester, we got lost. The Gloucester Royal Hospital is a big 1970s building with a huge chimney. I thought you couldn't miss it, but because of the new housing developments around it the road was obscured.

After driving around for a while and getting nowhere I said, 'Let's get out and walk.' Philip and I had to scramble over a wall to get into the hospital grounds.

We went to the reception area and asked for Isabella, but no one knew where she was. Eventually we found out she was in the Accident and Emergency ward, so we rushed there.

And that's where we found her. My heart went out when I saw her. She was propped up in bed, looking sallow, and wearing a thin white hospital nightgown. She was on a drip, and looked and sounded weak.

'Hi Det,' she said.

# CHAPTER TWO

## *Johnny*

Why did my wife, Isabella Blow, the fashion icon, the legend, the toast of glossy magazines from London to New York, want to kill herself? To answer that question I would have to go back to the very beginning of Issie's life, to her extraordinary childhood, to her relationship with her parents and to the great, central trauma of her life.

On 12 September 1964, her little brother Johnny, aged 2½, died in an accident in the garden when he fell into a body of water.

Issie was supposed to be looking after him. She was five years old.

'Everything went wrong for the family after the death of that little boy,' recalled Issie's now 94-year-old godmother Lavinia Cholmondley (pronounced 'Chumley') when she was interviewed for this book at Cholmondley Castle in 2009.

Confusingly, there are conflicting versions of the events that led to Johnny's death.

Issie had told me about it the first time we met, at a mutual friend's wedding in 1988. She told me that Johnny was chasing a ball and followed it into the swimming pool, which had been built by her father to celebrate a good harvest that year. After inhaling water, he vomited up a half-digested baked bean and choked on it. It was 'nanny's day off', Issie said, so dinner had been from a tin. She said that she

# LADY BROUGHTON AND HER YOUNG FAMILY

*In this after-the-christening picture, Lady Broughton is seen with the new baby and her two daughters, Isabella (centre) and Julia Helen.*

**A local press announcement about the birth of Isabella's baby brother. In the photograph is Helen Broughton with her new son, John Evelyn, Isabella and Julia.**

remembered the smell of the honeysuckle, and Johnny stretched out on the lawn. 'My mother went upstairs to put her lipstick on,' she said. 'That explains my obsession with lipstick.'

Issie knew this was a pivotal moment in her life, and, with typical disregard for the comfort zones of polite society, she would often describe the events of Johnny's death – the swimming pool, the ball, the honeysuckle and, above all, the lipstick – to relative strangers. She would even talk about it to newspaper interviewers, prompting her mother, Helen, to retort that the story about the lipstick was, 'An awful, unfounded lie.'

# JOHNNY

The version of Johnny's death told by Issie's stepmother, Rona, whom Evelyn married just under a decade after the accident (he and Helen were divorced in February 1974) is very different. Rona related this account at a meeting in the Sloane Club in London 2009:

> Helen went inside to do something, not put on lipstick; that was a very cruel thing for Isabella to say. But she went in to do something, I don't know what. And when she went inside, she said to Issie, 'Keep an eye on Johnny,' or 'Watch out for Johnny'. So Isabella was playing with John, but then somebody who was coming down the lane stopped at the gate and called Issie over to the gate. Issie went over, and while she was over there – it happened. He choked on a piece of dry biscuit and suffocated, and then fell in a small pond, not a swimming pool. And then everybody blamed each other.

Had Issie felt responsible for what happened to Johnny?

'No,' replied Rona. 'There wouldn't have been anything she could have done anyway. She was five years old.'

But such rational reasoning doesn't always stop people, especially small children, from feeling the emotion and burden of guilt, does it?

Rona conceded, 'She felt blamed.'

By who?

'She wasn't blamed by her father,' was all Rona, now 70, and cautious to the end, would say. 'By someone else.'

Memory, of course, plays tricks on us all, but it is quite extraordinary how Isabella's story and Rona's story (presumably relayed via Evelyn) diverge. Isabella very deliberately painted her mother as self-centred and vain by constantly reiterating the detail about her not being present because she was applying lipstick. When she told me the story of Johnny's death, it was always portrayed as a result of him falling into the swimming pool. Indeed, she added more and more detail to the story – how the pool had then been filled in by her grief-stricken father and another built to replace it. I was therefore amazed when, after we were married, Evelyn used to tell me that Issie swam like a fish as a child in the pool.

Never did Issie tell me about being called over to the gate, or about being asked to watch Johnny.

As her husband, I, of course, believe Issie's account unquestioningly over that of her stepmother, which I never heard until researching this book. Rona was not there at the time and would have heard it second-hand, years and years after the event. And yet, when I recall how Issie recounted this horrific, defining event of her childhood, it is impossible not to notice the foundation stones on which Issie built both her personal myth and her dark aesthetic.

All the elements of the black fairy story that she told to and about herself are there: the indifferent, heartless mother, the father more interested in his drinks and his friends than his son, and the terrible irony of the fatal pool being built to celebrate the harvest.

Isabella remembered her mother blaming Evelyn, her father. Helen once told the story of Johnny's death to a cousin of Isabella's who herself had just been bereaved. Later, the cousin told Isabella and I that Helen blamed Evelyn – despite the fact that, even in her telling, the death of Johnny was clearly an accident.

When I was researching this book I discovered a contemporary report of the accident from *The Times*, dated Monday 14 September, 1964. It was headlined 'Heir to Baronetcy found Drowned':

> John Evelyn Delves, aged two, heir of Sir Evelyn Delves Broughton and Lady Broughton, of Doddington Park, near Nantwich, Cheshire, was found drowned on Saturday in a shallow ornamental pool which was being built in the garden of his home. The boy was heir to a baronetcy dating back to 1660.
>
> Mr Giles Tedstone, farm manager to Sir Evelyn, said today, 'Sir Evelyn and Lady Broughton had been having tea with their children and friends on the lawn and the children wandered off afterwards to play. Lady Broughton missed young John a couple of minutes later and he was found dead in the pool.'
>
> Artificial respiration was tried and Sir Evelyn then drove the boy to hospital but it was too late. The pool was only 18 inches deep and has now been filled in.
>
> Lady Broughton is expecting another baby in a few months time. They have two daughters aged five and three.

The following day an inquest was held in Nantwich. Evelyn attended the inquest, and *The Times* also reported on it. At the inquest it was ruled that his son and heir had died of asphyxiation.

# JOHNNY

Dr John Heppleston, pathologist, said that a post-mortem showed that the death was due to a blockage of the windpipe by food, caused by vomiting which had followed immersion in water.

Questioned by Sir Evelyn, Dr Heppleston said it was possible that the boy slipped or fell into the water and the shock made him vomit. He could have been dead within part of a second.

Mr Leonard Culey, West Cheshire deputy Coroner, recording a verdict of accidental death, said by a chance in a million the shock of the water made the boy sick and he asphyxiated. It was a case that could not have been foreseen.

**Isabella looking down at the grounds of St John's Church, Doddington Park – the church where her brother John Evelyn is buried.**

Whatever the exact sequence of events, there is no disputing that Johnny's death, as well as traumatising Issie for life, destroyed the family utterly.

Evelyn's reaction to Johnny's death was extraordinary. Rather than trying for another son, he apparently became convinced that the death of John was a sure sign that the Delves Broughton line should come to an end with him.

The death of John, he appears to have decided, was to be the end of it all. It was a resolution from which he never wavered.

Johnny was buried in a small leather casket in St John's Church in the grounds of Doddington Park, next to General Sir Delves Broughton, who built the church in 1837. Helen and Evelyn commissioned a stained-glass window in memory of their lost son. Isabella thought the window was 'ugly but along the right tracks'. She respected their gesture of love.

# CHAPTER THREE

## *The Curse of the Delves Broughtons*

Tragedy ran deep in Issie's family, and the stain on the Delves Broughton name went back to Issie's grandfather, Jock. Sir Jock Delves Broughton had committed suicide, injecting himself with morphine in the Adelphi hotel in Liverpool after being accused of a notorious murder of a fellow aristocrat who was having an affair with his beautiful young second wife in Kenya in the 1940s (the subject of the book and film *White Mischief*). He was acquitted, but could not escape the smears of the press and his contemporaries, and many saw his suicide as a posthumous admission of guilt. Issie believed she had inherited her depression from Jock and was later to base one of her own unsuccessful suicide attempts closely around Jock's successful one.

Isabella's childhood was, by any normal standards, enormously privileged. It was, however, simultaneously defined by the economic anxiety of her father who was permanently terrified that what remained of the family fortune was about to slip through his fingers. As a boy, and later as a young man, Evelyn had watched helplessly while Jock spent, gambled and otherwise lost almost all his money.

Conversions into today's money are notoriously unreliable, but by any reckoning the fortune Jock inherited in 1913 was staggering. In various family trusts, Issie's grandfather was bequeathed not one but two stately homes (Broughton and Doddington Hall) and a collection of paintings, furniture and *objets d'art* accumulated over six centuries. There was also the not-so-small matter of 15,000 acres of prime farmland in three counties, a London residence, and a multitude of assorted stocks and shares. Isabella's grandfather was the fortunate beneficiary

**Jock and Vera at Royal Ascot in the 1920s.**

of the aristocratic British tradition of concentrating all of the family wealth in the hands of the eldest son. The reasoning behind the right of primogeniture was – and is – to keep intact the great family homes and seats, the income from the land being used to 'keep the title up'. This allows the title holder, if he so chooses, to cut a dash in society, thereby adding to the lustre and importance of the family.

Jock most certainly chose to do just that.

Doddington Hall was a grand house and Jock ran it on a correspondingly grand scale, retaining a large household staff. Oranges, melons and other exotic marvels issued forth from the laboriously tended (and heated) hothouses year round, and the Hall's splendidly stocked cellar ensured the finest wines were served at dinner every night. He entertained lavishly, and his extravagance was legendary in society circles: a jazz band would frequently be engaged to play his weekend guests up on the 3½-hour train journey from Euston to Crewe.

The aristocracy were the celebrities of the day and the Broughtons enjoyed their fame. Vera – Issie's grandmother whom she knew and adored – made particularly good copy for the era's social diarists: amongst her many claims to fame, she held the record for the largest tuna ever caught in northern waters. She hooked it off Scarborough, in Yorkshire. Her fish weighed 317.5kg (700lb).

In Jock's extravagance, some people discerned a desire to eclipse the events that overshadowed the beginning of his reign as the 11th baronet. For, just a year after he had inherited, in August 1914, the First World War broke out. Jock had supposedly been a professional soldier in the Irish Guards for over a decade, but was taken off the boat sailing for France to halt the invading German armies. The cause?

Sunstroke.

Jock sat out the war years at a desk in London, returning only occasionally to Doddington Hall. The Hall – which today is boarded up and languishes in a sorry state of disrepair – is a neo-classical fantasy built by Samuel Wyatt in 1770. The Hall was surrounded by a 500-acre park designed by 'Capability' Brown, with red and fallow deer and a 55-acre lake to the south ornamented with swans and birds. The lake boasted a banqueting hall on an island in the middle of it, which was subsequently demolished on the orders of a Broughton on account of his suffering too many hangovers. There were elegant stables designed by Wyatt, well stocked with fine horses to ride and take hunting, a tennis court and a croquet lawn.

The front of Doddington Hall. *Country Life*, 1950.

Doddington Hall's circular salon with its huge chandelier. Isabella always loved the circular design – she had, at one time, a flat in London with a circular room. *Country Life*, 1950.

**The rear of Doddington Hall.** *Country Life*, **1950.**

Things began to go wrong for Jock when the money started to run out. Since the late nineteenth century, the British upper classes had been feeling an economic chill owing to the invention of refrigeration for container ships, which allowed imports of cheap food from abroad. In a speech in 1920 in the billiard room at Doddington to some of his angry and bemused tenants whose farms he was selling to raise £150,000, Jock explained to them that he believed that the land-owning class was finished and he had no alternative but to sell their farms and look to the future.

He was far from alone in these views. The First World War had destroyed the political power of the European aristocracy and over-thrown many monarchies. In Russia, Germany, Austro-Hungary and Turkey there had been revolutions deposing tsars, kings and sultans. Revolution was in the air, even in England.

During the 1920s and 1930s, Jock continually sold off land, investing heavily in commodities and what Isabella's father Evelyn would later derisively refer to as a 'tin pot gold mine'. In addition there were large, often unsuccessful horse-racing bets and other gambling debts. Broughton Hall was sold early on to a family that had made their

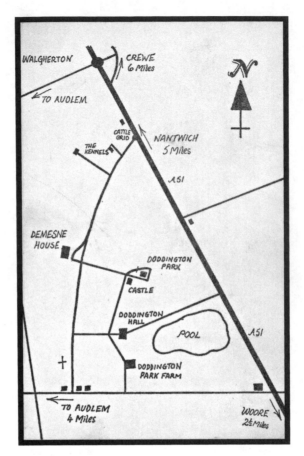

**A hand-drawn map of the Doddington estate.**

money from reinforcing concrete with steel mesh. The economic depression of the 1930s only exacerbated Jock's deteriorating financial situation, and, in desperation, towards the end of the decade, Jock started to make a series of fraudulent insurance claims. On one occasion he arranged for an out-of-work soldier to break into the Hall and steal some of the paintings whose insurance value he had recently increased. There were also claims on alleged thefts of jewellery, including one from the glove compartment of his car in the south of France. When Isabella was a child, a farm worker found a string of black pearls her grandfather claimed had been stolen wrapped around a branch in some farm woodland. Evelyn, his son and Issie's father, handed them back to the insurance company.

# THE CURSE OF THE DELVES BROUGHTONS

By the outbreak of the Second World War the Delves Broughton family estates had been reduced to just over a thousand acres: the deer park around Doddington Hall and one nearby farm.

In 1940 Vera divorced Jock. In her divorce petition, Vera cited Jock's affair with Diana Caldwell – a glamorous blonde divorcée, almost 30 years younger than him, who would become his second wife. With Britain desperately fighting for survival against Nazi Germany, Jock and Diana decided to leave England and go to Kenya, where Jock had acquired a beef and coffee estate.

Jock believed that his colonial adventure was going to give him a chance not only to make a fresh start with his beautiful young wife but also to allow him to contribute to the war effort with his farming. It did not hurt that it was also immensely cheap to live very well in Kenya. Jock and Diana were soon partying with the freewheeling 'Happy Valley' set of decadent colonials who drank heavily, took drugs and slept with each other.

Diana fell in love with Josslyn Hay, the Earl of Errol, a famous seducer of other men's wives, who had been married three times himself. Diana and Lord Errol started a passionate and very public affair. Three months later, Errol was found, shot dead in his car, just

**Stag beside the lake in the park at Doddington.**

2½ miles from Jock's house outside Nairobi; earlier that night, at 3 a.m., he had dropped off Diana.

Jock, the humiliated and cuckolded husband, was the obvious suspect and he was subsequently charged with Errol's murder. At the trial he put in a witty and polished performance in the witness box – and was acquitted. But the blanket coverage of the trial both in Kenya and the United Kingdom and the associated scandal destroyed him. After the trial, he headed back home, and when he arrived at the dock in Liverpool he was met by agents investigating his dubious insurance claims.

A few months after his return to England, in December 1942, Jock committed suicide at the Adelphi Hotel in Liverpool with a morphine overdose. He left behind a tangled legacy – and, as Issie often noted, 60 pairs of shoes.

# CHAPTER FOUR

## *Evelyn*

The upshot of all this was that what should have been a huge inheritance for Jock's son, Evelyn (Issie's father), was massively reduced. The vast estate was less than 10 per cent of its former size, a 'mere' 1000 acres. If an estate that size was to continue to support even a much reined-in Delves Broughton lifestyle, a major rethinking of how the estate functioned as a business would clearly be necessary.

The park at Doddington had been occupied by over 1100 Polish refugees in Nissen huts during the war. They stayed on for a few years afterwards, providing Evelyn with a meagre but welcome income from the government. But with the army no longer requiring Doddington Hall itself, Evelyn leased it out to Goudhurst Ladies College and in 1946 most of the contents of Doddington were sold at auction. This was a common occurrence at the time, when many stately homes were turned into prisons for young offenders, schools – or simply demolished and the contents sold off.

After the Polish refugees left, Evelyn, who was brutally practical, set about turning his remaining land into a modern farm. He killed the 300 fallow and red deer in the park, cut down many of the trees planted by 'Capability' Brown, now mature and valuable as hard timber in the post-war reconstruction, and then ploughed the park up and turned it into farmland.

The decision paid off. Over the next 20 years he made Doddington Park Farm into a state-of-the-art dairy, beef, corn, sheep and potato farm – and a great commercial success. Isabella described it as being run on factory lines.

Evelyn's greatest agricultural success was growing potatoes. They became a very successful cash crop, especially after he won a contract to supply potatoes to Walkers Crisps. Once, he told me, a manufacturer desperate for potatoes had paid him £9000 in cash for a large pile of spuds. Evelyn, who had a pathological aversion to paying tax, did not pay the money into the bank, thereby obviating the need to pay any levies on the sum, which gave him great pleasure. The local bank manager in Nantwich mournfully commented, 'Sir Evelyn, we have not seen you in here for such a long time.'

On other occasions he flew with Issie to Switzerland, where he would deposit the potato money into his Swiss bank account and return the following day. For the night Issie and her father would stay in luxury at the Palace Hotel. A Swiss bank account was a not unusual accessory for a rich man at the time – my father, far less wealthy, opened a Swiss account and deposited £250 – but it was illegal.

Evelyn's austerity drive complemented his miserly streak. Once, Issie was invited to stay at Chatsworth, the home of the Duke of Devonshire. One of her best friends from Oxford, Anthony Murphy, had married the Duke's youngest daughter. Issie asked her father for some money to tip the butler at the end of the weekend. Evelyn reluctantly agreed – but insisted Isabella write him a cheque for the £10 he gave her. On her return to Doddington, Evelyn plied Isabella for details on the set-up at Chatsworth, particularly wanting to know how many footmen there were. When he presented Isabella's cheque at the bank to get his £10 advance back, the cheque was returned. Isabella recalled with glee that her father tried to re-present it several times before giving up.

Issie put a cheerful gloss on her father's penny-pinching ways, but his habits often made life difficult or socially embarrassing for her. In 1979 she was invited by her friend Mimi Lady Manton to stay with her at her home in Yorkshire. She had a special guest coming – the unmarried Prince of Wales. She told Issie, 'You have goofy teeth and will make him laugh.'

# EVELYN

When Issie excitedly told her father that she was going to the same house party as Prince Charles, she asked for some money to buy an evening dress, a not unreasonable request.

Her father's reply was, 'Beg, steal, or borrow.' And he meant it. He was not going to give her any money for mere fripperies.

Evelyn may have been stingy but he did have a sense of propriety – he rejoined Lloyds Insurance to pay off his father's frauds, he claimed.

His big cut-back was to move into what had been the head gardener's cottage, located about half a mile from the Hall. Isabella was to resent this all of her life.She described it to me as 'a hideous pink house' with a '1950s wing' and 'a carport' which her father built onto it. Evelyn had decorated it with pictures bought 'from Boots the Chemist', according to Issie. His favourite was a painting of a scantily clad

**Isabella's mother, Helen Shore.**

19

ST. JOHN'S CHURCH
DODDINGTON

Baptism
*of*
ISABELLA
*daughter of*
EVELYN *and* HELEN DELVES BROUGHTON

Thursday March 12th 1959

Isabella Delves Broughton

was Baptised
at ___ Doddington Church
by ___ The Vicar
on ___ March 12ᵗʰ 1959

SPONSORS
Lady Rocksavage: friend
Mrs Cooper-Key: friend
Major Cayzer: friend
Signed ___

S.P.C.K.—No. 171.

**Isabella's baptism certificate. She was baptised on Thursday 12 March 1959, at the age of four months.**

Caribbean girl weaving a basket – now in the possession of Isabella's youngest sister, Lavinia. Issie told me that she always knew her parents had 'bad taste'.

Evelyn admitted freely – almost proudly – that he was a cultural philistine, and this would bring him into sharp conflict with Isabella, who grew up as a child yearning for the lost beauty and glamour of Doddington Hall, ever-visible just across the fields.

By 1955, with Doddington running successfully, Evelyn, now aged 40, married Helen Shore. The daughter of a successful Manchester greengrocer family, she was ambitious and clever, and had been called to the Bar in 1951 at the age of 21. Evelyn had in fact been briefly married before, to Elizabeth Cholmondley, so he and Helen had to content themselves with a service of blessing at St Simon the Zealot's church in Chelsea in 1955.

At the time of Isabella's birth, Evelyn was 43 and Helen 28. Isabella was born three years after the marriage. Julia was born in 1961 – and then in 1962 the longed-for son and heir, John Evelyn, finally arrived.

# EVELYN

The birth of a son settled all the inconvenient questions of inheritance that had been lurking unspoken in the background following the birth of the two girls, Isabella and Julia. It was quite clear now what would happen to Doddington Park – it would pass to John on his father's death. He may not have been able to afford to live in the splendour of the big house, but the prospect of a male heir redoubled Evelyn's determination to work at his farm. After a generation of scandal and financial disaster, it seemed that things might finally be starting to turn the corner for the Delves Broughtons.

**Newborn Isabella at the London clinic with her mother, who has had her make-up and hair done, which Issie later strongly approved of.**

One can understand, then, why the loss of Johnny was so devastating. Evelyn belonged to an age and a class which valued males more highly than females. He did little to spare his grieving daughter's feelings on this account.

After Johnny's death, he considered leaving Doddington Park to his closest male relative, Simon Fraser, Master of Lovat, the eldest son of his sister Rosie, and himself in line to inherit from his father, Lord Shimi Lovat. But then Evelyn did some research on some family assets managed by his nephew and was not impressed. Simon was struck off the list.

Another possible beneficiary, he announced to Helen when he came down to breakfast one morning, was Trinity, his old college at Cambridge. He had known happiness there, he said. His three daughters, sitting there eating their cornflakes, were not considered at all.

There was a curious dichotomy in his relationship with Isabella – and all his daughters – for while, ultimately, he betrayed them and badly let them down, there were tender moments of affection. Isabella often accompanied Evelyn on his agricultural rounds, for example, an important ritual that bonded her closely to her father and allowed her to feel

**Isabella with her mother and father, at the gardener's cottage. In the background you can see the beef cattle.**

loved by him. From the age of 14 she would drive along the internal farm roads to pick him up for lunch every day in the battered old farm car. And Evelyn was, to his credit, not always quite as distant to his children as many upper-class fathers of the age. As her father's friend Major Peter Ormerod recalled, Evelyn would dress up as Santa Claus at Christmas parties at the house and distribute presents to the children – and to the mothers give 'out of his sack a half bottle of champagne'.

Evelyn was not a bad man. His great fault was that he was weak.

# CHAPTER FIVE

## *Poor Relations*

Even as a child, Isabella was bedevilled by financial insecurity. She undoubtedly picked up her almost existential anxiety about money from her father, who, when he wrote to her at boarding school, would put in brackets next to each person's name the total number of acres of land which they owned.

Issie measured herself against the wealth of others and found she came up wanting. She keenly felt the part of poor relation. While the Cholmondleys, for example, still lived in splendour in their very own castle, with a retinue of uniformed servants, the Delves Broughtons, by comparison, were holed up in the hated gardener's cottage while the main house was occupied by a school. There were butlers and gardeners, to be sure, but the set-up was all too obviously being run on a shoestring by comparison to their far richer neighbours. Evelyn's proud boast that the family had once been able to walk fourteen miles without straying off their own property made matters, if anything, even worse.

The gardener's cottage so despised by Issie was, in fact, a perfectly agreeable and spacious four-bedroom house. Yet even today, with the once-magnificent big house boarded up in the distance, it still looks out of place, a curiously suburban, almost hacienda-style structure, parked incongruously next to a tumbledown pink sandstone castle tower dating back to medieval times.

Issie loved to play in this perilous, weed-filled tower, conducting dramatic re-creations of medieval rites and myths with her sisters as

**The medieval castle in the grounds of Doddington Park, where Issie spent much time playing as a child.**

willing or unwilling participants, and it was an important part of the family's history. At the Battle of Poitiers in 1356, John de Delves fought valiantly and he was later knighted by King Edward III and granted a licence to crenellate and fortify the tower. The tower was a formative element in Issie's medieval aesthetic. Years later, the tower would be the inspiration for a 'castle hat' designed by one of Issie's most famous discoveries, the milliner Philip Treacy.

The Broughtons had an-old fashioned disregard for modern health concerns. Isabella grew up enjoying fresh, unpasteurised, creamy milk straight from the house cow. Their farm manager, worried about the risk of catching tuberculosis, had his milk delivered by the milkman in a sanitised bottle. Throughout her life, Isabella would insist on the richest, full-fat milk.

Another family indulgence was cigarette smoking. Evelyn and Helen smoked heavily, though Evelyn eventually had to give it up when he began suffering bad emphysema. Married to me, Isabella would start smoking at breakfast – sometimes chain-smoking five in a row – ignoring my pleas and entreaties that it was damaging her health.

'Detmar, you cannot talk, you smoke cigars,' she would say airily, clouds of smoke billowing out from under her latest Philip Treacy hat.

'But not for breakfast, Issie,' I would retort, gasping for air. 'And anyway, cigars are good for you – look at Churchill and Castro.'

Growing up at Doddington, Isabella often heard stories from the locals of her grandmother Vera's menagerie at Doddington. Vera had kept a dazzling array of exotic animals, including Carroway birds, ostriches and honey bears, which would often escape to the village from the cages that can be seen at Doddington Hall to this day. Once a bear had to be lured down from the church steeple with pots of honey.

Isabella's last memory of her beloved grandmother Vera was being with her while watching the news coverage of the assassination of Bobby Kennedy at her first-floor flat at 51 Eaton Square. Shortly afterwards, Vera died. When Issie and I were first married we lived a few hundred yards away from Eaton Square in Elizabeth Street, and when she was upset with me Isabella would go and sulk in the doorway at 51 Eaton Square, beneath Granny's old flat.

After Vera's funeral, Evelyn's sister Rosie suggested that their mother's ashes should be buried at the family church at Doddington. Evelyn flew into a rage and refused Rosie's request. He told his sister, 'If our mother had not divorced our father, none of the murder trial mess would have happened.' The scars and shame of Kenya ran very deep for Evelyn.

* * * * *

Isabella was six years old when Lavinia arrived, and was attending Nuthurst school, the local private primary school in Nantwich, a few miles from Doddington. The school, which has since closed down, was a red-brick Georgian house with a white portico doorway in Hospital Street. Isabella enjoyed it and was popular with the other children and the teachers.

Her friends remember Isabella for 'her mop of blonde hair', and described Issie enjoying doing the washing-up at a schoolfriend's party with her sister Julia.

Midway through Issie's career at Nuthurst, a new teacher started. Arriving for her first day, Isabella, seeing that she looked a bit lost, greeted her with the words, 'You must be new here. Let me show you

**Left to right: Julia, Helen, Lavinia and Isabella, at their home in Cadogan Square, London.**

**Young Isabella in her Nuthurst school uniform.**

around.' It was typical of Isabella's kindness and thoughtfulness to people, the teacher said.

Isabella was, she added, 'A little ray of sunshine.'

To occupy her children outside of term time, Helen, who had studied medieval history at school, encouraged them to look to their medieval roots. In addition to playing fantasy games in the tower, where she would make other children worship a plaque of a 'goddess', Isabella was often taken to nearby Audlem church, where she would make brass rubbings of her knightly ancestors' tombs.

Once they went on a trip to the former family house, Broughton Hall. This single visit left a lasting impression on the young Isabella. For the rest of her life, she remained intrigued by the place, a sturdy black-and-white timbered building constructed in the 1450s. During the English Civil War in the 1640s, a young Broughton boy declared to the entering enemy Parliamentarian soldiers, 'I am for the King!' He was shot instantly, his blood flowing down the ornately carved staircase as he lay dying. As Isabella was absorbing all this history, her mother told her, 'Well, Isabella, it is not yours any more,' and took her home to the former gardener's cottage.

**Two views of Broughton Hall.**

BLOW BY BLOW

In the inexplicable way of such incidents, this cruel jibe about the lost Broughton fortune became a focal point for Isabella's hatred of her mother. And in her escalating battles with her mother Isabella was to hone in on her mother's weak spot: her bourgeois background.

# CHAPTER SIX

## *Helen*

Isabella, I can say with complete confidence, loathed her mother. When Helen finally left Evelyn, she lined up her children on the gravel outside the gardener's cottage, and shook their hands goodbye.

This disgusting act of abandonment was the culmination of a truly dreadful mother–daughter relationship.

Issie actually looked down on her mother socially. Helen's grandfather had owned a successful greengrocery business in Manchester with several stores, so he had been able to afford to educate Helen at Roedean and King's College London, but she had no money of her own and never completely escaped her roots.

This would not have mattered, of course, had she not so obviously sought to. Helen's father died young and the business passed to Helen's brother, 'Uncle Mike', an alcoholic who had a bar in his lounge. Helen's mother – Isabella's maternal grandmother, Nancy – spoke with a broad Cheshire accent and lived in Wilmslow, an expensive, sought-after suburb beloved of Mancunian business families. Issie mockingly described Nancy's house as, 'A marble bungalow with electric blinds, fake Louis XV furniture and a Mercedes sports car in the driveway.'

This was all marvellous material for Isabella, for it was a long way from Helen's perception of herself as 'Lady Broughton'. She did not care to discuss her background, although once, after a few drinks, she let her guard down and told us her grandmother was Irish, from Dublin, and one of a large family. She hinted that she was connected to an Irish peerage. When I asked her whether she was in contact with any of her grandmother's relations, though, she drew up the drawbridge, and stared at me blankly. In the 11 years that I knew Helen, she always spoke in a clear, confident upper-class accent, but once or twice, she slipped. She caused Issie to howl with delight when she asked, 'Are you coming on then?' – Cheshire vernacular for 'Are you pregnant?'

Conclusive evidence of what Isabella would see as her mother's vulgarity were the family cars, which had personalised number plates: 'EDB1' for Evelyn's Jaguar and 'HDB1' for Helen's Volvo. To obtain these, Helen bought two cheap cars in the nearby county of Denbigh in north Wales and transferred the newly issued Denbigh number plates.

Isabella, did, however, believe that her interest in clothes and hats sprang from Helen. When she was around 6 years old, a photograph was taken of her standing on a chair in front of her mother's dressing-room table, trying on a large pink hat and looking, as she said, 'as happy as can be'. Helen would take Isabella with her to Chester to choose fur coats – and during her marriage to Evelyn she built up a large collection of mink and sable coats, which Isabella adored.

In the early 1970s Helen started to spend more and more time in London at the family flat at Cadogan Square. After 15 years with Evelyn she was becoming less and less satisfied with country life as Lady of the Manor in Cheshire: opening fêtes and sitting as a magistrate in Nantwich. Helen yearned for a more culturally and intellectually fulfilling life. Evelyn, a self-confessed philistine, was interested in little other than making money and horse racing. Apart from a shared enjoyment of parties, they had increasingly little in common. And Evelyn, neglected as a child by his socialite parents, feared loneliness.

In 1973, Helen had to go into hospital for a serious operation. Evelyn had already booked an expensive trip to the Far East, and decided that although his wife could not go, he would. After all, he had paid for it – and Helen could just get on with her operation. He was 58 years old.

Travelling on a bus in Hong Kong he met Rona Crammond, 34, a very attractive, intelligent and determined woman. Rona was born on 22 November 1939 in West Cardiff. Her father, Ernest Clifford Johns, was a bank manager – but Rona would have known who Sir Evelyn

**Six years old, trying on a large pink hat. 'As happy as can be.'**

Delves Broughton was. By a curious coincidence, she had been educated at Goudhurst Ladies College at Doddington Hall when the big house was leased to the school by Evelyn.

After leaving Goudhurst, Rona had trained as a nurse to work as a missionary in Africa. A beautiful young woman, she was pursued by several eligible young men, including a young Michael Heseltine, later the Deputy Prime Minister.

Rona subsequently married the flamboyant Old Harrovian property developer Donald Crammond and gave up her missionary ambitions in Africa. Like Evelyn, Rona had three young daughters, but, despite this complication, a romance between Evelyn and Rona blossomed, and developed further on their return to England. Before long, they decided to divorce their spouses and marry each other.

# CHAPTER SEVEN

## *Heathfield*

For most children of divorcing parents at boarding school, it is customary for the parents to come to the school and explain what is happening, but this was not to be the case for Isabella, who was at Heathfield in Berkshire. Her schoolfriend Rosie Pearson remembered the dramatic moment when Isabella discovered that her parents were divorcing: she rushed out of the dining room at Heathfield in floods of tears, holding a letter. Helen had written to Isabella telling her that Evelyn wanted to divorce her.

Up until this moment, Issie's days at Heathfield School had been among the happiest of her life. I hated my boarding school, but Issie was one of those who thrived in the system. She found Heathfield tremendously good fun compared to the boredom of being at home. Even more crucially, at Heathfield she also experienced the unfamiliar sensation of security, which she had not known since her own family had been thrown into turmoil by the death of Johnny five years previously.

Heathfield was, and remains, an old-fashioned school, but old-fashioned in the best sense of the word, with a disproportionate emphasis on manners. Issie's instinctive generosity and desire to help others were fostered here, developing into the generosity that would

**Issie (bottom row, second from right) during fun times in the sixth form at Heathfield.**

see her so ready in later life to devote such great time and personal energy to her discoveries and protégés.

When Miss Eleanor Beatrice Wyatt founded the school in 1899, one of her guiding principles was, 'My girls come here not to only to learn their lessons, but to learn how to live as well.' The school's main priority then, and still in Isabella's time, was the turning out of accomplished and marriageable 'gels'. Things have changed somewhat since then, but not too much. When I visited the school in January 2010, I was struck by the warmth and cosiness of the institution.

The school is not a big one and has 170 pupils spanning the ages of 11 to 18. Housed in an elegant late-Georgian building with white stuccoed walls and a Palladian colonnade, it is set in 36 acres of grounds with mature ornamental trees, rhododendron bushes, lawns, and the usual school facilities of science laboratories, art studios and playing fields. It is not a beautiful place, but its size and architecture give it a definite feeling of friendliness.

# HEATHFIELD

Academic achievement may not have been obsessively sought in Issie's day, but when it came to pass it was welcomed. When any student passed the Oxbridge exams, the school motto was invoked – 'The merit of one is the honour of all' – and the whole student body would be a granted a day off. Issie remembered this happening when Rosie got into Oxford – even though she had left Heathfield the year before and actually passed from Marlborough.

Heathfield is situated just 15 minutes by public bus from Eton College. This made for a handy supply of well-bred boys for the Heathfield girls, as the socially obsessed Evelyn noted. The close links between the girls of Heathfield and the boys of Eton were strengthened because the headmistress, Mrs Parry, was the wife of an Eton housemaster.

Issie made full use of this extra-curricular benefit, joining the Caledonian Society, which was invited for annual dances at Eton, providing an ideal excuse for illicit snogging. Issie's first boyfriend was her Cal Soc dance partner Cosmo Fry, an artistic scion of the Quaker Bristol chocolate family. She would go to Eton at weekends to watch him play soccer, yelling 'Come on Cosmo!' from the sidelines. Cosmo found that Issie's vociferous attention usually made him want to 'find somewhere to hide' on the pitch.

Issie also spent time with Cosmo watching plays at Eton in the Farrar Theatre, an ugly 1970s building that dominates the parade ground at the north end of the school. Issie and Cosmo would snuggle up for a whispered chat during house plays.

They corresponded with each other, and on one occasion Cosmo, who was also dating another girl at Heathfield, accidentally put his love letters in the wrong envelopes. The next time Issie met him she asked him knowingly, 'Am I your only girlfriend?'

She let Cosmo squirm for a few moments, then said, 'It doesn't matter, Cosmo – the other girl is my best friend.'

Staff at Heathfield turned a blind eye to romances with Eton boys, especially as such affairs were usually strikingly innocent. Issie and Cosmo's relationship involved nothing more sexual than a few snatched snogs. Issie and Rosie even took a schoolgirls' vow not to have sex before marriage.

Issie's other big crush at Heathfield was, somewhat bizarrely, on the school chaplain. Climbing up a ladder to change the hymn numbers in chapel, Issie would deliberately raise her skirt hoping to entice the poor chaplain, the Reverend Dick Stride. Reverend Stride, however, was an upstanding and decent man who remained true to his calling, and nothing improper ever occurred.

But Issie's interest in religion was piqued by her attraction to the hapless vicar, and she was immensely proud when, in her final year, she was appointed Head of Chapel.

This was a real expression of trust in Isabella by the school authorities, because religion was important at Heathfield, which is a High Anglican institution. The chapel is visually very impressive: a Gothic building with stained-glass windows, with a white timbered vaulted ceiling lit by flickering electric candles mounted on iron chandeliers, each decorated by a cast fleur de lys, the school emblem. The high pews face each other and have the names of all the pupils of the school, past and present, formally carved into them. The chapel is attached to the main building by a covered brick and timber passage, simply adorned with a pale-blue enamelled classical ceramic circular plaque of the crucifixion.

Girls attended chapel twice a day, and whilst the regular gatherings were informal, more like a school assembly with prayers, full-length services on Sundays were steeped in ceremony and sacrament. On saints' days the girls dressed in long white dresses, with white tights and lace caps, and incense was often burned in the chapel. Issie had the job of cleaning the incense censers during the summer holiday, a responsibility that triggered a lifelong love of incense and the associated paraphernalia.

The mystical and medieval rituals of the church as practised at Heathfield left a lasting impression on Isabella. In the vestry she would drink the blood of Christ, and then await a terrible punishment to befall her.

Heathfield nurtured Isabella's taste for glamour. Socially the school was exclusive and international. Isabella's contemporaries included a niece of the Shah of Iran (Nazak), daughters of Indian industrialists from Bombay (Aswani), a daughter of a major Greek shipping tycoon (Maria Niarchos), the offspring of a Hollywood actress (Liza Todd-Burton, Elizabeth Taylor's daughter) and the daughters of several earls, including Warwick (Charlotte Greville) and Yarborough (Sophia Pelham). The wealthy and successful of England and its admirers were represented at Heathfield, and it was a world in which Issie – who was just 5ft 2½ inches tall and nicknamed 'Titch' – felt comfortable, as did Evelyn. According to Issie, 'My father enjoyed coming to functions at Heathfield as there were so many people he knew.'

Another reason why Evelyn liked Heathfield is because he didn't have to pay for it. Vera had left money to pay for her Broughton grandchildren's education.

I have just one of Issie's school reports, from the Lent term in 1971. Although it was written just a year after she went to Heathfield, I recognise acutely the depiction of her personality. The teachers speak constantly of her effort, her desire to please her teachers, her helpfulness and good-natured character. I particularly like two comments. The English teacher remarks:

I am very pleased with the improvement in Isabella's work. While losing nothing of her gaiety, she has behaved in a more mature way in class.

And her geography mistress reports, 'She has been much more controlled in class.' That must have been a real effort for Issie!

Isabella was reported to be making 'excellent progress' in both her fencing class and her ballroom-dancing classes. The headmistress wrote:

Isabella has an enchanting character. She is one of the most genuinely good-hearted people in the school and although occasionally she talks too much, it is always in a good cause. She is always doing good to others and generally being a little ray of sunshine.

A little ray of sunshine. That phrase again.

Isabella kept only one other school report in which the headmistress wrote that she would make 'an excellent lady of the manor'. She would show it to me and laugh about her teacher's prescience after we married, as she set about restoring and reviving our 'manor' in Gloucestershire.

Heathfield has a system of awarding 'bows' at the end of each term. These are coloured badges worn by the girls on their jumpers, given out for 'Striving to maintain the high tone of the school, forgetfulness of self, readiness to help others, and self control at work, at play and in conversation.' A blue bow could be awarded to girls in their first three years at school, and Isabella was awarded a blue bow in the summer term of 1971 and then re-awarded it in the Michaelmas term of the same year. In 1972 Michaelmas term, she won the Senior Cheerfulness prize.

Issie was clearly very happy, but there was another, more vulnerable side to Issie as well. As Rosie observed, Issie 'crumpled easily, and people didn't always see that'.

The whole school ate together in the dining room at Heathfield. As with most boarding schools in the 1970s, the food was not up to much. Each week there was the ordeal of finding out who you were sitting next to or whether you would be 'floating' – meaning you could sit where you liked. At lunchtime the girls would receive with excitement their letters and communication from the outside world. One lunchtime in 1974, Issie opened that bombshell letter from her mother saying that Evelyn wanted a divorce. As her parents' marriage broke messily apart with much recrimination on both sides, Issie developed a tendency for melodrama. Teresa de Chair remembers that Isabella had difficulty getting to the dining room for breakfast and that she would get hysterical when cockroaches were found in the dining room and scream about their size. She dropped the nickname Titch and earned a new one, 'Huffy'. She became increasingly temperamental, theatrical and dramatic.

Issie was to win no more prizes for cheerfulness at Heathfield, as her world imploded.

# CHAPTER EIGHT

## *Rona*

If Issie's relationship with her mother had been bad, her relationship with her new stepmother, whom Evelyn married in 1974, was catastrophic.

Things got off to a bad start when Issie was evicted; Evelyn installed his stepdaughters in his daughters' bedrooms. The next time Isabella came back to Doddington, she found she had been turfed out of her bedroom; the swan wall paper and glam-rock posters of *Ziggy Stardust* had been torn down and thrown out. She recalled that they were moved out of their bedrooms and installed 'above the car port' in the guest wing her father had added on to the house in the 1950s.

Evelyn was not a bad man but he was thoughtless and weak, and the saga of the bedrooms was typical of the way in which Evelyn now treated Isabella. Coming just months after her parents' divorce and with that trauma still very much ongoing, it left her feeling unwelcome at Doddington in school holidays, and became a focal point for Isabella's teenage rage and despair. It is the moment when Isabella began to feel rootless and that she belonged nowhere. This demon would develop into an obsessive fear that she would end up a home-less bag lady – a belief that would haunt her for the rest of her life and contributed to her eventual suicide, despite the fact that at the time of her death we manifestly were not homeless, with a flat in Eaton Square and also occupied Hilles, the wonderful Blow family seat on a thousand acres of land in Gloucestershire.

There was another problem with 'The Steps', as she called her young stepsisters; they were extremely good looking. She was particularly concerned that boys she was interested in would prefer her oldest stepsister, Louise, who was the closest in age to her.

Like many teenage girls, Isabella was very unsure about her looks. She liked her figure; she was petite, sexy and curvy, with wonderful 32B bosoms. She had huge, flashing, green-blue eyes, described by Rupert Everett as 'mad' and by Rosie as 'beautiful'. She had slim hips, great legs and elegant feet.

But she felt strongly that her face was very ugly. She hated her protruding, 'goofy' teeth. She blamed her parents for being too mean to spend money rectifying these 'combine harvesters' when she was a teenager.

A father of some friends of hers who lived in Gloucestershire remarked to his sons that her face was 'hideous' but with a figure like hers she'd be 'great in bed'.

Such callous remarks irrevocably coloured Issie's view of herself. She once said to me, 'When you're poking the fire, it does not matter what is on the mantelpiece.'

I told her when I met her that she was beautiful – but it was too late. The damage had been done. She was convinced she had 'an ugly face'.

A decade later in New York in the 1980s, Isabella visited a dentist who looked after Frank Sinatra's and others stars' teeth. The dentist told her it was too late for her to do anything about what she called her 'yellow fangs'. Her habit of smearing her lips and teeth with lipstick was in part to deal with this perceived disfigurement. Her hatred of her face was another demon Issie carried with her for life.

Rona found Evelyn's children hard to deal with. Rona believed in nannies, mealtimes, bedtimes, bath times and strict routines while Evelyn's children more or less did what they liked, grabbing a bite to eat from the fridge when they felt hungry and going to bed whenever they pleased. Although 'Baby' Lavinia appeared to like the new structure, enjoying trips to the museum and organised activities, Rona and Issie battled each other. Rona recalls one occasion when Issie was going to a party. When Rona asked her what time she would like to be picked up, Issie brushed the request off and said she would make her own way home, which Rona found 'ridiculous' and completely unacceptable.

Issie was only 20 years younger than Rona, so when Evelyn told Rona, in a typically offhand fashion, that his three daughters had their own mother and that she was not responsible for them, it must have come as both a relief and a confirmation of what she already knew.

Isabella saw everything that Rona did as evidence that her stepmother was trying to drive a wedge between herself and her father. For example, one change introduced by Rona and resented by Issie was how she earned her pocket money. Issie had learned to operate the potato machine but Rona felt it was 'beneath (her) dignity' for Issie to work for her father. Instead, Issie had to 'bicycle to the local Bridgmere nurseries' to earn her pennies.

Lavinia remembered Issie crying in the morning and being very upset at having to go to Bridgemere.

Despite the sometimes brash exterior, Issie was still very much a little girl and the presence of her young stepmother created a rival and competitor for her father's love. The battle for this love would cause Isabella terrible emotional pain, hurt and despair, and become another demon.

Isabella would never overcome this demon, or accept her stepmother. In later life she took to describing her as hurtfully as possible in public interviews, once referring to her in a profile in the *New Yorker* as 'a creature my father met on a bus in Hong Kong'.

But her father had a love and a need for her stepmother, and he was about to become more dependent on Rona than ever.

# CHAPTER NINE

## *Evelyn's Leg*

J ust under a year after their marriage, on 4 February 1975, Evelyn went into the private block of the North Staffordshire hospital at Stoke-on-Trent hospital to have an operation to remove a varicose vein and some lumps on his left leg. On 5 February 1975, he had the operation. A day later, he had swollen up like a balloon – gas gangrene had broken out in the hospital and three other patients in the private wing died. Fighting for his life, Evelyn was prescribed morphine, hydrocortisone, diuretics and antibiotics to reduce the swelling.

Five days later, to try to stop the spreading gangrene, the surgeon amputated his leg below the knee.

Issie firmly blamed Rona for the disaster claiming that Rona pushed him to have the operation because she thought his varicose veins looked unsightly on the beach.

It was unfair of Issie to blame Rona for the operation, for her father medically required it. But, by 24 March 1975, death was a real possibility, and Evelyn signed a new will in the North Staffordshire hospital, witnessed by the orthopaedic surgeon and a nurse.

In fact, Evelyn survived, but the change to the will was permanent. The dramatic secret of what he had written would not be revealed until his death in 1993.

# EVELYN'S LEG

On 9 April 1975, Evelyn had a second operation amputating his leg above his knee.

There was some discussion of suing the hospital for negligence. But Evelyn was having none of it. The hospital had far more money than he did to fight in court. Besides, the surgeon was a friend of his; they shot together in Staffordshire.

Indeed, the shoots after Evelyn lost his leg were one of Issie's happier memories. With his artificial leg, he needed Isabella to hold him in case he fell over while shooting a 'left and a right' bird. For Isabella, it was a special time. She had her beloved father to herself.

With his leg stub rubbing against his artificial leg, Evelyn was to be in constant pain for the rest of his life. The pain and handicap were borne by him bravely and with dignity and there was rarely any complaint or fuss. Emotionally he may have been a weak man, but physically he was brave. Isabella inherited her father's physical courage.

What really irked Isabella was the fact that Rona had not allowed her to see her father when he was in hospital. Thirteen years later in 1988, when Isabella took me for the first time to meet her father and stepmother for dinner at their home in Kensington Square, the subject came up. Rona explained to me that, in her judgement, Isabella was too young to deal with the sight of Evelyn in hospital with gangrene. I disagreed. Isabella was over 15 years old at the time and, I felt sure, old enough to have witnessed the admittedly distressing scene. Issie and I had both been brought up in the countryside where blood, gore and death are very much part of life. Rona had grown up in the city and town, and had the sensibilities of a city dweller.

But Evelyn had lost his leg. In less than a year, Rona's fairy-tale marriage to a rich, older, titled man had turned into a nightmare – she now had six children to look after and a husband with one leg in a wheelchair. Despite his efforts to carry on as if nothing had happened, Evelyn was now severely handicapped and heavily dependent on Rona, and she was to care for him for the next 18 years until his death.

# CHAPTER TEN

## *Eighteenth Birthday*

Most of Issie's contemporaries were given a special present of some value for their eighteenth birthday – a pen, a piece of jewellery or maybe even a car.

Evelyn gave Issie a Bible. It was inscribed, 'Follow in thy father's footsteps', and accompanied by a birthday card telling her she was 'Off the books'.

It was a joke, but a bad one at Issie's expense. Evelyn did, of course, continue to pay for certain expenses for his daughter, but he was letting her know in typically brutal fashion that she was now financially responsible for herself. Isabella's early life had been very privileged, with cooks and staff to look after her things at home, and for Issie this was financial abandonment by the man she loved. She always remembered that thoughtless birthday card – it fed her demon of financial insecurity.

But now that she was 18, her arguments with Rona cooled somewhat, especially when she managed to persuade her father to lend her the farm Ford Fiesta. Despite the fact that the farm car 'had straw sticking out of it', she loved being able to drive herself around the country as she pleased. As she had been driving the car on the farm roads for years, she was a good driver and never had any accidents.

# EIGHTEENTH BIRTHDAY

Even as a teenager Issie was the life and soul of any party, and she loved parties, particularly if they were grand and glamorous ones. Because she was so funny and lively she swiftly became much in demand on the stately home circuit even though, or perhaps because, her behaviour was so outrageous. Hugh St Clair, whose father was a Gloucestershire MP, remembers Issie dancing 'semi-topless, howling with laughter in front of my stuffy father at Gloucestershire teenage parties'.

Because of Issie's precociousness, she was often invited to the same parties as Evelyn and Rona, and, wittingly or not, Issie often embarrassed them at these events. At the famous Sitwell home of Renishaw, at a party for Alex Sitwell, which they all attended, Issie was thrown naked into the swimming pool. Issie told me that Evelyn and Rona ignored the scene. I understood by the way she told me the story that she was actually trying hard to get their attention and love by her provocations.

One of Isabella's party pieces involved performing 'feats of extraordinary strength'. Issie was petite – just 5'2½" – and her strength astonished unsuspecting onlookers. When she stayed with her Heathfield friend Lady Sophia Pelham at Brocklesby Park, she carried her father, the 18-stone Lord Yarborough, twice around the long dining-room table. She particularly enjoyed arm-wrestling much bigger people, as well as humiliating fitness fanatics who, unlike her, worked out. Much later in Paris, in the late 1990s, at an exhibition of 'Sex and the British' at Thadeus Ropac's gallery, I watched with amusement as serried ranks of tough, tattooed YBAs lined up to arm wrestle Issie – and were easily beaten by her one after the other.

Although the debutante season was in the process of becoming an anachronism, it still existed in the late 1970s and early 1980s. But, to Issie's great disappointment, there was no suggestion by Evelyn and Rona of Issie becoming a deb, still less of her officially 'coming out' in society with a big party. Needless to say, Rona made quite sure that her stepsisters, by contrast, were given lavish coming-of-age parties in the castle at Doddington.

# CHAPTER ELEVEN

## *The Lovats*

When Issie left Heathfield, she spent the summer working at Laura Ashley, where, as her shop-floor colleague Phil Athill recalls:

> She was utterly incapable of measuring the materials we were selling and gave people as many metres as they liked. Likewise wallpaper – anyone asking for advice as to how many rolls they needed for a certain space was in deep trouble and I can imagine that 'Laura Ashley' is a black name to this day with most of the customers who fell on us.

From Laura Ashley in Sloane Street to her mother's flat at 17 Cadogan Square is a short 10-minute walk. But for Isabella there was a problem getting inside. Her mother, as her friend Charlotte Greville remembered, treated her 'like a child' and refused to give her a key to the flat.

When Isabella caught pneumonia, her mother offered to take care of her, but was then called out of the country. Hearing of this situation, her father's sister, Aunt Rosie, invited Issie to convalesce with her at Balbair, their cosy Highland house next to the river Beauly, 10 miles from Inverness in the Highlands.

Evelyn was never once invited to any of Rosie's homes, but Issie jumped at the chance, keen to spend some time with Rosie's husband, Lord Shimi Lovat, her beloved 'Uncle Shimi'.

Lord Lovat had become a legend for his exploits in the Second World War. He had been a leading figure in the Commandos, and an inspirational leader

Lovat sacked Evelyn Waugh from the Commandos – and was satirised by Waugh in his brilliant *Sword of Honour* trilogy about the war.

At D-Day, Shimi had led his Commandos on the first wave at Sword Beach in Normandy, armed only with his sporting Winchester rifle. Accompanying him was his 21-year-old personal piper Bill Millin. To encourage his men, Lovat ordered Millin to play 'The blue bonnets from over the border'. The Germans ignored Millin, thinking him a lunatic transvestite. It was an exploit worthy of Hollywood, and in 1962 Darryl Zannuk produced *The Longest Day,* in which Lovat is played by Peter Lawford.

Lovat was famously handsome and vain. It was said that he would admire the reflection of his beauty in the silver cutlery.

In the mid-1960s, Uncle Shimi had suffered a series of heart attacks. Afflicted by that perennial fear of the British upper classes, the payment of death duties, he had made over the Lovat estates, which stretched across 165,000 acres of Scotland from the east to west coast, to his eldest son Simon, Master of Lovat and Isabella's first cousin.

Isabella was to develop a close and loving relationship with her aunt and uncle, and they with her. When out walking with Uncle Shimi, he would ask her to be silent and then name all the birds that were singing. In the House of Lords, Uncle Shimi had urged potential explorers to stop irritating 'Nessie', the Loch Ness Monster in which he professed to believe.

Before traveling up to Inverness to stay with her aunt and uncle, Isabella found time, despite her pneumonia, to have her hair frizzed to look 'more Fraser'. During her childhood, the Lovats' youngest son Andrew Fraser had once stayed at Doddington to go to a local ball. On his return after the ball, the tipsy Andrew had demolished a stretch of post and rail fencing in his car, but what Issie really remembered was his frizzy hair.

Flora Fraser remembers meeting Issie on her first trip to Inverness:

She was staying with Uncle Shimi and Aunt Rosie at Balblair and Uncle Shimi was tickled pink by her, especially when she asked for crème de menthe to put on her porridge. I have an image of her hearty laughter at a picnic up the glen. Huge pale eyes, pale hair and scarlet mouth, nursing a bloody Mary in a tartan mug. She was recovering from pneumonia, so she had a Fraser hunting rug hung round her shoulders.

Benjie Fraser remembered his first meeting with Issie during this stay. It was at Kiltarlity church during the midnight mass Christmas Eve service. As the youngest member of the Fraser clan, he had the task of taking around the collection plate in the church. Dressed as a punk in his neon green jeans and leopard stripes and a nose ring, he passed Issie, who whispered to him, 'I hope you're not keeping any of that for yourself?'

Uncle Shimi, Aunt Rosie and the rest of the extended Fraser clan were to be emotional rocks for Isabella throughout her life. They became a surrogate family, which made it even harder to bear when, later, they were engulfed in tragedy themselves.

# CHAPTER TWELVE

## *Wolf*

In the autumn, after her convalescence in the Highlands, Issie went to the Oxford and County secretarial college in Oxford – aka the Ox and Cow – to take a secretarial course. Evelyn, of course, made it clear that he was paying for this course only because it would enable her to earn her own living.

The Ox and Cow was located at 34 Giles Street, a Georgian terrace in the centre of Oxford. According to her roommate Christine Selby, Issie had a penchant for wearing dresses from the 1920s, set off with a red or green beret. She also smoked cigarettes through a cigarette holder.

Evelyn may have hoped Issie would meet a nice suitor at Oxford – instead she met Wolf.

Wolf was a dark-haired, Old Etonian history scholar at Christchurch College, whose wildness is legendary amongst their contemporaries. He is described by one Eton friend as 'coming from another age – a buccaneer Elizabethan'. He seems to have been always in trouble: he was expelled from Eton a couple of weeks before the end of term for drinking beer, and then later from Oxford for setting alight the curtains in the rooms below his own. A friend says that Wolf never considered that 'actions have consequences'.

Issie fell head over heels in love with Wolf and lost her virginity to him at 17. She said it was an unpleasant physical act, but it was an important milestone in her life, breaking her schoolgirl vow to save sex for marriage. Issie, when telling me about the event, pointed out with a certain pride that she was not 'pumped and dumped'; she and Wolf were to remain together for the next two years. It was for Issie, her friend Mosh Gordon-Cumming remembered, an important relationship into which Issie channelled her love.

Wolf was given to stealing cars – 'he invented joyriding' one contemporary recalls – and his nefarious activities also included siphoning off petrol from cars parked on Oxford's streets in the dead of night, helped by Issie. One of Issie's Heathfield girlfriends remembers:

> Wolf was rather like a pirate; totally wild and unpredictable and
> rather dangerous and frightening. When you got to know him
> he was adorable, though. I think he was probably slightly mad.

One night riding on his motorbike in London, they went to eat at a restaurant called 'Up all Night' on the Fulham Road. The restaurant was closed, and Wolf, incensed at the false claim contained in the name, threw a brick through the window before roaring off through the quiet streets of Chelsea. Issie, riding pillion and clinging to his waist, loved every moment of her new life.

Wolf was a rebel, but his love was also a wonderful escape for her from the hurt and sadness of home. She only once invited Wolf to stay at Doddington. Evelyn loathed Wolf – understandably, especially when he later went out with Issie's sister Julia. When he would ask his daughter how she planned to get to Doddington, Issie would reply, 'By motorbike.' Wolf arrived after the long four-hour journey from London and, to Issie's thrilled delight and her stepmother's great annoyance, trampled motor oil into all the carpets.

At the end of her year at the Ox and Cow, she and Wolf moved into a grim basement flat in Oakley Street, Chelsea, with her friend Christie Saunders and her boyfriend. Christie remembers that there was almost nothing in the flat. With no money, and egged on by Wolf, Issie set about furnishing it by theft.

When, years later, Issie bought her 4.10 shotgun, I helped her fill in the form. It asked if she had any criminal convictions and she told me the story of the stolen sofa for Oakley Street. After dinner with her friend Minnie Scott at Minnie's mansion block off the King's Road, Issie asked Minnie if she minded if she took the plastic sofa in the block lobby. Minnie told Issie that she had no objections. Issie and her two friends in their high heels were halfway up the King's Road with the sofa when a police van arrived and they were all arrested and taken to Chelsea police station. Issie merrily recounted to me how her rather shocked, pale, girlfriends spoke in low voices to give their names – with titles and grand addresses in Scotland and Wiltshire.

The girls got off with a warning – though Issie mentioned something to me about probation. To her irritation and complaints, I insisted that she put this into her shotgun-licence application form. It proved to be no bar to her getting her shotgun licence.

Issie was not totally faithful to Wolf. At Oxford she had a fling with Tim Hunt, curator for the Andy Warhol Foundation of the Visual Arts, who later married Tama Janowitz, the author of *Slaves of New York*. When he and Tama got married, we went to the party they gave in London. Her 'relationship' with another Oxford student was even more fleeting. Aghast at learning that he was still a virgin, Issie, ever the fixer, said, 'Well, we'd better get that sorted', and promptly sorted it out for him.

Issie also had a casual affair with the gentle son of a Viscount, a brother of one of her schoolfriends. It was a relationship of which her father approved. He knew the family well. From this pleasant man, Issie learnt how to go duck shooting and tread in the divots between polo chukkas. When we were married, Issie would sometimes wonder if she would not have been better off marrying him and settling down to a quiet life.

'But Issie, would he have married you?' I would ask. Issie would sigh and think it may have been a possibility – and then we would move quickly on to the next drama in our lives.

To support herself when she was living at Oakley Street, Issie resorted to many odd jobs. She worked at a telephone switchboard, and when she worked as a cleaner with her friend Camilla Uniacke they both dressed up with hankies on her head. Once as a dare she went to a porn magazine and showed them her bosoms but, thankfully, she was not taken on.

The King's Road played a large part in her life at this time. She drove up and down it in a friend's blacked-out mini looking at boys and listening to Barry White.

Although Isabella had a punk-inspired look at the time, she was not into the music of punk. Issie went to her first concert aged 19 on 15 July

1978 at Blackbush Airfield in Fleet, Hampshire. 'The Picnic at Black-bush', as it was billed, was attended by some 200,000 people. Bob Dylan headlined, with support from Eric Clapton and Joan Armatrading.

I was there too, aged 14. It was my first rock concert and it was the first time I know of that Issie and I were in the same place. I walked the several miles from Fleet railway station to the gig, where I was intrigued by the sight of old hippies frying up sausages for their small children in the sun. This was not what I had expected of a rock concert. I was into punk music. The same year I went to see the Ramones.

After two years together, Wolf told Issie that he did not love her any more. She threw her things together in a tearful scene and moved out of Oakley Street, but, as she told her friend Mosh Gordon-Cumming, who found her sobbing in the Kings Road with a suitcase, 'she had nowhere to go'.

Issie's greatest demon – the fear of homelessness – was already hard at work.

# CHAPTER
# THIRTEEN

## *Nicholas*

In early 1980, Isabella fell in love with Nicholas Edward Taylor, a slightly older, mature student, who was studying Politics, Philosophy and Economics at Merton College, Oxford. Nick was the incredibly handsome third son of Dr Keith Taylor, a lecturer at Oxford University, and Ann Jones, a Physiology don and later lecturer in Biochemistry at St Edmund's Hall, Oxford. Like many of the offspring of Oxford academics, Nicholas attended the Dragon prep school in Oxford.

What threatened to be an entirely conventional British upper-middle-class childhood was transformed in 1963, when Nicholas's father was offered a job as Professor of Medicine at Stanford in California. After some soul-searching, Nicholas's mother gave up her job at Oxford, and moved the young family – four brothers and a sister – to Palo Alto, in the San Francisco Bay Area of north California.

The Taylor brothers enthusiastically embraced the entrepreneurial spirit of Californian life. Nick's elder brother Sebastian became a professional backgammon player, and today both he and the youngest brother, Daniel, are successful financiers.

Nicholas, however, was more academic than his brothers and headed back to Oxford to complete his studies after school. On his return to England he quickly became bored by his conservative contemporaries. He told his friend Robert Murphy, a scholar at Oxford, that he wanted to meet some 'more exciting' new people. Robert knew exactly who to introduce Nick to: his elder brother Antony's friend Isabella, who was constantly flashing her bosoms and at the centre of an exciting, destructive, law-breaking set with, as he puts it, 'no sense of modesty, decorum, or respect'.

Isabella was without a boyfriend following Wolf's dramatic announcement that he was no longer in love with her, and Robert's introduction worked well. Nicholas and Isabella soon became an item. Isabella told me that sex with Nicholas was fantastic.

Flora Fraser, then at Oxford studying for a history degree at Wadham College, knew Nick well because she was living in his parents' old house in Jericho, which Nick now occupied, renting out spare rooms as student digs. Flora recalls:

> When she and Nick went out, I used to hear she did a fabulous striptease after dinner. It was part of her personality at that time. She had a fabulous figure. Her bosoms were generally on show in some way. We were all quite on top of each other and Nick found it difficult working when Issie was around, so one day he suggested she go to the Museum of Modern Art and look at the Kandinskys. She went back again and again, more excited each time.

Nick's brother Sebastian first met Isabella in the King's Road in London. It was a darker side of Isabella that he encountered: she was chasing the dragon – smoking heroin in tin foil.

Drugs were a big part of Isabella's generation, which had been hit from the late 1970s by what her friend Colin Cawdor remembers as a 'wave of heroin'. Isabella, Wolf and many of their contemporaries were into 'hard drugs' – heroin, coke and speed. Isabella was one of the few in her circle not to become addicted, a fact of which she was proud. Issie smoked grass now and then throughout her life, but hated hard drugs.

The Taylor brothers were very handsome and they became popular members of Isabella's circle, but tragedy was to strike the family. Nicholas's eldest brother, Mathew, was killed outright riding a motorbike in London, only a short time after qualifying as a doctor. Also travelling on the motorbike was Mathew and Isabella's friend Cristina Zilkha, a half-French, Harvard-educated lyricist who had success with the dancefloor anthem 'Disco Clone'. She survived the crash with barely a scratch on her. Cristina said that her life was saved by the protection afforded her by the fur coat she was wearing.

# CHAPTER FOURTEEN

## *The Disposal of Doddington*

Around the same time as Isabella was falling in love with Nicholas Taylor, her father, Evelyn, was reorganising his life. Evelyn decided that the time had come to retire after 35 years of farming. He resolved to sell up and move permanently to London. With a family history of over 600 years as landowners, it was a controversial decision, and his friend Major Ormerod and some other Cheshire landowners were dismayed. They let him know that they felt he was letting the collective side down.

But, practically, of course, Evelyn's reasons made sense. Evelyn was 65 and, with one leg, life in the country was increasingly becoming a struggle for him and Rona. He told the Major that moving to London would enable him to see more of his daughters, but the decision to sell was also bound up with his failure to produce a son and heir. Had Johnny survived, Evelyn's attitude to the future of Doddington Park would have been very different.

However, when the crunch came, even bottom-line obsessed Evelyn could not bear to cut the ties to Doddington completely. His land agent advised him to retain the profitable farming business and get shot of the big house itself, a liability that was ruinously expensive to maintain. Evelyn, contrary as ever, did the opposite, selling the farmland, the farm units, the 1950s cottages that he had built and the hideous pink house that Isabella had grown up in, for £1.3 million to Malcolm Harrison, who had a successful haulage business in north Staffordshire.

Evelyn retained the Hall, the lake, the castle, the woods he had planted in the 1950s, and 20 Arts and Crafts cottages in the park. The way Doddington was disposed of was an extraordinary decision by Evelyn and a rare example of Evelyn allowing his heart to rule his head. Without a farm to support it, the Hall, boarded up since the school had left, would never be able to pay its way. Evelyn would certainly never be able to afford to live in it again – a fact he implicitly acknowledged by keeping a small black-and-white home for himself and Rona on the estate.

In a bizarre twist of fate, Harrison got into financial difficulties in the early 1990s, and, after Evelyn died, Rona bought back the land from Harrison. She runs the estate as a commercial farm today, spending weekends in Cheshire, and is engaged in a project to restore the Hall, which is still boarded up although the exterior is open for viewing by the public.

Issie's friend Hugo Guinness told her how lucky she was because now she would be inheriting money instead of property, but for Issie the sale was a cause of great sadness, as the land that she had known and walked over was no longer her family's. Another root had been cut.

# CHAPTER FIFTEEN

## *Texas*

Evelyn also had an offshore family legacy abroad, which needed sorting out. He was vague to the point of secrecy on the details of this money, but he did reveal that the fund had been badly managed. The real estate had been sold and replaced with high-risk, speculative investments that had largely failed. What could have been worth several million stood at under £100,000, and, to receive anything at all, and escape the hated taxman, the beneficiary had to live permanently abroad.

Isabella, Evelyn decided in typically autocratic fashion, was the most suitable candidate to receive the money. Julia had health problems and Lavinia at 15 was too young, and both of the younger sisters were temperamentally unsuited to exile anyway. And Evelyn made clear that exile was what was involved, warning Issie darkly: 'I don't care if you marry a waiter – you have to live abroad. If you return to this country with that money, you will go to prison.'

For Issie, the timing could not have been more propitious. Nick, on the slender basis of a conversation with a stranger on an aeroplane, had decided that he was going to make his fortune by 'wildcatting' for oil in Texas. Wildcatting was a highly speculative enterprise, which involved buying the rights to vast tracts of barren land – the kind of places where only wildcats lived – and then drilling, more in hope than expectation of striking oil. Through his father's professorship at Stanford, Nicholas had the necessary permits to live and work in America. When he got lucky, Nick would tell Isabella as they hatched their plans in pubs and parties in Oxford and London, he would be able to buy back for her the life into which she had been born – a big house in the country, a townhouse in the city and private education for their children.

It was a beguiling fantasy, and in 1981 Nicholas, 26, and Isabella, 22, moved to Midland, Texas, the hot and dusty capital of the west Texas oil fields.

Midland had started as an oil town in the 1920s and still supplies one-fifth of the total oil and gas for the United States. Isabella and Nicholas would have their breakfast at the counter at the local diner next to George W. Bush, who was then running his father's oil company Arbusto – which means 'bush' in Spanish. They rented an apartment in a condo on what Issie described to me as 'a road with oil juggernauts roaring past, leaving the taste of dust in your mouth'.

As Anna Wintour observed, it is hard to imagine Issie in 'unfashionable' Midland, Texas. Issie, who hated being idle, found a job at Guy La Roche in Midland, but oil-rich Midlanders preferred to fly to Paris in their private jets to do their clothes shopping. Issie decided to put the time she had on her hands while minding the empty shop to good use, reading, among many other classics, *War and Peace, Les Liaisons Dangereuses,* books by the feminist Simone de Beauvoir and the Beatnik poets. In literature, as in all her creative inspirations, Isabella's enthusiasm for the progressive and the new was balanced and set in context by her knowledge and understanding of what had gone before.

One night, Nicholas telephoned her from an arid corner of Texas, and warned her that unless they got married she was going to be deported. And so, on 22 April 1981, Issie, wearing a T-shirt and Fiorucci jeans, went to the town hall with Nicholas and were married by the sheriff. The sheriff tried to kiss Isabella. She slapped him and went home, got drunk on champagne and telephoned home to tell her parents what she had done. Her furious mother told her 'Isabella you were a pain when you were born and you are a pain now.'

Evelyn was kinder. He bought Isabella a pair of aquamarine and diamond earrings and noted her marriage in Debrett's and Who's Who. When we were getting married eight years later, Issie criticised her father for making these entries without her permission.

# BLOW BY BLOW

It was far removed from the romantic church wedding she had dreamed of and expected for marriage.

Isabella always insisted that she had not been married 'in the eyes of God', and that it was a 'visa wedding', but she was clearly in love with Nicholas. Thanks to his fantastic appearance and physique, Issie also regarded him as good genetic stock for children, which she wanted desperately.

But they were not ready. Isabella told me that she had one abortion when she was with Nick and that a second time she became pregnant the foetus aborted naturally. But to her old friend Emily Dashwood in England, who she would call out of the blue from Texas, sometimes in tears, she said she had 10 abortions. The truth is probably somewhere in between.

Later in England, working at *Tatler*, she would confide in her friend the writer Mary Killen, a doctor's daughter, her sadness and regret about her abortions. When Issie and I became engaged, Issie had herself checked out and told me everything was OK. But she didn't go into details and I always sensed a niggling doubt about her own fertility, despite the beautiful baby clothes she bought and stored in cupboards in readiness for the happy day that would never come. By another coincidence a cousin of mine had a cottage in Sussex next door to Nicholas's father, Dr Keith Taylor. Dr Taylor told my cousin that Isabella could never have children.

I suspect Dr Taylor formed this opinion because while in Texas, Isabella had a serious case of Crohn's disease, an inflammation of the intestines. She was operated on and had 18 inches of her perforated intestines removed. From then on, her friend Natasha Grenfell remembered, her famous stripteases involved carefully shrouding with material the 18-inch scar on her stomach.

But away from the sadness of the abortions, there was a glamorous, petrodollar-fuelled side to Texan life that Issie enjoyed immensely. While Nick went off for weeks on end, covering vast expanses of Texan desert in his hunt for oil, Isabella visited places like the enormous King Ranch, the largest ranch in America, which extended to a million acres. She had Uncle Shimi to thank for her introduction to King Ranch, and she also had contacts from her friend Lucy's father Patrick Helmore, who insured racehorses for a number of Texan owners. Soon Isabella was flying around Texas on private jets visiting the homes of wealthy Texans, pretending to admire their collections of crystal animals and having her nails and hair done by manicurists and hairdressers who were drafted into these opulent and unre-strained homes by the day.

The wealth generated by the American oil boom in America in the eighties was staggering and Issie and Nick wanted a slice of it.

But it was not to be.

'All Nick ever found was few rusty old coke tins,' Issie said.

By March 1983, the love affair with Texas, which she had taken to describing as a 'den of doom', was definitely over. She and Nick made plans to head to New York and Issie was 'over the moon'.

She would need some new armour for New York, however. She asked a friend back home to send over her 'Piero de Monzi skirt' and 'insure it for £150,000'.

# CHAPTER SIXTEEN

## *Issie ♥ NY*

In the end, Issie – along with her Piero de Monzi skirt – made the trek to New York on her own. Issie may have given up on striking oil, but Nicholas was not so easily discouraged. He decided to stay in Midland, looking for luck. Issie was sad to leave Nicholas, but the blow was softened by the fact that they had not spent much time together anyway, as Nicholas had spent most of their time in Texas on the road – or in the air – hunting for that elusive 'gusher'. Although she had done her best to make the most of the state, she eventually accepted that for her own sanity she had to escape Texas and its desperate millionaire housewives measuring out their days with mani-pedis. Issie knew her future lay not in the South but on the East Coast.

Issie had formed a plan to use her family legacy to go to Columbia University in New York, but as for any other new arrival in the city, there were practicalities to organise first. Issie's first priority on landing in New York was to find somewhere to stay. She found a room in a flat in the Midtown area of New York, sharing with Catherine Oxenberg, daughter of Princess Elizabeth of Yugoslavia, then working as a model but soon to find fame playing Joan Collins's glamorous daughter in *Dynasty*.

Issie's decision to go to Columbia had not been made lightly. Although Issie had not been particularly bothered about her A-level results at the time, a few years out in the world had left Isabella conscious of her lack of a formal higher education. Her father had refused to send her to study art in Florence, but the family legacy she received by living abroad now made it possible for her to pay for her higher education herself.

Money was only half the battle, however. To get into an American university, there was the small matter of Issie's A-level grades, which needed improving. The improvement was achieved with the aid of a photocopying machine and Tippex. Her deceit paid off – she was accepted to do a degree in Chinese Art at Columbia.

Issie enjoyed the Chinese Art course, studying ancient Sui and Tang pottery and, as she said, 'looking for hours at the Buddha's ear lobe'.

After a year, however, Issie decided to drop out. Her decision, she told me, was precipitated by a fellow student being stabbed to death on campus. In the early eighties, New York City was a dangerous and lawless place recovering from its bankruptcy in the 1970s. It was also, however, a seething cauldron of creativity. Issie's interest in fashion and the individual way she dressed may have protected her – she attributed the fact that she was never mugged or attacked to the wild way she looked and behaved.

She continued her practice of flashing her bosoms. At Nicola's, a homely restaurant popular with authors on the Upper East Side, her friend Michael Zilkha, the Oxford-educated, Lebanese heir to Mothercare, recalls that she volunteered to the owner Nick that she would expose her breasts in return for a bottle of champagne. The transaction was 'duly consummated'.

Flashing her breasts became Issie's calling card. The artist Hugo Guinness recalls:

Issie was incredibly attention seeking and demanding of attention and an exhibitionist – but that was what was fun. She was a performer, she was this eccentric, crazy girl who, basically, if anyone wasn't paying attention to her, she would flash her boobs. That was what she did. That was her party turn. That was her thing. If you were not interested in talking to her, woop! Out they'd come. She'd play with them, she'd squeeze them, that was what she used to get attention – her boobs. It was pretty radical.

That's why she'd be invited everywhere. We'd all be waiting to see till she did that. And she wouldn't have to be pissed to do it. Her boobs were her secret weapon from the age of 17 to 27. That is what I remember most about Issie. The boob flashing.

Another reason for dropping out of Columbia was simply that Issie found being tied down – to a desk, an employer or a course – stifled her creativity. It helped as Issie herself admitted that at the time it was fashionable to 'drop out'.

By the time Issie left Columbia, Nicholas had finally had enough of his fruitless quest for oil in Midland and came to join Isabella in New York, where he swiftly landed a job at the investment bankers Salomon Brothers. Financially savvy Nicholas told Issie that they needed to use the capital of her legacy in order to buy a flat in New York.

The flat Issie bought was a first-floor walk-up on the corner of Charles Street and West 4th in Greenwich Village. It had two bedrooms, but Issie knocked them together to create a big bedroom. In the kitchen she put down industrial rubber, which was then unheard of. *Vogue*'s André Leon Talley, who visited the apartment, remembered:

It was a beautiful flat, very neat and fastidiously clean. She had one big painting on the wall by some fantastic artist she had discovered. It was huge. I don't recall who the artist was, but I remember she told me that the painting cost £700 – and £700 was a fortune then.

André also remembered that the flat was dominated by 'a big wrought iron bed'. There was no central heating in the flat, so when visitors – such as her cousin Aeneas Mackay, who was at Brown University in Rhode Island – came in the winter, they would sleep with Issie in the bed with all their clothes on to keep warm.

New York was kinder to Nicholas than Midland had been. The bond market was booming and he started to make some serious money. But Issie was not getting to the one place she wanted to be in fashion: *Vogue* magazine.

Issie had applied to personnel at American *Vogue* but been turned down by the then fashion director Polly Mellen. So Issie was again working odd jobs. One of them was at a coffee shop called La Manga on 57th Street. 'I dressed and looked so unusual that they would not let me serve the customers, and kept me downstairs working the cappuccino machine,' Issie said. Out of pride, she would have her lunchtime sandwiches delivered to her there – from another sandwich shop.

She also worked the coat check in an Ian Schrager club. Aeneas remembers that at this time Issie was frustrated in her career and was increasingly tempted to ignore her father's dire warning about the tax implications of the legacy and return to England.

Then, at a stroke, Issie's luck changed. Her old friend Lucy Helmore had married Bryan Ferry, who was one of the hottest and most celebrated rock stars in the world at that moment, effortlessly straddling the worlds of art, fashion and music. Bryan and Lucy came to New York and rented Anna Wintour's brownstone in Greenwich Village. Issie hung out with the glamorous pair constantly. It was a triangular friendship that would endure over the years. Hugo Guinness explains:

> Issie was the one friend of Lucy's that Bryan actually liked. Lots of relationships have someone in the middle and for them it was Issie. Issie would always try and make peace between them so they could carry on. Bryan – who is a creative, talented person – loved Issie's energy and style. Issie was absolutely incredible. She was a real upper, she was the person who made the party fun.

Issie told me that Bryan could not believe that she worked in a coffee shop and came to check it out. He told her, 'Issie, this is ridiculous, you love clothes – you should be working at *Vogue*.' (Bryan says he has no recollection of telling Issie this.)

Bryan was able to arrange for Issie to have an interview with Anna Wintour, then creative director of American *Vogue*. Independently, Anna had heard from her friend, the British restaurateur Brian McNally, about 'a fabulously eccentric creature who worked as the coat check girl in one of Ian Schrager's nightclubs'.

Issie's foot was in the door of *Vogue*. Her interview in 1984 with Anna at the old Condé Nast office at 350 Madison Avenue was to change her life. In February 1984, Issie wrote excitedly to her friend Liza Campbell in England saying she had 'lied like the devil' and falsely claimed to have attended London University.

But Issie's qualifications didn't really impress Anna – her literary tastes did. Anna recalls:

Issie was transfixed by the copy of Vita Sackville-West's biography that was on my desk. She said to me, 'I've cried each of the three times that I've read it.' 'Issie,' I told her, 'There's nothing to cry about.'

Issie's reference for her job was Michael Zilkha. Anna asked Zilkha about Issie. 'Well, Anna, I can recommend Issie for making the best roast potatoes,' he replied.

Issie got the job as one of Anna's two assistants. It was the break she needed. Ever after, Issie would say, 'I owe everything to Anna.'

# CHAPTER SEVENTEEN

## *Anna*

I ssie was the ultimate Voguette.
  As Anna Wintour's new assistant, she created something of a stir when she started at American *Vogue,* the most influential fashion publication in the world. Or rather, her outfits did.

The pages of American *Vogue* at the time rarely featured daring, avant-garde designers of the kind Issie loved and would go on to champion, and the dress code at the office was similarly conservative. The palette was predominantly grey and beige and the unofficial 'house designer' was Calvin Klein. While the American *Vogue* uniform was undoubtedly chic, it rocked no boats.

Then Issie came along. Anna says:

> People would stop by my office just so they could see what Issie was wearing that day. One morning she might be in full East Village punk regalia like she'd just stepped out of the Mudd Club, which she may well have done, the next dressed like a Maharaja, dripping in jewels and sari silks.

On one occasion, Issie wore an elaborate sari creation that unravelled as she exited the Condé Nast building on Madison Avenue. She didn't notice – or didn't care – and hopped into a cab, only to get the fabric caught in the door. The last anyone saw of Issie that day was a silk sari streaming in the tail wind from a yellow cab heading uptown.

Anna explains: 'There has never been a shortage of glamorous, stylish, well-connected young women working for *Vogue*. Issie undoubtedly brought all those qualities to the magazine too, but in her own utterly idiosyncratic way. And while her eccentricity and flamboyance made her stand out amongst all of the elegantly and quietly attired girls, she also needed them to be as discreetly chic as they were. Their presence only served to amplify Issie's every look, her every gesture.'

Anna was surprised to discover that, despite the extravagant outfits, Issie could actually type, thanks to the Ox and Cow, but from the outset it was clear that Issie had no time for anything humdrum, banal or mundane – to the extent that cleaning her desk every night was done with a bottle of mineral water and a few squirts of Chanel No. 5.

She'd often tie her hair up in a floral headband, like a fifties American housewife, while undertaking this task. It was all part of making her job an event. Says Anna:

> Issie elevated everything she did, no matter what it was. She could make the most boring or pedestrian task into something so fabulous – otherwise, for her, what was the point in doing it?

Issie put a different slant on this in later years, sighing nostalgically to friends and colleagues when editors of cash-strapped British publications balked at her extravagant budgets: 'At American *Vogue,* we had so much money we used to clean the desks with Perrier.'

Anna found that, despite her other qualities, Issie was not a great administrator.

> For all of her voluble, excitable personality, Issie had a strong work ethic – for some things, at least. Ostensibly, she was my assistant. But while she would fully engage with whatever interested her – going on appointments, arranging shoots, producing thick and exhaustive dossiers of research for a sitting I was working on – she'd studiously avoid doing anything she didn't like. My expenses, for instance: I'm probably still owed money by the company because she rarely, if ever, did them.

# ANNA

Not all the staff in the highly competitive world of American *Vogue*, however, appreciated the outrageous creativity of the new arrival. 'The American girls didn't know what to makes of Issie,' says Anna.

There was conflict with Anna's other assistant, who was climbing the greasy pole of fashion in a far more professional manner than Issie, and the two girls didn't get on. Anna, however, British-born herself, appreciated and understood Issie's Anglo attitude and sense of humour. Unsurprisingly, Anna came to value Issie for her creative output and the inspiration she provided.

> I've always believed it is important to have people around you who challenge your perspective on things, who can bring new ideas, new people, new talents. You don't get that by sitting behind your desk all day – or, for that matter, staying at home all the time. You need to be out there, looking, seeing, engaging with the world. Of course, Issie spent her entire time working for me doing just that. Unlike so many people, Issie wasn't frightened of the shock of the new; in fact, the more it shocked her, the more it captivated her imagination. Others might choose to run away in the opposite direction from it – Issie, on the other hand, not only ran straight towards it, she fully embraced it.

Anna took Issie's inspirations and discoveries seriously, which may have been another reason that some others in the office who played more by the rules liked her less.

> Every day Issie would leave *Vogue* and it was as if her working day was only really beginning. She'd come to the office the next morning, almost every morning, and I would hear her relate with a breathy excitement about the new artist, the new designer, the new photographer, the fabulous girl we absolutely must work with. And she had a habit of bringing them to the office, and letting them stick around, to the point we *did* end up working with them – or packed them back off to wherever they'd come from.

> One discovery she brought in was the painter Jean-Michel Basquiat. He was Andy Warhol's collaborator and turned up at the immaculate office wearing the paint-splattered, $1000 Armani suits he wore while

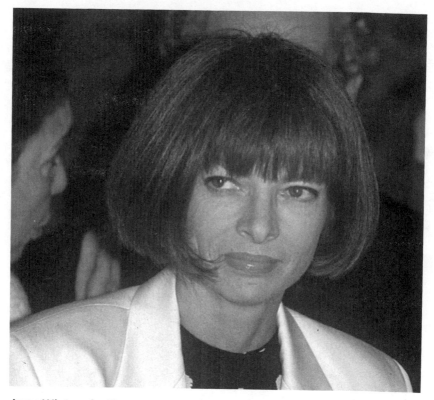

**Anna Wintour by the runway.**

working on his canvasses. Both Warhol and Basquiat ended up doing assignments for *Vogue* as a result of Issie's introductions.

Issie met Andy Warhol at a party where she was wearing a silver shoe and a purple shoe by Manolo Blahnik of the same style. Warhol came up to Issie and said, 'Gee you had to buy two pairs of shoes to get that look.' They became friends.

There is a photograph by Andy of Issie in a New York restaurant in a black satin blouse and dark puffball skirt with piratical earrings, taking a drag from a joint.

Issie was put off Basquiat by his heavy use of heroin, which she no longer touched, but she deeply admired the uncompromising nature of his artistic and creative vision and his disdain for the demands of the market. Issie said that both Andy Warhol and she were in love with Basquiat and they would all go together to eat at the Russian Tea Rooms on 57th Street. But one day Issie told Basquiat she hated his

Comme des Garcons duffle jacket – and he was so hurt by this criticism that he stopped seeing her.

The first story Anna let Issie work on was to style a photograph of a roast chicken for the food pages, but Anna gave Issie more assignments as time went on. She once asked Issie to go down to the Factory and talk to Andy Warhol about doing something for *Vogue*. Warhol agreed – and then, right in front of Issie, over the course of just a few hours, did a painting of the legendary *Vogue* editor Diana Vreeland. It was called *Diana Vreeland Rampant,* and was based on the portrait *Napoleon at the Saint-Bernard Pass* by David, replacing Napoleon on a rearing horse with Vreeland. The painting, which last changed hands in New York in 2008 for $42,000, was the centrepiece of a December 1984 story called 'Bridled Passion'.

# CHAPTER EIGHTEEN

## *André*

Shortly after Issie was hired, Anna made a second inspired hiring, recruiting André Leon Talley, a hard-working New York City fashion journalist, who would rise to become one of the most powerful African-American men in fashion.

Flamboyant, outrageous and with an extraordinary biography of his own, André, the grandson of a sharecropper, was immediately drawn to Issie, and recalls the first time he encountered her:

Isabella was seated at a typewriter in red chinoiserie, a Chinese dress with brocade and black gloves above the elbow. She was pecking at a typewriter. She really wasn't typing, but she was pretending to type. Isabella was not there to type letters. She was there to give an atmosphere. But the outfit was so extraordinary. I thought it was so glamorous. And we became fast and close bonded friends.

I remember one day while she was still in Anna Wintour's office, I didn't know her well, but she was known for her beautiful outfits and her eccentricities, and she was on the phone at 4.30 in the afternoon and she was whispering. She was saying, 'Darling, darling, are you in your jammies? You're still in your jammies? Go to make yourself a cup of tea. It's 4.30 in the afternoon.' And I said, 'Isabella, may I ask who on earth are you talking to?' 'My husband.' I said, 'Your husband?'

André was shocked to learn that Anna's blithe assistant was married. Nicholas, in the grip of one of his periodic bouts of depression, was struggling to get out of bed.

André and Issie were kindred spirits, and André would visit the Charles Street flat. It was while visiting Charles Street that he first met Rupert Everett, the actor. Issie had known Rupert since her teens in London, and he had suddenly struck the big time at home with his starring performance in the film adaptation of the play *Another Country*. But his fame was not translating across the Atlantic. André explains:

> He was very young and very beautiful. But Rupert was nervous that he wasn't getting the kind of press he should be getting. So we went back to Isabella's house [after an event]. And Rupert and Isabella jumped on the bed and we started talking. And Rupert said, 'I've got to get publicity. This isn't working. What else should I do? I think I should go around in tattered clothes and look more like those SoHo downtown artists – like I've just slept in the same outfit for five days and not taken a bath and been smoking joints.

As André and Issie became closer, it became increasingly apparent that they had similar ideas about what constituted great fashion. Recalls André:

> One day, maybe nine months into my first year at *Vogue*, Isabella came up to me. She said, 'Darling, darling, I've decided I have to come and work for you.' So she moved her office from Anna Wintour's office into my office and became my assistant and it was a wonderful time.

Through Andy Warhol, Issie had met his business manager, the elegant and suave Texan Fred Hughes, who at one time had been engaged to her friend Natasha Grenfell and lived up on the east 90s. André Leon Talley remembers that, 'Issie was always at Fred Hughes's house. He was one of the great, great catalysts.'

Fred Hughes ran Warhol's studio and found wealthy people to commission Andy to do their portraits – a very lucrative source of income for Warhol. Issie admired Fred and Andy's trick of imbuing wealthy sitters with glamour in return for a fat fee. It was a skill that Issie would later copy, asking wealthy people to invest in the creativity of her fashion and fine-art protégés.

Andy was a voyeur and took Issie around to the apartment of a successful actress to watch her masturbate with a vibrator. Andy softly suggested to Issie that she might like to put on a performance herself. Issie declined. She was beginning to tone down her exhibitionism – she was even flashing her breasts less – and wanking for Warhol was not her idea of art.

# CHAPTER
# NINETEEN

## *Divorce*

Eventually Issie told Nicholas that she could not go on living with his depression.

Although Issie was later to suffer from and be formally diagnosed with chronic manic depression herself, which played a huge part in the troubles she was later to endure, she did not at this stage in her life identify herself as a sufferer of the condition. It is clear in retrospect, however, that manic depression was with her from an early age. Nudity and sexual disinhibition – as in her stripteases – for example, are classic symptom of mania. Matters were further complicated because it was when Issie was in a manic phase – fizzing with energy, working day and night on a new project – that she was most inspired and did her best work. But hanging over her was the horrible knowledge of what would come next – another crashing low.

Nicholas said, 'OK, let's get divorced, but you will have to pay for it.' He picked up the Yellow Pages and found a divorce lawyer.

Nicholas packed his clothes and returned to England. Ross & Matza, the lawyers Nicholas found, of 29 John Street, New York, acted for Isabella. On 18 June 1985 at the Courthouse at 60 Centre Street, New York, Isabella was granted a divorce by the Hon. Thomas J. Hughes, a Justice of the Supreme Court, on the grounds of constructive abandonment for a period of one or more years.

The Judge ordered that Isabella was authorised to resume her maiden name Isabella Delves Broughton.

The background to all this was that Isabella had fallen in love with a Scots aristocrat named Colin Emlyn, heir to the Thaneship of Cawdor, the anachronistic title made famous by Shakespeare in *Macbeth*.

Alex Cohane remembers:

Issie was absolutely obsessed and bewitched by Colin. Colin was studying architecture in New York and had a Spanish girlfriend Ana Corbero, who studied art in Philadelphia during the week – returning at the weekend to New York City. This allowed Issie to pursue Colin during the week.

In secret, Issie once commissioned a shooting suit made from Cawdor Campbell tartan.

In 1986, with her obsessive love for Colin going nowhere, Isabella started to think about leaving America and returning to England. The money from the legacy was all spent now anyway – and she was afraid again of homelessness as she had had to sell Charles Street to pay her debts.

Events were precipitated by a bounced cheque to Manolo Blahnik. André recalls what happened:

One day Isabella said to me, 'I've got to go away to a hunt in Scotland. I've had this wonderful shooting suit made in beautiful tweed' – with Isabella it always began with the clothes – and she described the tweeds and said, 'You know it's just the most beautiful jacket, a beautiful hunting jacket with an hour glass shape, with a tweed skirt and it's perfect. And I'm going off to a shooting party. I just need to be away for a week. Do you think it's okay?'

I said, 'Of course, Isabella. You must go to this party.' 'Darling, I'm going to go to Manolo to get tons of shoes.' And then Manolo Blahnik, well, the owner of the business, in fact, George Malkemus, he called me and said, 'Darling ... Isabella's check bounced for all the shoes!'

So two weeks later Isabella comes back and I said, 'Isabella, we never heard from you. It's been two weeks. You've been away for two weeks. What were you thinking?'

# DIVORCE

She burst into tears. And I felt so bad but I said: 'Isabella, I can't have you work for me. You didn't even respect me enough to say where you were. Two weeks later you were still somewhere in England on a pheasant shoot. I didn't know where you were. You never called.'

I didn't say, 'You're fired ...' like Donald Trump, but I did let her know that this was not going to work. And I wasn't being mean to her, but I just thought, 'You can't just go away for two weeks, and then come back and say, "Darling, I've had a wonderful time."' But then in the end you could if you're Isabella Blow, because you were doing your things your way.

There was a big row. She broke into tears. Then she decided she was going to go back to England anyway. Anna gave her a going-away party and she wore a Gaultier suit she loved, a fitted navy blue suit with the back cut out like a halter dress, but the front was a very serious business suit.

And then she did move back to England and then the next thing I know – I haven't heard from her in a long time – I wake up one day and read this most extraordinary article in the *New York Times* that Amy Spindler had written about how Isabella Blow was responsible for discovering Alexander McQueen!

# CHAPTER TWENTY

## Tatler

I ssie may have been fired by André, but it is as much testament to the esteem in which he held her as it is evidence of the idiosyncratic rules of the fashion business that he nonetheless recommended her for a job to his friend Michael Roberts, fashion director at *Tatler* in the United Kingdom.

The timing was fortuitous. Michael's assistant, Charlotte Pilcher – Char – had expressed a desire to go travelling for a couple of months, and, as Michael recalls, 'I was needing someone.'

And so it was that one day in 1986 Issie turned up for her first day at work at the offices of *Tatler* in Hanover Square, London, 'looking extraordinary, as she always did'.

During her first few days at *Tatler,* Michael recalls, he was asked to draw her picture for the magazine, which favoured caricature bylines. It was early in the morning, but the hour meant little to Issie. Says Michael:

> She was wearing a feather cocktail hat, a very short pouffe cocktail dress, and a pair of very worn-down Manolos. She'd had a very bad time on the bus, and complained passengers on the bus had been staring at her.

*Tatler,* first published in 1709, is a society magazine that is, as its title implies, overweight on tittle-tattle and gossip. Evelyn, when he heard about his daughter's new job, shuddered that *Tatler* was 'a magazine for drug dealers'.

In truth, *Tatler* was, and remains, a product primarily of interest to privately educated upper-middle-class and upper-class families, but Evelyn's criticism was perversely perceptive. *Tatler* was changing. It was not becoming particularly democratic – blue blood still coursed through its veins – but it was honing a more mischievous voice that persists alongside the sense of entitlement to this day.

This subtle shift was largely thanks to its visionary and discerning editor, Mark Boxer, who had made *Tatler* a crucible for emerging talent. The cast of characters included many names who would come to dominate British journalism over the next two decades: Alex Shulman (current editor of British *Vogue*) and the critics Jonathan Meades and Craig Brown were all on the masthead. Michael Roberts would go on to some of the biggest – and most cerebral – jobs in fashion media, becoming fashion editor first at the *New Yorker,* then at *Vanity Fair* in America.

Mark Boxer believed talent could flourish anywhere, and when a glimpse of it was spotted it was pounced on. Char recalls that Mark 'actively encouraged work-experience people to write pieces'.

*Tatler's* stock-in-trade was wry commentary on the rapidly changing social landscape of Thatcherite England. The magazine was particularly up on the shifting demographic movements of London neighbourhoods. The rich 'trustafarian' bohemians of Notting Hill Gate sneered at Peter Yorke's 'Sloane Rangers', the Sloanes sneered at the 'loadsamoney' City 'yuppies' (young urban professionals) – and *Tatler* sneered at and satirised them all, in a way they all quite enjoyed.

Thanks in large part to Boxer, Michael Roberts and Alex Shulman, however, *Tatler* did take fashion and art seriously. This made Issie a natural fit for the magazine, as André had perceived. *Tatler* stole a march on its rivals by being the first mainstream publication to spot the importance of the emerging artistic movement that was beginning to establish itself in the empty industrial buildings and squats in the East End and which would eventually become the YBAs (Young British Artists), taken up and made famous by Charles Saatchi and Jay Jopling in the 1990s.

Issie, who was firmly a West End girl, was not sure how to behave out east. Taken to a café in Hackney Wick by the photographer Alastair

Thain, she asked, 'Do I leave a tip?' If she wanted to leave 20p, Thain replied, that would probably suffice.

Once again, however, it was quickly observed that Issie was not cut out for administration. Shortly after Issie arrived in the assistant role, Char left to go travelling for three months as planned, and Michael told her to get in touch with him when she returned to England:

> When I did call, there was a sense of relief in his voice saying, 'Do you want to pick up where you left off?' Michael adored Issie, but the fashion room was too small to accommodate two such large personalities. Mark Boxer, quite rightly, saw what she brought to the swinging *Tatler* party in the 1980s and gave her control of four pages a month. So everybody was happy.

Michael was to be a massive influence on Issie's creative and professional life, and they remained very close friends for the next 21 years. She particularly admired Michael for his lack of interest in money. In the decade of conspicuous consumption, 'greed is good' and the City's 'big bang', Michael would leave his cheques uncashed in a

MY JOB.

cooks well, m...... ....... .....and lists his hobbies as 'worrying about money and trying to achieve Sybaritism on a budget'.

**Isabella Broughton** (left), when asked at dinner parties what she does at *Tatler*, is apt to reply through a veil of ostrich feathers and a lipstick slick: 'I do historical research, I find unbalanced people, I choose photographers and places to shoot them.' Designer: Balenciaga. Period: Middle Ages. Tip: always accentuate the head and feet.

**Alastair Thain** lives to photograph artists in moody black and white. When they are camera-shy he sometimes makes do with their offspring. His portrait of 'Stash' de Rola – son of Balthus – is yet another triumph in the life Thain describes as 'a regular self-assessment with themes ranging from sex to death'.

**Issie's handwritten label on a profile piece about her job at *Tatler*.**

drawer, and lived in a room provided by the cigar-smoking fashion designer and entrepreneur Joseph Ettedgui. Later, Michael recalls, as he climbed the fashion ladder, Issie would furiously berate him for 'selling out' when he knocked back her less-publishable ideas.

# CHAPTER
# TWENTY-ONE

## *Independence*

Issie was 26 when she was given the job title Associate Style Editor and four pages of her own to commission and shoot each month. Creatively they were a huge success, but she was often at war with the 'suits'. When Issie complained to Michael about the problems of working with editors, Michael told her, 'Issie, you just listen to them and say "Yes, yes, yes" – and then go off and do your own thing.'

Unfortunately for Issie, doing her own thing usually meant spending vast amounts of her own money on shoots, money which she would then struggle to get back off the company. Her very first story, 'Place Your Pets', was a case in point. Inspired directly by her beloved grandmother Vera Broughton, the shoot featured her cousin Laura Mackay (sister of Aeneas) with a monkey, a 13-year-old Mexican tarantula and a parakeet. She knew it was easier to get forgiveness than permission, so she paid for all the 'pets' on her credit card. Mark subsequently wanted Issie to reshoot the photographs and Mary Killen found Issie crying, as she had to pay for the hire of the pets again.

After some grumbling from accounts, the expenses were usually repaid. As Rebecca Fraser, who had the desk next to her, recalls, 'She had frequent meetings with the Managing Editor Chris Garrett about

**PLACE YOUR**
# PETS

A nation of animal-lovers poses for
**ALASTAIR THAIN.**
Styled by Isabella Broughton. Text by Kate Bernard

'Delilah is a spider of simple tastes,' declares **Joanna Heyworth** of her thirteen-year-old Mexican tarantula. She is often found in her favourite restaurants with the poisonous beauty perched on her shoulder 'to spy out potential prey'. In order to keep Delilah in cockroaches Miss Heyworth spends her days slaving for Sir Humphry Wakefield's reproduction furniture business in Kensington. Twenty-three-year-old **Rosie Cornwallis**, daughter of Lord Cornwallis, cares little for parakeets, despite her close relationship with Isabella (above). As a child, her parents showered her with exotic chickens, so parakeets seem 'rather standard'. Isabella lives like a Regency belle in a cage made by her mistress who works for Scott Crolla – he shares her interest in birds.

**Lady Fisher** has a reputation for being animal crackers. She is pictured above with her pet marmosets: Dandelion and her children Peanut, Cap and Jumper. Lord and Lady Fisher have been running their wildlife park since 1973. Some of her other pets have been two jaguars, and a spider monkey that slept in silk sheets and shopped at Harrods. 'I always keep my favourites in the house until they start biting my husband.' **Laura McKay** has always had a passion for monkeys, which has been handed down through generations of Broughton women. 'My great-grandmother kept gibbons for years, and was famous for her fierce ostrich.' Pictured with Valentino, Laura seeks a career in the theatre and an enormous garden littered with apes.

117

**Issie's first story for *Tatler*, 'Place Your Pets'.**

her expenses bill.' However, 'Her charm and talent, indeed genius, meant no one could ever get really cross with her.'

Issie has the distinction of submitting the highest expenses claim in the history of Condé Nast for a single item, writing on the expenses form that she was claiming, 'Just £50,000 for a very small ruin which was really a must.' It went unpaid.

Issie's striking dress sense earned her attention on a national level – the *Sunday Times* ran a feature on Issie entitled 'Girl in a Brouha-bra' shortly after she returned to the UK – and her clothes were also a talking point in Vogue House, much as they had been in New York.

Issie was a natural fit for *Tatler* in 1986. As Char says, 'In the six years I was with Michael, nobody knew what sex anybody was in the smoky little fashion room that invariably had Tina Chow, Manolo Blahnik,

Ninivah Khomo, Rifat Ozbek and Robert Forest all lurking in the recesses amongst the androgyny and peroxide crew cuts of the various second, third and fourth assistants.'

But even in this mix, Issie, who usually wore evening clothes more appropriate to a cocktail party than work, stood out. The only time she ever wore trousers, she wore velvet knickerbockers. In particular, her ever more elaborate hats became famous. Once, she got into the lift with Nicholas Coleridge, the Managing Director of Condé Nast in Britain, and inadvertently trapped him in a corner of the elevator with the horns of one of her headdresses.

Issie rediscovered her exhibitionist side in London. Issie, Char and another *Tatler* colleague Gabe Doppelt all lived in the same area in Chelsea. The three girls often shared a cab home to catch up on the daily gossip.

The feature The *Sunday Times* ran about Isabella shortly after she returned to the UK in 1986.

# INDEPENDENCE

The rides could be eventful, as Char recalls:

On one occasion, Gabe was the first out. She shrieked at us in
the cab, as it pulled away, lifting her top and bra and flashing
her perfect bosom, which was incredibly unlike her, but I think
Issie brought it all out in us.

Then, the next stop was Issie, and she got out and shrieked
at me – she was wearing an orangey-yellow, see-through
chiffon mini-crini skirt, and velvet signature-boned bustier
designed by Vivienne Westwood – and she lifted her crini in a
*Folies Bergère,* Can-Can sort of way, revealing that she was
wearing no knickers and flashing her bush. Finally the taxi
pulled into my destination. I got out to pay and the cabby said,
'Please, love, don't take all your clothes off.'

Issie also approved of wild behaviour in others. The photographer
Dan Lepard recalls:

The night before I was to meet Issie I was carried out of The
Ritz completely drunk. I arrived to see her at Vogue House with
a bad hangover and sick in my hair. Issie told me, 'On that basis
alone I will work with you.'

# CHAPTER
# TWENTY-TWO

## *Andy*

In 1986 Andy Warhol came to London and took Isabella to see a Jeff Koons exhibition at the Anthony d'Offay gallery. There is a photograph of them together – a hatless Issie with dangling earrings and a happy smile, and Andy looking on like a proud father.

During this visit her half-Bolivian friend Simon Ortiz-Patino remembered an evening with Issie and Warhol. He had been told by 'an intermediary' to meet Issie at 'a particularly obscure Chinese restaurant off the Earls Court Road', but when he arrived Issie was not there.

I proceeded to my designated table, where I sat next to Alana Hamilton, Rod Stewart's previous wife, who was the most statuesque of creatures with long legs and long arms, and she looked on in amazement as this dark-haired foreign chap sat down at her left. I was gobsmacked to be sitting next to such a stunning women and was wondering what my purpose was.

All of a sudden I saw Issie's graceful hand come around the front entrance of the restaurant, signalling my attention to join her in the street outside. I did as I was told; and she pushed me into a cab and there, inside, was Andy Warhol. Next to him was a reporter from the *Today* magazine, a supplement of the

**Polaroids of Issie in her former office at Condé Nast, in her Bill Blass suit, before she went to Andy Warhol's memorial service at St Patrick's.**

*Daily Mail*, who was giving him an interview while the cab was heading full steam ahead. Andy Warhol, when asked a question by the journalist, would never answer the question. For instance, the young journalist would ask him, 'What do you think of the Queen?' and Andy would reply, 'I like her Corgis.'

Issie and Simon were reduced to helpless giggles by Andy's merciless teasing of the hapless writer. Eventually the cab pulled up at Café de Paris, where they bundled out and joined a large party of celebrities including Tina Turner. 'After a few hours, Andy vanished with some young effeminate man,' Simon recalls.

When Warhol died in 1987 Issie flew back to New York for his memorial service at St Patrick's Cathedral. Issie slept on Fred Hughes's sofa. For the service she wore a black-feathered hat and her Bill Blass two-piece black jacket and skirt. After the funeral, many of the mourners went to a Steve Rubell club, where Issie wrote in our photograph

**An Andy Warhol postcard, which Issie kept as a memento of his memorial. Her invitation to his memorial was hand delivered to the Condé Nast offices.**

album, there was 'Delicious food, champagne, silver balloons, and the Velvet Underground played'.

Issie found the party boring and staid for such an important Warhol moment – and, partly drunk, she proceeded to take her clothes off and do her striptease dance in front of Warhol's family and friends.

# CHAPTER
# TWENTY-THREE

## *Inspiration*

The ideas for Issie's stories came more from her own interests and heritage than from editorial meetings. One writer she was excited about at that time was Mervyn Peake, author of the Gothic trilogy *Titus Groan*, *Gormenghast* and *Titus Alone*, which describe the life of Titus Groan, the son of the 77th Earl and Countess of Gormenghast. His mother, the countess, has birds nesting on her shoulders.

On a visit to Germany with Alastair Thain, the pair went to some brothels in Mannheim because 'Issie was interested in researching the fashion of German prostitutes'.

But not all her influences were so pariah. 'Det,' she once told me, 'my secret source of inspiration is *Country Life* magazine.'

Issie's interests can clearly be seen in the stories she commissioned. 'Apparel of Fun' had girls coming out of dressing-up boxes, including her friend Lady Sophie Vane Tempest-Stewart, who wore her ancestor's nineteenth-century military uniforms; 'Femme Fatales' included my first cousin Catherine Blow, a painter, who was pushed over a cemetery wall for the shoot and wore a peacock blue Antony Price cocktail dress; 'Flower Girls' featured Isabel Bannerman, who lived in a baroque house in Chippenham and grew in her garden borders cabbages and roses, artichokes and rhubarb.

# INSPIRATION

Issie did have an enviable reputation for always getting the job done. Dan Lepard recalled:

> We went to do a shoot at Canterbury Cathedral. Initially we were not allowed to shoot. Issie said, 'I want to speak to whoever is in charge' and spoke to the Dean. 'I am from *Tatler* and I want to do a fashion shoot – which I am told is not possible. How much Dean? You must have a price?'

She pulled it off in return for a modest donation to the cathedral coffers. The resulting photographs, 'Under the Arches', are fantastic. Sophia Woolton is pictured in the Prior's Chair in the chapter house; Issie's young fashion assistant, the beautiful 17-year-old Sophie Thynne, is shown in the chantry chapel of Henry IV; and a local Kent girl, identified only as 'Audrey' and found by Issie on the day, is photographed in front of the one of the miracle windows of Canterbury Cathedral. Accompanying the photographs is a story by Jonathan Meades, which mentions the Black Prince, whose body lay in state in his black armour at Canterbury and whose sword and armour are still in the crypt. The story itself was a homage to the stone statue of the Black Prince at the castle at Doddington.

She once organised a shoot of crime writers to accompany a series of interviews. Rebecca Fraser recalls,

> She managed to coax these very distinguished Baronesses like P.D. James and Ruth Rendell into revealing a little bit of their more sinister authorial side in a series of striking gothic portraits. But you could not really have told from what she was doing what she was up to; it was all whispered collaborations, in an instinctively directorial way, with the photographer. She had an amazing ability to comprehend people's essential being in a flash.

The huffiness in her character remained. Michael Roberts recalls her 'imperiousness' and her assistant Sarah Hamilton says that Issie could be 'bossy and difficult to work with when she was in an artistic mood'. But, says, Sarah, her generosity of spirit flourished too:

> Issie was always trying to help people. She had me moonlighting, working to help Benjie Fraser rent Eilean Aigas.

Eilean Aigas was a 60-acre island 'dropped' in the fast-flowing river Beauly in the Highlands of Scotland, which Issie's cousin Benjie had inherited from his father Sir Hugh Fraser. As a politician, Sir Hugh had little money. The island's lodge had been saved in the 1960s by the commercial success of the biography *Mary Queen of Scots* by Benjie's mother, Lady Antonia Fraser.

The house required substantial repairs and Benjie, encouraged by Issie, set about renting it out to her friends:

> These friends included Grace Coddington [fashion director of American *Vogue*], and the Ferrys. I was always included as the paid host. Perfection if you're a broke laird. Eilean Aigas reached a new height and Issie re-introduced the Highlands to the outside world by these means.

On one occasion Issie rented the island herself, and invited some of the people who had helped her in London. She dressed up her friends in Fraser kilts she had had made, and took them over for tea to uncle Shimi and aunt Rosie at Balblair. Lovat walked out of the house and was obviously angry. Issie followed him into the garden and asked him what was wrong.

'Issie, I may have made over my estates to Simon but I am still head of the clan. No one has the right to wear my tartan without my permission.'

Issie, thinking quickly, replied, 'Uncle Shimi, Benjie is renting out the tartan to help pay for Eilean Aigas.'

The 'renting' of the tartan by Benjie was completely untrue, but Uncle Shimi was at least somewhat mollified by this reply and returned to the house to meet Isabella's friends for tea. Ever after when I met him, the first thing Uncle Shimi would crossly ask me was whether Benjie was still renting out the family tartan.

There was undoubtedly some chaos in Issie's life, but things were going well for her. One Saturday morning in September 1988, she set off with Benjie and – as luck would have it – my sister Selina, to the wedding of her friend Emma Roper-Curzon in Salisbury Cathedral.

# CHAPTER TWENTY-FOUR

## *Meeting Issie*

I was there too, and Emma's wedding was the first time I ever met Issie.

Emma was my sister Selina's best friend. She gilded furniture for a living in a studio in London off the Pimlico Road. Robert Murphy was also well connected, so although there were only about 200 guests, it was nonetheless a society wedding of sorts.

I went to the wedding with my younger brother Amaury (pronounced Aimerry), driving for three hours from Hilles, our family house in Gloucestershire, through narrow winding country roads. We found a place to park outside the cathedral and rushed across Cathedral Close to get there in time for the service. We entered the cathedral and sat down in an empty pew at the back of the congregation in the nave. I was quite exhausted by the journey and relieved that we had made it in time.

Salisbury Cathedral is part-Norman and very beautiful, Gothic in places where it was rebuilt in the fourteenth century, with a 404-foot spire soaring into the skyline like a wimple. To the south and east sides of the cathedral lie the green pastures of the Bishop's Grounds, almost unchanged since they were painted by John Constable in the 1820s, and to the west the quietly flowing river Avon.

My invitation to Emma and Robert Murphy's wedding, 24 September 1988. The wedding at which Isabella and I met.

It felt ancient, religious, theatrical, ultra-romantic – and the perfect place to meet somebody special.

As we stood to sing the first hymn, Issie walked into the cathedral. I was dumbstruck by her appearance – but then again, I imagine everybody in the whole cathedral was. She was wearing an enormous hat festooned with giant black ostrich feathers, bright-red lipstick and a purple Katherine Hamnett coat dress. She came in with her cousin Benjie Fraser and my sister Selina. Selina had done a photoshoot styled by Issie the day before for *Tatler* magazine – it featured Selina sitting on an old-fashioned push-bike surrounded by Christmas presents. Issie, was always very keen on putting people together, and she also wanted an escort for the wedding, so she phoned Benjie and told him, 'I've got this great girl for you to meet and I've got a free Condé Nast town car left over from the shoot. Come to this wedding in Salisbury Cathedral.'

Issie and Selina swept straight past us on the way in, because my sister wouldn't acknowledge Amaury and me. I was slightly hurt but not surprised. We were in the midst of one of our many family arguments at the time, and Selina has a very possessive streak. She never wanted me to meet any of 'her' friends, but as they made their way down the aisle, I did catch a closer glimpse of Issie.

She had extraordinary eyes. They were quite shockingly blue. I also thought that Issie looked rather pale and sallow, as if she were ill, like a heroin junkie. But she was very sexy as well, with a great bust and a petite figure that gave her a delicate, rather fragile air, like a little song bird. From the extraordinary way she was dressed, and the cautious way she carried herself, I suspected she was rather highly strung.

Although Amaury and I were sitting about four pews behind Isabella and Selina, and on the other side of the church near the back of the cathedral, I noticed that Issie talked to Benjie throughout the service, which amused and rather shocked me. The fantastical ostrich feathers were sticking up above everyone else's heads and hats, amplifying her every movement. I could not take my eyes off her.

As I watched Isabella chattering away excitedly to Benjie, I tried to work out who she was. Sometimes it can seem like the English upper classes – even hillbillies like the Blows – are all known to each other and connected in some way. That was certainly true in the case of Isabella and I. Although we had never met, Issie and I knew each other's names because my sister Selina was having a relationship and was very much in love with Nicholas Taylor, Issie's first husband.

I had heard from Selina about Isabella, this extraordinary woman who had once been Nicholas's wife. Issie, I heard from Selina, was extravagant, exciting, capable and, my sister hinted, a bit cruel. She was also the granddaughter of Sir Jock Delves Broughton and I had read *White Mischief* when staying at a girlfriend's house that summer while studying for my bar exams.

While we sang the first hymn, I recalled that I had found Fox's story about Isabella's grandfather intriguing. Here was a man who on the surface had it all but managed to lose everything; in just over 20 years, he managed to squander over £70 million in today's money. And then to be tried for murder and to ultimately commit suicide! One could easily imagine the anguish and despair of his descendants.

**The moment that Isabella and I met for the first time, at Emma and Robert Murphy's wedding.**

Issie's father, Evelyn, was also quite well known, of course, because he only had one leg.

After the marriage, we all filed outside and people were greeting and talking happily to each other as one does at a wedding. It was an early autumn day, not raining but cool, and the leaves were still on the trees. I was wearing my Sri Lankan grandfather's ambassador's coat, a knee-length black *sherwanee*. It is a striking article of clothing, with gold buttons emblazoned with the Lion of Sinahla and gold leaves embroidered on the collar. My grandfather had worn it in the Elysée Palace for the ceremonial receptions of presidents de Gaulle and Pompidou. It had a reputation as a lady-killer coat, and I always wear it at weddings and funerals out of respect for the occasion. It is elegant and graceful, and in England it makes something of a statement about my exotic ancestry.

The coat also made me feel confident and although I am by nature shy I went straight up to Isabella and said, 'I love your hat.'

She said, 'I like your coat. I wish I was wearing my violet shoes for you, but it's rather muddy, and I left them in the car.'

# CHAPTER TWENTY-FIVE

## *Falling in Love*

The moment that Issie opened her mouth, I was utterly captivated by her voice. It was gentle, musical and mischievous. And she had such a striking look, a combination of that very pale face and bright red lipstick. She was clearly very theatrical, but I also thought she seemed quite insecure. I was pretty certain that Issie was quite a few years older than me – in fact, she was 29 and I was still just 24. But the age difference didn't bother me.

It was only later I would discover how very unlike Issie her restraint regarding her shoes really was. If Issie wanted to make a statement, I would learn, she would wear her stilettos in the mud and to hell with the consequences. Maybe that's why she was particularly sorry she had bowed to convention and wasn't wearing them this time.

We walked separately to the reception, in the garden of the Teynham home in Salisbury Close, but when I got there I was bored and lonely because I simply wasn't interested in speaking to anyone other than Isabella and she was surrounded by other guests. Everyone wanted to speak to her. I waited patiently for my slot. Eventually the opportunity arose and I was able to sit and talk to her.

In English society you are supposed to be discreet, and there is a convention that at such social gatherings one should talk about nothing very much – and certainly not about death. But Issie and I were quite the opposite.

In that first meeting I told her about the central trauma of my life; my father committing suicide when I was a boy.

My father, as I told Issie, went to the local farm shop and bought paraquat poison on the farm account. He came home, went into the kitchen and drank a pint of milk from the fridge to line his stomach, and then went into his gardening room to drink the poison. He went back inside his beloved house, Hilles, and walked through the ground-floor rooms – with their portraits of Stuart kings hanging from Elizabethan panelling on the walls, and floors of flagstones and polished elm boards covered by intricate William Morris carpets – bidding them farewell. Then he climbed the oak staircase and collapsed on his bedroom floor as the liquid burned out his insides.

His fists, I told Issie, were clenched in pain.

Amaury, my dark, curly-haired 12-year-old brother, was in the house at the time, and tried to give him the kiss of life. When the police arrived they had to drag him away from the body.

To this day neither my mother, brother, sister or I have fully recovered from this terrible event.

I was 14. I can still remember seeing the bill for the poison afterwards.

I told Issie how my mother then took off to Sri Lanka and abandoned us.

Issie told me how her parents had been hoping for a boy, and that she, their first born, as a girl, was the wrong sex.

'There's plenty of time for a boy,' Evelyn had brightly told the local paper in Cheshire when she was born. Their disappointment had then been made all the more intolerable by Johnny's death.

Despite the darkness in both our histories we were both also very lively, energetic people and there was a great deal of laughter in our conversation too. While I thought even then that Issie and I were going to have an enormous amount of fun together, there was a sense of foreboding as well.

I told her that we seemed like court jesters, and recounted the story of the poor court jester who, having ceased to amuse, was kicked to death. It was an unusual chat-up line.

Issie and I connected very quickly on the dark stuff. There was an immediate empathy because we had both suffered tragedy and hurt, and neither of us sought to hide that from the other. I wanted to be with her immediately, so I said, 'Come back to Gloucestershire with me after the wedding.'

'You're a cheeky boy,' she said and declined my offer. 'I'm breaking up with my boyfriend,' she told me very dramatically.

Her boyfriend was a journalist called Tim Willis and she was meeting him that evening to go and watch the new Rolling Stones movie *Cocksucker Blues* (which was never actually released). But she was quite amused by me, and despite the intensity of some of our conversation we had actually spent the rest of our time at the wedding laughing and drinking and flirting, so I was bold enough to ask for her number. She gave me her number at *Tatler,* which I could easily have found anyway, but that was a little touch which struck me as very dignified and not overly keen. This was the time before mobiles, of course.

The extraordinary thing was that despite the brevity of our meeting, I knew that I had fallen in love with Isabella. Every time I thought of her my heart would race and I would fantasise about what I would say to her, or what I should have said to her. And when she saw Tim Willis that night she told him she was breaking up with him, and when he asked why, she just said, 'I've found someone else.' So she must have known too.

The break-up had a severe effect on Tim:

Issie and I had been together for a couple of years, and chucking each other every couple of months. It was my turn to be the chuckee – so at first, I didn't feel too bothered. But when I heard she was engaged, I felt I'd made a big mistake. Suddenly, I missed her terribly. I think I was in slight shock. I'd assumed that our soap opera would limp on for ages, and now the show was over. I sent a weekly armful of lilies to Maria St Just's house in Gerald Road, where Issie was staying. I was so distracted at work that the editor sent me to Australia, which seemed to help, as did getting a job in Scotland – and an encounter with Lady St Just. 'It's a *coup de foudre,*' she said. 'You'll never get her back. But don't stop sending the lilies. They make the house smell lovely.'

# CHAPTER TWENTY-SIX

## *Courtship*

On Monday, two days after the wedding, I called Issie for the first time and we arranged to have dinner on the Thursday at my family house in Elizabeth Street in Belgravia. Isabella first told me that she could not come for dinner as she was already booked to have dinner with her friend Geraldine Ogilvy, the eldest daughter of the press baron Lord Rothermere, who owned the *Daily Mail* and *Evening Standard* newspapers, but I pleaded with Isabella to come and she eventually agreed. This gave me a foretaste of things to come. It was never easy meeting up with Issie – even when you were married to her. Issie was always a busy girl.

In the intervening days, Issie did a bit of research about me. A great friend of hers, Nadia La Valle, had a shop on Beauchamp Place called Spaghetti, a fun place where Isabella used to go and smoke and talk about her problems and order clothes on account. Nadia and her husband Suomi knew the Blows because she had rented Kimsbury Farmhouse on the estate at Hilles for years. Nadia said to her, about Amaury and me, in her strong Milanese accent, 'Issie they are like characters from D.H. Lawrence, these brothers, they wrestle naked in front of the fire.'

This was true.

# COURTSHIP

Isabella arrived for dinner that night in a short silver lamé mini-skirt, silver stilettoes, a purple top and a silver bandana around her head – and then dramatically announced: 'I can't stay. I've got to go to dinner with Geraldine [Harmsworth].'

'Oh please stay, Issie darling,' I said. I was standing there in a starched cooking apron over some especially flamboyant articles of clothing, which I thought was quite a cool, ironic look. 'I have marinated this lamb in honey and apricots especially for you,' I said, and she relented.

For dinner I had invited my beautiful first cousin Catherine Blow, who was a painter. Catherine knew Isabella because it was she who had been pushed over the cemetery wall for the photograph in *Tatler*.

She had brought as her date Anthony Belmont, a children's illustrator. Ant's sister had been at Heathfield with Isabella. His father had been called 'Boss Belmont' and had been the head of Cazenove, the stockbroker. He flew around in a helicopter in the 1970s and was a friend of President Nixon's. Ant's mother was a Tate sugar heiress.

I was going out with a handsome blonde artist called Kate, who drank in the Chelsea Arts Club and was in her mid-40s. She was permanently furious with her teenage daughter who was going out with an unsuitable man. Kate lived in Cirencester (about 15 miles from Hilles) in a rambling farmhouse with a charming large bearded man who had the biggest market garden in the Midlands in Nottingham. Kate was a fantastic cook and she made a fruit salad to have after my lamb.

The house on Elizabeth Street was built in the 1830s and had once been a doctor's house and surgery. Elizabeth Street was the high street of Belgravia, with shops including a delicatessen, a good greengrocer and a good wine merchant, all of which was useful for entertaining and made it an ideal place to live. The house had been found by my late ex-stepfather Rajah Ratna Gopal, a Sri Lankan Tamil businessman whom my mother Helga had married in Las Vegas in 1979 at the Little Church of the West. The house was structurally fragile, but my mother had made it into a very elegant space. She had created one large drawing room on the first floor, which she painted a black-blue colour with the cornices in gold, and installed a grey marble fireplace that she had bought in Bath, a cream carpet and an opulent nineteenth-century Chinese golden drinks cabinet on a baroque-style base. The room had two long windows looking on to Chester Square, with dark blue and gold Fortuny blinds.

But this evening we sat down to dinner in the pillar-box-red basement dining room below.

I can still picture the scene. Isabella talked throughout dinner about Tim Willis, who divided opinion violently; Ant thought he was wonderful and my cousin Catherine thought he was 'a jerk'. Kate, my girlfriend, didn't join in the conversation at all, but just sat there staring daggers at Isabella.

After dinner Isabella went up to the drawing room on the first floor to call Geraldine, whose dinner she had cancelled to arrange to meet up.

I was in quite a state. Hearing from Isabella about Tim Willis made me very jealous, and I followed Isabella into the room. I kicked the door shut and wedged it closed with a huge marble cannon ball stolen from Brompton Oratory and left as a house gift by some junkie friends of mine. She was standing by the long windows, next to an eighteenth-century chair with a high back. She was on phone, walking around holding the handset and dialling, and I just grabbed her and declared, 'I can't stand you talking about your ex-boyfriend – I am in love with you!' I flung myself on her and kissed her to make sure that she understood.

Isabella wriggled out of my grasp and shouted, 'Get off you silly Sri Lanki!' and then got on with her call to Geraldine while I just stood there feeling that at least I had made my point. I knew she had enjoyed the flamboyance and passion of my lunge.

Meanwhile, downstairs, my sister had turned up and joined the party. So then Selina, Isabella, Kate and I piled into my white Fiat Panda, which Issie instantly christened 'the bread bin', and I drove to Geraldine's house off the New King's Road. Inside there were not enough chairs around the dining table and I asked Kate if she would mind if Isabella sat on my lap. She did – but I didn't care any more what she thought.

I was in love with Isabella.

We dropped Isabella off on the Fulham Road that night, and from there she caught a taxi to stay the night with Lucy Ferry. Back at Elizabeth Street, Kate went mad, slamming doors and storming around the house. Selina and I stayed together in our mother's bedroom like small children cowering away from the angry adult. In the morning, Kate left – and I never saw her again.

# CHAPTER TWENTY-SEVEN

## *Engagement*

I was more convinced than ever that Issie was the one. So the follow-ing weekend I invited her to stay at Hilles with Catherine and her boyfriend, the art dealer James Birch.

James recalls, 'Issie plied us with questions on the train.' As well as other details, such as whether or not I was gay, she wanted to know at which party they had last seen me.

I collected them from Stroud station and took them to Hilles and let them in by the North Hall door. Isabella put her suitcase down in the hall in front of a painting of Charles I hunting – a good copy by a pupil of Van Dyke – and, she told me later, thought to herself, 'I am not leav-ing here.' She saw the painting of Charles I as a sign that Hilles was where she belonged. She was much drawn towards the elegant and artistically inspired monarch, not least because they both shared the same birthday, 19 November.

That night I cooked moules marinières and brought steaming bowl-fuls into the candlelit Long Room, pulling out all the stops to impress Issie. I had set a huge log fire blazing in the grate and lit candles to draw attention to the massive 1680 Mortlake tapestries, depicting Raphael's *Acts of the Apostles,* commissioned for the entrance to the Sistine Chapel. The tapestries were acquired by my grandfather and the dimensions of the house had been specifically tailored to accommodate the tapestries – they take up one whole wall of the hall. The atmosphere was like a medieval banquet.

Hilles was very impressive illuminated by candlelight – but the place didn't bear closer scrutiny so well. The truth is that, back then, the house was in a very run-down state. My mother had abandoned it (along with her children) for Sri Lanka in the mid-1980s, and it was very dirty, because there was just one unreliable cleaner who turned up only occasionally or not at all. The cleanliness situation was not helped by my brother's deerhound, whose messes festered in revolting piles throughout the building – one good reason for us to fight naked in front of the fire. The roof was leaking, the house was freezing because the central heating had broken down, and in the kitchen – where the family lived – all the electrical appliances were wired up to extension cables, which lay on the floor like giant spaghetti.

But although managing and trying to maintain the place was a nightmare, Hilles remained a magical and romantic place to visitors. I had put Isabella in the best room, the Red Room, with a four-poster bed decorated with orange Byzantine Sanderson material from 1968, turquoise walls and a folding leather screen. I called into her room to check she was comfortable before bed – and she invited me to sit down.

We stayed up talking for the whole night.

As morning broke, I fell asleep with Isabella in the bed – but there was no kissing or any sexual contact.

In the morning, after a lazy breakfast, we watched Woody Allen's *Manhattan* in the kitchen, and then we all went for a walk. James Birch recalls:

> It was a wet and rainy English weekend and everybody insisted we went for a walk. I am not crazy about walks anyway, but instead of gumboots Issie made me wear a pair of red cowboy boots that were so tight and so uncomfortable I have never been for a walk in the countryside since.

Above Hilles in the Spoonbed valley which I loved so much, I asked Isabella, 'Do you like living in the country?'

My mother had told me that I needed to make sure whoever I married liked living in the country.

# ENGAGEMENT

She replied that she did, and told me more about her childhood on her father's estate in Cheshire.

'And what do you think of Hilles?' I asked her pointedly. I knew she would be quite at home in Gloucestershire.

'I think it looks like it could pay off my overdraft,' she said with a mischievous grin, and we headed for home. Issie wanted to go into Spoonbed Farmhouse, but I refused. It was almost derelict, having lain unoccupied since 1975 when the tenant farmer had died. I didn't know it then, but restoring Spoonbed was to be Issie's first big project on the estate.

That night the rest of the house party returned to London by train. I, however, stayed in Gloucestershire.

The next morning I called Isabella at work.

'Isabella, I am coming up to London tomorrow to get my hair cut,' I said, 'and I want to ask you something that I have never asked anyone else before. Can you come round to Elizabeth Street at 7 p.m.?'

Isabella knew what was coming and spoke to Rebecca Fraser at work. 'Rebecca,' she said, 'I think Delmar is going to ask me to marry him.'

On Tuesday afternoon I drove up to London in the bread bin with my brother Amaury. As we rattled down the M4 I told him that I was going to ask Isabella to marry me.

He went ballistic, shouting and screaming at me, 'You're fucking mad, you hardly know her, you're too young, you've only known her for two weeks, you fucking idiot.'

We got to London quite late. I parked in Elizabeth Street and went inside – Amaury went off on his own in a sulk somewhere.

Waiting for Isabella, I was extremely nervous. I had a bottle of red wine, so I opened it and had a couple of glasses to calm my nerves. Amaury might have thought I was an idiot, but that didn't bother me. I had never been more sure of anything in my life. I knew exactly what I was doing. Isabella was everything I wanted for a wife; she was clever, funny, sexy, sensitive, well connected, and I knew that she would connect with my brother and sister, and that my mother would be impressed by her sense of style.

Eventually the bell rang, and there was Issie, wearing a long velvet coat to her knees, fishnet stockings, Manolo Blahniks and a dress coat because she was going to a party afterwards at Leighton House in Holland Park.

She came in and we went up the stairs.

Then, before she could say anything, I said, 'I don't want to have an affair with you. I want to marry you.'

She just stopped, looked me in the eyes and said, 'Yes.'

And that was it. Off we went to the party and told everyone there. Catherine was furious; she said to Issie, 'I've been living with James for two years now and he hasn't asked me.'

That party was very much my first taste of Issie's world. It was an opening for Piers De Laszlo, an Old Harrovian society artist, and the crowd was a very camp, dramatic mix of actors, artists and high-fashion people. There was champagne, of course, and Issie was running around telling everyone, 'Detmar and I are getting married!'

I didn't have a ring, but Issie already had one picked out at her favourite jewellers, S.J. Phillips. It was a shield, a big diamond with six small diamonds around it, three on each side. It was made in 1760 as a mourning ring, which was typical of Issie's dark side. It cost £6000, which was a lot for my frugal existence, and I was a bit doubtful about it. My mother, though, said to me, 'If that is the ring she wants, she must have it.' I borrowed the money off Amaury, which just goes to show that even fucked-up families can do the right thing once in a while.

After the party we actually went our separate ways. Issie lived just round the corner from me anyway. Then the next day I had to rush back to Gloucestershire, as the family feud had erupted again. Like Vesuvius, it just does from time to time.

As I was running from my lawyers to Elizabeth Street to get the bread bin, in a dreadful panic, I met Issie on the street. She had just taken Maria St Just out to lunch, to celebrate her engagement, and she said, 'Hi, Det!'

I said, 'Hi, darling. I have to rush off to Gloucestershire. I'll see you when I get back.'

But the moment I was out of earshot, Maria said to Issie, '*Coup de foudre!* Don't let him out of your sight!'

A few minutes later, I was shocked when Issie appeared at Elizabeth Street with a suitcase.

'What are you doing?' I asked.

'I'm coming down to Gloucestershire with you,' she said, throwing her suitcase into the back of the car.

And she did. It was October 13. We had first met 20 days previously.

We would be together for the next 18 years.

# CHAPTER
# TWENTY-EIGHT

## *The Blows*

As Issie and I drove down to Hilles in the bread bin, I started to explain to Issie the bitter battle that I was involved in – trying to remove my mother and stepfather from the trust my father had set up in 1969 to save tax on his death.

My father had placed into trust the farms, cottages and 1100 acres of farmland. After living the legally required seven years to make the trust effective, he had felt free, in 1977, to kill himself.

My cousin Simon Blow has lately taken to airing the theory that my father killed himself because he had murdered his mother and was consumed by guilt, but the truth, I believe, is more prosaic. For the last three years of his life, my father had sunk into a deep depression, which he self-medicated with heavy drinking.

My father had gone to Eton and then to Balliol College, Oxford, in the late 1930s. At Balliol his contemporaries were the future prime minister Edward Heath and the leading politicians Roy Jenkins and Denis Healey. During World War II he had served in the Coldstream Guards in the Middle East and in Italy, and had ended up in Berlin as Aide-de-Campe to General Templer, head of the British zone of divided Germany. My father and Templer lived in one of the former homes of Hermann Goering.

# BLOW BY BLOW

My father told me that the best parties given by the Allies were the Russian ones, where vodka and caviar were served. The worst were the ones he had to arrange, because these, under the somewhat puritanical Labour government, consisted of tea and scones. My father, who spoke German, interrogated Hanna Reitsch, who obeyed Hitler's direct orders to fly the last German plane out of Berlin on 28 April 1945 as the city fell to the Russians.

My father had an elder brother, Purcell (Simon's father), who had died of Huntingdon's chorea in 1963 before my birth. My uncle was disinherited by his mother for being a drunk, ironically enough, and Hilles and the estate therefore went to my father.

After the war, my father got a job as a journalist with Kemsley newspapers, which then owned the *Sunday Times* and the now defunct *Daily Graphic*. My father's boss at the *Sunday Times* was Ian Fleming, the creator of James Bond. After three years of journalism, my father took a sabbatical to write a book on the Middle East called *Horns of Hattin*. But when Hilles burnt down in 1951 (it was rebuilt) he lost his manuscript, and his creative and mental decline set in.

In 1955 he stood unsuccessfully for Parliament, and from then on buried himself in farming and managing Hilles. In the 1960s he wanted to write a biography on Louis XVI and Marie Antoinette's only surviving child, the Duchesse D'Anglouême, but did not do so, terrified as he was of failure and mockery. He had been out of touch with the literary world for almost two decades and started to drink heavily to deal with his growing sense of inadequacy.

My beautiful mother Helga, 25 years younger than him, bravely and determinedly struggled to help him in his depression with the support of her parents, who came from Sri Lanka to live with her at Hilles.

He made, as far as I know, two unsuccessful suicide attempts over the course of his life. As a young man, he had put his head in a gas oven, and in the late 1960s he cut his wrists. With great difficulty my mother had managed to get my father to go for treatment in various hospitals in Gloucestershire and Northamptonshire, and to the Priory in London. I greatly admired my mother's courage and determination in refusing to give up hope of saving my father. The doctors explained to my mother and myself, a very adult 13-year-old, that, in spite of our love, pleading and tears, it was ultimately up to my father whether he was going to stop drinking and save himself.

After my father's suicide in 1977, my mother, aged 33 – lonely, depressed and exhausted – was desperate to rebuild her own life as quickly as she could. She was strikingly beautiful, enjoyed dressing dramatically, had a lively personality and an excellent sense of humour.

As a young girl in Ceylon in the 1950s, my uncle had sold photos of my mother to his lovesick friends in their hometown of Kandy, some of whom would get their drivers to collect them at school and drive past my grandparents' home to get a glimpse of my mother wandering in her garden. After attending boarding school in the Isle of Wight – which was believed in Sri Lanka to be warmer than the rest of England – my mother had been a model in London.

On his marriage, my father had been advised by a cousin to keep my young and beautiful mother 'pregnant and in the country'. By the time she was 21, my mother had produced three children. But she had lost touch with her own friends and was isolated at Hilles. Her life revolved completely around my father. After my father's death, her parents returned to Sri Lanka, and she was alone. She was not really interested in looking after us, her children, who were then 14, 12 and 11. My mother felt somewhat bitterly that she had wasted her twenties at Hilles, looking after my father and, to a lesser extent, their children.

The man she subsequently decided to marry was a Sri Lankan businessman friend of my grandparents called Rajah Ratna Gopal. In the 1950s, my Sri Lankan grandparents had tried to rent a flat in London and had been refused. The owner told them she was not renting it to 'coloured people'. So they, and most Sri Lankans visiting London during that time, stayed with Rajah in his rather squalid boarding house in Queensgate Gardens. As a result Rajah had prospered and had acquired three properties in good addresses in Hyde Park and Belgravia, which he soon let run down. It was into one of them in Eaton Terrace in Belgravia that we had moved in 1977, when my mother had left my father to try and frighten him into giving up drinking.

Initially my mother's marriage to Rajah at the Little Church of the West in Las Vegas in 1979 had been very exciting for us all. We had all flown to Los Angeles and driven across Death Valley, arriving at night at the famous neon city in the desert. We stayed at Caesars Palace and listened to Frank Sinatra. But things soon started to go wrong. My mother, in an attempt to 'keep' Rajah, involved him in the business affairs at Hilles. It was a disastrous decision. Soon my father's trustees resigned because my mother, who for a while was the trust administrator, had, under the advice of her new husband, refused to produce any accounts.

My mother and stepfather then installed themselves as trustees, just as agriculture was booming in the 1980s. My mother, still emotionally fragile after my father's death, was subject to a cruel campaign by my stepfather to undermine her and our self-confidence. He mocked us for having 'inherited wealth' while he himself was self-made. In order to try to please her new husband, my mother started to sign over to him chunks of trust capital and income to pay the deposit on my stepfather's property purchases in Cheltenham, Colombo and Menorca. When a farmhouse burnt down at Hilles, half the insurance money was paid into my stepfather's Swiss bank account.

As a young man, I wanted only to escape from the horrible life at home with this crooked, lunatic stepfather and to have some time for myself. Rather than challenge my mother and stepfather, I threw myself into the history degree I had started at the London School of Economics.

I had originally been keen to do a history of art degree in London but, out of a sense of filial duty, followed my father who had read history.

In 1985 I graduated from university. I spent a few days doing a book-keeping course at my mother's behest, as she thought I could do the family accounts when qualified. Then I started a law conversion course, at what is now the University of Westminster, to become a barrister, following in the footsteps of six generations of my family in Sri Lanka.

My heart was not in the law – I knew that I wanted to work in the art world – but my mother and grandfather had urged me to follow in the family tradition. There was an unspoken concern that creative careers were likely to lead to doom. My grandfather, though successful in many ways, had died a broken man, and my father had failed to prosper in his chosen career as a writer.

By early 1987 the trust finances were in a terrible state. No accounts had been produced since my mother's marriage in 1979. On 7 April 1987 I opened a letter from the Inland Revenue to my stepfather regarding the family trust, telling him that his 'promises of attention can no longer be regarded as satisfactory' followed by a demand for £55,000 in 10 days' time.

I knew I had to act. I went to see a solicitor in Cambridge, who wrote politely but firmly to my mother and stepfather that I wanted them to resign. If they would not do this in a spirit of co-operation, then I and my brother and sister would ask the court to protect our interests.

*Daily Telegraph*, 15 December 1986.

I carried on with my legal studies and passed the Bar exams in 1988, a couple of months before I met Isabella.

When Isabella had seen me in Elizabeth Street that afternoon, I was in an emotionally agitated state as my stepfather was delaying his resignation as trustee.

I told Issie, as we drove down to Hilles at high speed, to be wary of my mother. Issie was, I sensed, looking for a mother figure. My mother was glamorous and would love Issie's clothes and hats, but I warned Issie that she would not get what she was looking for from my mother.

Issie completely ignored my warnings, and within weeks began trying to sort out my mother's financial problems. My mother had been speculating in property in London and, just as the market crashed in 1987, borrowed £350,000 to buy a house in Pimlico. The house went to auction and did not sell. Isabella chatted up an interested bidder who offered £250,000. My mother would have lost £100,000 but she could have managed that.

Rajah told us that the neighbour was going to buy the house. Issie went round to see the neighbour who had just moved in. He knew nothing of my stepfather's story and told Isabella that he had no intention of buying my mother's house.

After more than a decade in which I had given my stepfather the benefit of the doubt, Issie had in one stroke revealed him to be a liar, a fantasist and a cheat.

I knew then that Issie was going to be the saviour of Hilles.

# CHAPTER
# TWENTY-NINE

## *A Church Wedding*

Our engagement was announced in the newspapers on 19 December, and we spent Christmas 1988, our first together, at Hilles. My mother was still in England because her marriage to Rajah was breaking down. She was full of good intentions on Christmas Eve and said she was going to cook Christmas lunch – but, in the end, she was unable to get out of bed because she was so severely depressed. Rajah had worked hard to break her nerve over the years and had finally succeeded. She was terrified of divorcing him.

In the end, Issie rustled up a fried English breakfast for Christmas lunch. It was, in a way, symbolic: Issie would now arrange Christmas and other important meals at Hilles; my mother's influence was waning and Issie was the stronger woman. Issie, as previously demonstrated, was the only one of us able to stand up to Rajah anyway.

Before this rather disgraceful Christmas lunch, we had been to church at Gloucester Cathedral.

After the service I had pointed out to Issie the famous Crécy window – the largest stained-glass window in the country, which depicts the coats of arms of the families of Gloucestershire who fought at the Battle of Crécy in 1346 during the Hundred Years' War against the French. Two of my grandmother's Tollemache ancestors

Our official engagement photograph, taken by the local photographer for the *Gloucester Citizen*. The caption read: 'I don't think they'll be dressed like that at the wedding.'

had fought in the battle, and it preceded by just a decade the Battle of Poitiers in which Isabella's ancestor John de Delves had distinguished himself.

Like Salisbury Cathedral, where Issie and I had met, Gloucester Cathedral was begun in the eleventh century by the Normans. The cathedral prospered in the fourteenth century when the abbot brought for burial the body of King Edward II, who had been murdered at nearby Berkeley Castle. The cathedral became a major pilgrimage site, and the alabaster effigy of the dead king has an exquisite ornamental canopy.

The plan to get married at Gloucester Cathedral was already forming in our minds. I had asked Issie about marrying at Broughton – Rona had suggested a marquee in front of Doddington Hall – but Issie did not want to return there. The place had at that time too many bitter memories.

Fortunately Issie was sufficiently impressed by Gloucester's medieval grandeur and agreed we could be married there.

There was only one problem. Issie had been married before. We were going to have to get a special dispensation if we wanted to fulfil Isabella's romantic vision of a traditional church wedding, steeped in the ritual and drama of religious ceremony.

In the new year, I wrote to the most senior churchman I knew, Eric Evans, who was the Dean of St Paul's Cathedral in London, asking for an audience to plead our case. He had been a friend of my father and had conducted his funeral at Gloucester Cathedral.

He agreed to see us, and Issie and I were invited to his home in Amen Court next to St Paul's in London. As we made our way to see him one bright afternoon in February, Issie worked herself into a state of righteous indignation. She told me that she knew 'exactly what to do' to get permission from the Dean to marry at Gloucester. Despite my pleading, she would not tell me what she planned. But when we got into the Dean's quarters, Issie looked him straight in the eyes and told him, 'Dean – the marriage was unconsummated.'

Inside, I was squirming with embarrassment, but I knew how much it meant to Issie, so I said nothing and stared straight ahead. After a long moment, the Dean, who had two daughters himself, solemnly replied, 'Isabella, on your conscience be it.' With that, he agreed to give us a full church wedding at Gloucester Cathedral.

Isabella was ecstatic. Her parents, however, were not so enthusiastic. Helen told us that as she had enjoyed only a blessing – since Evelyn had been married before – she did not see why Isabella and I should have a church marriage.

Such grumblings rumbled on for a few months. Things took a turn for the worse when we went to stay with Evelyn and Rona in Cheshire in May for the Chester Races.

The trip started happily enough. The May Festival at Chester, which takes place on the Thursday, Friday and Saturday of the first week in May, is traditionally regarded as a pre-Derby trial. The racing was excellent, and Evelyn was in top form, able to show off his extensive knowledge about horses. As we arrived at the racecourse on the Thursday, there was a man with a sandwich board telling people to repent of gambling and follow Jesus. Evelyn walked up to him, tapped him with his walking stick and jovially advised him, 'You won't have many takers here!' The prophet of doom took Evelyn's comments in good part.

Issie, who literally hung off her father's arm the whole day, wore a smart Katherine Hamnett dress coat and a hat adorned with so many feathers that her father said she had killed a cockerel. He had arranged for a cook to prepare a nice picnic for us to take to the races, and a good dinner when we returned.

On the Friday, we snuck back to Doddington before the last race, and Issie took me around the childhood haunts I had already heard so much about. She showed me the empty Hall, the church where poor dead Johnny was buried, the castle where she had played with her sisters, the two-acre walled kitchen garden and her father's farm buildings, where she had queued up to collect her wages with the other workers. Although the park had some evidence of its new owners – several large container lorries, and some unfortunate daffodil planting along the roads – it was still possible to feel what her Uncle Shimi had described as the 'land of milk and honey' in the 1930s. She could not face going to the ugly pink house where she had grown up and Johnny had died.

But on the last night of our stay, the Saturday, Evelyn got very drunk and told us that we were not going to get married in the cathedral and that Issie should be called Mrs Taylor on the invitation. It was something Helen had already raised – and I suspected she had pressurised Evelyn to say this.

I was very hurt, and shocked at the cruelty and thoughtlessness of her father. I went up to bed, deeply disturbed about the family I was marrying into. Issie stayed downstairs and calmly explained to Evelyn that in her divorce papers it stated, '... that it is further ORDERED, ADJUDGED AND DECREED that plaintiff is authorised to resume her maiden name, to wit Isabella Delves Broughton'. Issie had to send this document to both her parents before they would desist with their bizarre insistence she use the name Taylor on the wedding invitations. Uncle Shimi shook his head in disbelief when we recounted to him the story at his wife Rosie's house in Montpellier Street in London, opposite Harrods.

'The church has been very understanding to you, Isabella. I wish your parents would be the same.'

During the stay, Evelyn also became agitated about the cost of the wedding, for which he had agreed to pay.

I had heard about his legendary meanness from Issie and seen evidence of it myself when Issie and I met both her parents for dinner for the one and only time in our lives. Evelyn asked me to suggest a restaurant to go to. I suggested a Russian restaurant off the Fulham Road, which served caviar and vodka, called Nikita's. It was not, I confess, a particularly sensible choice, as it was in a basement and Evelyn had to climb gingerly down the stairs with his artificial leg. During the dinner, Issie had ordered a box of cigarettes which was put on her father's bill. When Evelyn came to pay, he scrutinised the bill and queried it. For a moment, I thought Issie was going to have to pay for the cigarettes herself. In the end, he grudgingly coughed up.

Evelyn flatly told us that he was going to give Issie £500 towards her dress and no more. Issie wanted a party after the reception – Evelyn refused. At one stage I was so frustrated that I told Rona, 'Look I have some cash from my father and I will pay for the wedding myself. I am finding it very hurtful and upsetting dealing with Evelyn.'

Rona was sympathetic and told me, 'Keep calm, he will come round in the end.'

Because of Evelyn's financial contribution to our wedding, Isabella's parents seemed to feel they had the right to be involved in every element of it – even our wedding list.

Isabella had put our wedding list at the fine china shop Thomas Goode's in South Audley Street, which was established in 1827. Isabella's grandparents had ordered in the 1920s many things from Goode's, including a china service, and Issie was determined that we should have our own china service, decorated with crests and mottos of her own design, her shield set on the Blow Coat of Arms which had been devised with the assistance of the College of Arms. It meant our guests

**London's living guide**
Feb 18-25 1998 No.1435 £1.80

# Time Out

Plus
**30-page**
**TV**
guide

## LONDON FASHION WEEK

# WILD THINGS

Behind the scenes with superstylist Isabella Blow,
wonderboy Tristan Webber, queen of the catwalk
Vivienne Westwood, and our supermodel supergrass!

**PLUS** Jerry Sadowitz • Neil Jordan
• The Wombles • **WIN** a £500 shopping spree

ISABELLA BLOW PHOTOGRAPHED BY GAVIN EVANS

08>

0049 391087

**p1** The *New Yorker*'s Mad Muse of Waterloo: Issie in an Alexander McQueen dress and Philip Treacy's 'Arrows of Love' hat. **Francoise-Marie Banier.**

**p2–3** Issie and Alexander in a shoot for *Vanity Fair*. Issie was often inspired by her beloved castle at Doddington. **David LaChapelle.**

**p4** *(top)* Detmar and Isabella in front of Hilles for *Vogue*'s 'Over the Hilles and Far Away' feature in 1992. **Oberto Gili.**

**p4** *(bottom)* 'When Philip met Isabella' exhibition, a collaboraton of work between Philip Treacy and Isabella Blow. **Design Museum, London.**

**p5** Issie on the cover of *Time Out*, February 1998. **Gavin Evans.**

**p6** In homage to his formaldehyde shark, Issie put Damien Hirst in a Perspex box for *Vogue*. **Lord Snowdon.**

**p7** Dressed as Joan of Arc for *Vanity Fair*, this was Issie's final shoot before her death. **Tim Walker.**

**p8** Issie's dark violet wedding dress was designed by Nadia La Valle and her medieval headdress was made by Philip Treacy. **Julian Broad.**

**Full credits p278**

could either buy us a teacup or a soup tureen, and spend as little or as much as they wished on a present.

Evelyn and Helen were furious, insisting that we went to Peter Jones like 'sensible' and 'normal' people.

We ignored them. We were not children.

Our friends were extremely generous and by our wedding day we had a full service for 20 – plates, bowls, side plates, coffee and tea sets, serving bowls and gravy dishes.

Isabella's relationship with her father was hard to follow. Sometimes they seemed like the best of friends, and he could be tender and loving, but at other times the relationship was unpleasantly formal. It was a confusing dichotomy.

For instance, Isabella could only go to see her father at Kensington Square when she had an appointment. Casually dropping in on him was not allowed.

Nor, she told me, was helping yourself to anything in the fridge acceptable. I put this to the test when I was let in by a maid one time; I wasn't hungry but I went straight to the kitchen and wolfed down a pork pie before going upstairs to the drawing room on the first floor and announcing what I had done to see what would happen. Sure enough there was a row. Over a pork pie!

Once we were invited to a drinks party at Kensington Square, which Rona organised to support her subsequent successful election to the council of Lloyd's of London. I asked Evelyn about the Lloyd's insurance market, which was at the time paying out huge claims in America for asbestosis and widely reported to be ruining many aristocratic families. In the good years, it had been an easy way for people with capital and little income to make large sums of money annually. However, members had to agree to 'unlimited liability'; if things went wrong, they would have to pay up everything they owned.

Evelyn told me, 'Only join if all your money is tied up and they can't get it.'

After the drinks there was a buffet dinner. Evelyn came up to me during the drinks and asked me whether Issie and I were doing anything for dinner afterwards. If we were not, would we like to stay for supper? The invitation was kindly meant, but I found it curious that a child had to be formally invited to eat in their father's house.

Another person who spoke to me at this party was a very successful property developer called Eric Hopton, who owned a string of properties in Chesham Place in Belgravia. He had known my father during the war because they had been stationed together in Salisbury. My father had arranged a great party – he had got all the nurses from the local hospital to attend, abandoning, so Hopton told me, their sick patients.

Hopton added, 'Be kind to Isabella. She has had a very hard life.'

Rona always demanded that Evelyn treat her daughters identically to his own. But he could on occasion break the rules. When Isabella came round to see him and he was alone, he would open a bottle of champagne for her – and tell her to take the empty bottle away with her as her stepmother would be upset and jealous if he did not do the same for her daughters. When Rona's youngest daughter married, Evelyn gave her a £1000 cheque. This was what he was meant to give Isabella, but he secretly gave her an extra £1000 – £2000 in total – telling her, 'You are my daughter.'

# CHAPTER THIRTY

## *The Restoration of Hilles*

As well as falling in love with me, Issie had fallen in love with Hilles, a troublesome love affair that was to last the rest of her life. The love was not always requited by my mother, who still, to this day, actually owns Hilles. In the first few months of our engagement, Issie set about what would be her life's work – restoring Hilles. Furniture was repaired, gutters untouched by human hand for decades were unblocked and long-neglected roofs were fixed – all paid for out of Issie's own money.

Hilles had not had such love – and financial resources – lavished on it for a generation. As my brother Amaury recalls:

> We'd spent our lives living frugally. Life at Hilles was one perpetual austerity drive. As children it had been impressed upon us that economy was the greatest of virtues. So Issie coming in on that was extraordinary. She was described to me by one of her friends as the most extravagant woman since Marie Antoinette. I remember I was working in the fields one day, and I looked up and saw two Harrods vans snaking their way down the lane. I'd never seen anything quite like it before.

# BLOW BY BLOW

The Harrods vans contained Issie's latest purchases for the house: a washing machine, dishwasher, fridge and cooker.

As well as physically fixing the place up, Issie began to inject life back into the four walls of Hilles by inviting interesting and exciting people down to stay at the weekends, which frequently stretched from Thursday to Monday. Says Amaury:

> Suddenly the house was full of glamorous people from every
> part of the world, and also with the most extraordinarily
> beautiful women. It was a fantasy, but, amazingly, it was real.

In March 1989, for example, we had Malcolm McLaren to stay. Issie and my sister Selina had been working with Malcolm, on a shoot in Norfolk at Elveden House for his new pop song called 'Something jumpin' in my shirt', about a girl who discovers her bosoms. The girl with the bosoms was the model Lisa Marie, who would later go out for a decade with Tim Burton and become a good friend to us and a supporter of Modern Art, the gallery that we set up in 1998. It was a memorable weekend: on the bank holiday, we had a meet of the Berkeley Hunt at Hilles. The riders and foot followers came for drinks before setting off on their hunt. There were also several hundred saboteurs running around, trying to disrupt the hunt.

Malcolm was in his element, loving all the anarchy. He told us that we would probably find a number of pop stars amongst the saboteurs. It was hard work for the saboteurs: Hilles is on a hill, and running up and down is exhausting work. Amaury and I joined in the anarchy. A good day was had by all – and no foxes were dispatched.

Isabella conspired to make much of her work for *Tatler* revolve around being down at Hilles. One story, 'Rags to Witches', was photo-graphed by Nitin Vadukal and featured a photograph of a guillotine made by my brother Amaury. It was the 200th anniversary of the French Revolution, and a ghostly head with a Marie Antoinette-style wig floated in the foreground, while my brother, dressed in a medieval helmet, held under his arms the rest of the body, which was an Antony Price dress.

There was another shoot on the Painswick golf course, all the girls dressed in Galliano. One photo is of Lavinia, Isabella's youngest sister, lying in a bunker with a golf ball in her mouth.

In April 1989, Issie commenced a thorough sartorial make-over for me. Apart from my grandfather's ambassador's coat, some saree brocaded waistcoats, a cloak of Detmar Blow's and some military trousers, I had a very limited wardrobe. The first person I went to see in London was Scott Crolla in his shop in Dover Street, where Issie ordered me some elegant trousers and we bought one of Scott's Sherwanees and some gothic ties. Scott was charming: intelligent, kind – and, oddly, straight. Jack Nicholson came into the shop while we there, but Scott stayed with us. I needed some decent suits and Issie took me to Demi Major in Dawes Road, Fulham, a brilliant tailor originally from the Ukraine. Issie told me that Demi had made the suits for The Who in the 1960s. I would spend many happy hours with Demi in the coming decades, and, now that he is dead, I go to his son.

For shirts, Issie bought me a dozen cream shirts from Hilditch and Key – my father had worn their shirts – which made sense as a barrister. For shoes she took me to Johnny Moke in the King's Road, and then bought me several pairs of brothel creepers with large platforms from a Manchester-based shop in Carnaby Street. For eau de cologne, she bought me oil from Truefitt and Hill. Later I would buy shirts and ties from Richard James, and when I became an art dealer I added Comme des Garcons, Junya Watanabe and Prada to my wardrobe, with some punk-inspired jackets and shirts from Brick Lane.

Issie began to deal with the financial problems at Hilles. A property on the estate called Bacchus House was sold to Mike Foster, CEO of Courage brewery. He was also a good friend of Lavinia's husband Douglas, a builder who now got on with the job of refurbishing the main house. By autumn 1989, Issie had rented out three houses, and commissioned Julian and Isabelle Bannerman to design a garden for the derelict walled garden at Spoonbed Farm.

# CHAPTER THIRTY-ONE

## *Philip*

While all this activity was going on, Issie was also preparing her outfit for our wedding. She had originally wanted her friend John Galliano to make her a dress in chain mail, but became anxious that our wedding on 18 November (the day before her 31st birthday) would clash with John's commitments to his own spring/summer catwalk shows and that he would not have the time. Instead she asked Nadia La Valle. The dress was a dark violet and there was a necklace embroidered with faux stones made in India and based on a Moghul design. The dress and the colours were to match Gloucester Cathedral's stained-glass windows.

Helen was aghast. In a particularly offensive letter, she wrote to Issie criticising her 'shabby appearance' and warning her she would go 'bankrupt' and telling her she looked 'frightfully down and out'. She concluded by appealing to Issie to dress in 'nice, simple clothes'.

'Nice, simple clothes' were, of course, anathema to Issie, as even Helen would have known.

With the dress sorted, Issie's thoughts turned, over the summer, to what she would wear on her head. Inspiration struck in the form of a visitor to the offices of *Tatler*, a friend of Char's, a millinery student called Philip Treacy. He had been asked by Char to make a hat for a

story Michael Roberts was shooting called 'The Green Hat', based on
a book of the same name from the 1920s. It was one of those occasions when the high-concept idea for a story had leapt ahead of the
reality – and high or low, no decent 'green hats' could be found. As the
result of winning a competition, Philip was designing hats for Harrods.
He recalls:

> Charlotte phoned up and asked if I would make a green hat so I
> made a green hat. It was for the girl from Shakespears Sister.
> So I made a green hat, I took it to the shoot and I didn't really
> think anything of it. I didn't even know who Michael Roberts
> was. I didn't know the whole fashion scene. I didn't really think
> in terms of the scene.
>     When I went to collect the hat from *Tatler,* I went into the
> art department and Isabella came in. She was wearing a John
> Galliano transparent see-through knitted cobweb top and a
> little skirt and beautiful shoes and lipstick that was crooked,
> that was on her teeth. This was at a moment in the late 80s
> when most people on those magazines were wearing a suit.

Philip recalls that Issie was 'not overly-friendly', so he didn't particularly expect to hear from her again. He went back to the Royal College
of Art.

Then the phone calls started.

A receptionist at the Royal College of Art told him: 'This woman has
been on the telephone and it's very, very unusual. She wants to know
what your schedule is like for the next six months.'

It was Issie. She told Philip she wanted him to make her a medieval
headdress for her wedding.

'I couldn't believe that I'd hit upon the one person who didn't expect
tulle and veiling and pearls and all that for her wedding hat,' Philip
recalls. He and Isabella quickly developed an intense and creative relationship. 'It was like having an affair with no sex,' he says.

The creation he finally came up with demanded that Issie's head
and neck be bandaged in pale pink chiffon, with just her face exposed.
The hat or headdress has sometimes been described as a wimple –
part of a medieval nun's habit – but really it was more like a golden
crown with delicately cut gold lace filigree on the sides of her head.

Philip was baffled as to how much he should charge Issie for his
work. He erred on the side of caution. He explains:

**Issie and her good friend Philip Treacy. Philip used this photograph on the front of his Christmas cards the year that Issie died.**

Sometimes people were trying to charge Issie the most extreme prices because they thought of her as a rich girl. She had a very gentle way of trying to make people understand that she just didn't have that kind of money. I can't even remember [how much I charged her for the wedding hat] but it was not a great deal. It was maybe £60 or something like that. The money wasn't really important, the experience was priceless. I got much more out of it than she did. And I didn't have any 'clients' anyway. Isabella was my only client.

# PHILIP

But in fact the relationship, Issie knew, would work both ways. For in Philip, Isabella confided in me, she had found not just the creator of her wedding headdress – but the greatest discovery of her career so far.

# CHAPTER
# THIRTY-TWO

## *Duggie*

By a quirk of fate, Evelyn and I shared the same birthday – on 2 October 1989 he was 74 and I was 26. We had a merry joint birthday party with Rona, Isabella and her sisters at Kensington Square.

The next day the curse of the Delves Broughtons struck again. Lavinia's husband Douglas had been to the dentist in Swindon, but his old banger of a car overheated when he was returning to have dinner with Lavinia. He parked on the hard shoulder of the M4 motorway, waiting for an emergency service to come to his rescue.

As he was sitting there, a lorry driver who had been away on holiday for two weeks had fallen asleep at the wheel and ploughed straight into his parked car. The only mercy was that Duggie was killed instantly.

Issie had just got home from work at about 5.30 p.m. when she received a call at Elizabeth Street telling her what had happened. She tried to call her father at Kensington Square, but the line was engaged, so I drove her there. Of course, the rush-hour traffic in Kensington High Street was terrible, and in the end Issie got out of the car and ran down to Kensington Square to tell her father what had happened.

When Issie urged him to go and visit Lavinia immediately, he replied, 'I cannot because I am having dinner with Diana Ford at the Berkeley.'

# DUGGIE

He was, of course, in shock, like we all were, but still it was a very strange thing to say, and he did actually go for the dinner that evening, discussing Duggie's death throughout it. A few days later, he arrived at Lavinia's door with some social-security leaflets and the callous suggestion that the answer to her financial problems was that her two children, aged three and one, should go into state care.

Isabella and I drove directly to Lavinia's home In Camberwell. She was, of course, utterly distraught. Helen arrived with £500, which she left for Lavinia.

Evelyn did arrive later that evening – maybe Diana told him to go – and Lavinia sat on his lap weeping. But overall he was unsurprisingly unsupportive financially. He felt that Duggie's family should step in.

In the end, Aunt Rosie paid for Duggie's funeral.

# CHAPTER
# THIRTY-THREE

## *The Wedding*

We never questioned whether our wedding, scheduled for December, should go ahead following Duggie's death in October, but the tragedy hung darkly over our preparations.

Amazingly, on 8 October, just days after this terrible tragedy, when she might have been focused on comforting her daughter, Helen sent an absurd letter to Amaury, attempting to take control of the cathedral seating plan. I tore her ridiculous missive up and put the Lovats in the first row, next to the Delves Broughtons, as we had planned.

On 11 October 1989, we attended Duggie's funeral at St Barnabas Church in Dulwich. The church was packed out with over 400 mourners and his coffin was draped in the Union Jack.

On 3 November, Isabella and I went for marriage counselling with the Dean. He told us that if Isabella and my mother were both drowning in a river on the day before we married, I should save my mother first. As soon as we were married, however, the reverse was true: I should leave my mother to drown if that were necessary to save Isabella. It would take me several years to understand this. My mother had trained me well to look after her: Issie had been stunned when she had seen me buy my mother's sanitary towels. As Amaury commented perceptively in the *Sunday Times'* Relative Values column, 'My mother used Detmar to take charge of us and, I think, as a surrogate husband for a time.'

The night before the wedding, I gave a dinner at Hilles with my mother and new stepfather present. Earlier in the year my mother had, without letting any of her children know, remarried on the very day her divorce came through from Rajah. My new stepfather was Desmond Perera, a retired tea planter. None of us had met him before but we liked him – he was kind and gentle and appeared calm. His father had been the first psychiatrist in Sri Lanka and he had grown up in Angoda, the mental asylum outside Colombo. He was fascinated by my mother's mental states.

After the dinner I drove Evelyn and Julia back to the Snooty Fox pub where they were staying. We met Isabella's first cousin Andrew Fraser, whose daughters Daisy and Laura were bridesmaids. We chatted for a while. I noticed that Evelyn did not buy his nephew a drink.

While I was making the 40-minute trip back to Hilles, I decided, on the spur of the moment, that I would stay with Isabella at Yew Tree Mount (Geraldine Harmsworth's house). I suddenly just couldn't face my mother – although it was my wedding, I knew that she would be demanding that I make her tea, fetch her things, iron her saree and the like.

There was a bit of a stir when I arrived, but Issie was happy that I had decided to break with convention and spend the night before the wedding with her. We needed each other's support.

The next morning, the day of our wedding, I returned to Hilles. I was full of nerves. I knew that at 26 I was young to get married, but I also knew that it was the right thing for me to do.

My mental state was not helped when a helicopter, lent by a friend of Isabella's who was abroad in tax exile, landed in one of the fields. On board was Philip Treacy and others involved in dressing Issie.

Helen was giving a lunch at the Painswick Hotel for the older generation – and, sure enough, my mother asked me to drive her and her new husband to it. Of course, I wanted to focus on my own preparations – the wedding was scheduled for 2.30 p.m. in Gloucester, which is half an hour away from Hilles – but in the end I opted for the path of least resistance and just took my mother to Painswick to be done with it.

My ushers' lunch was a quiet affair – Ant Belmont cooked, Amaury was my best man and Benjie Fraser was the head usher. It was going well until the ushers told me that unless they had a brandy none of them were coming to the ceremony. I felt angry but also strangely amused as I ran around trying to find the bloody bottle. The day was getting more and more surreal.

I had feared it was going to be a nightmare for our guests to find their way through the new one-way systems in Gloucester to the cathedral, but to my relief there were people in pews in the choir. I smiled to myself when I saw the Lovats in the front row on Isabella's side, in defiance of Helen's diktat.

At Kimsbury Farmhouse, I was later told, there was a merry atmosphere with champagne flowing as Issie dressed. When Evelyn arrived Isabella came up to him in her elegant underwear and said, 'What do you think?'

Evelyn told her, 'Darling, you look beautiful.'

After dressing in Nadia's elegant dress, and having her head wrapped in pink chiffon like Eleanor of Aquitaine in *The Lion in Winter* and her wimple placed on it, she was carried across some mud and put into the hired Daimler car by Rifat Ozbek and Manolo Blahnik. Manolo had given Issie a pair of pointed silver shoes as a wedding present. They were a size too small.

Amaury had gone to check that all was well down at Kimsbury farmhouse. It was a good thing he did. Parked in the driveway, blocking in the bridal party, was a large cattle truck. The farmer had gone out into the fields to round up some cows to take to market.

Amaury, despite having no experience of driving such a large piece of machinery, jumped instinctively into the cab. 'All I remember is the truck lurching forward and then down as I bedded it into a ditch, but the cars moved and Issie was freed,' he recalls.

Nadia, who travelled in the car with Isabella and her father, remembers that they spent the whole journey talking about the battle of Poitiers.

When Issie arrived at Gloucester Cathedral, Philip Treacy recalls, the growing crowd outside the cathedral, drawn by the procession of Rolls-Royces arriving, were stunned when the bride emerged in a violet dress with a wimple on top. Helen was so disgusted by Issie's flouting of tradition that she did not speak to us for the rest of the day.

Inside the cathedral, meanwhile, I was waiting nervously for Isabella's arrival. As soon as I saw her, I was thrilled by her wimple – the dress was beautiful and elegant with its train – but the wimple was incredible.

# THE WEDDING

**Issie and her father arriving at the cathedral. Issie caused quite a stir.**

Holding her right hand in his left was Evelyn, who made it successfully the 300 yards up the nave before sitting heavily into a pew.
Behind them were the six tiny bridesmaids and two knights, Issie's
godson Otis Ferry and his brother Isaac. They had been told by Issie
to keep their visors down to look more warlike.

A stirring improvisation of the Agincourt song was played loudly by
the organist as the procession made their way into the choir.

Issie had chosen 'Praise, my soul, the King of Heaven', and then
we had 'Veni, Creator Spiritus', which had been played by the first
Crusaders when they had triumphantly taken Jerusalem in 1099 (and
massacred the city's occupants). More appropriate was what followed:
'Pray for the Peace of Jerusalem' by John Blow.

We were married in front of the congregation, who saw Evelyn
shakily give Isabella's hand to me. Some thought the shakes were to
do with supreme emotions – in reality, he was nervous of losing his
balance and falling.

The page boys and bridesmaids in the nave of Gloucester Cathedral.

Coming out of Gloucester Cathedral after being married.

# THE WEDDING

We left the cathedral to Widor's happy, fast and uplifting Toccata.

The reception was about an hour away at Chavenage House, outside Tetbury. Of course, we had wanted to have our reception at Hilles – but my mother had refused.

Amaury – whose Rudolph Valentino good looks were much admired – made a funny speech without notes. He teased Issie about having as many shoes as Imelda Marcos, and then said how much he loved Issie and appreciated how much she had helped us since joining our family.

# CHAPTER THIRTY-FOUR

## *Morocco*

The next morning we drove back to Hilles, and then set off by helicopter to London, where we caught a plane to Marrakesh. We arrived very late at night in La Roserie in the Atlas mountains. Issie and I went off riding after breakfast on strong Arab horses. I had not done much riding since my father died 12 years earlier – but Issie insisted we start galloping as soon as we hit the flat. Then we climbed single file high into the Atlas mountains, and the valleys beneath us became smaller and smaller.

At a high point, Issie's horse reared up. It was terrifying. After dismounting, she changed horse with our guide and we headed down the mountain. When we reached the bottom, we rode along a dry river bed. Issie's horse then fell, and Issie jumped off, as it rolled on its back in the river bed.

We were meant to spend a week riding, but Issie was too shaken to ride any more and La Roserie was not really a place for us – there was no glamour or buzz. Instead we headed back to Marrakesh, where we stayed in a small hotel run by a large shaven-headed French lesbian just outside the main Souk, which cost $10 per day – including a breakfast of fresh croissant and coffee. It was perfect.

In Marrakesh, Issie wanted me to meet a local character named Moulay Kebir, who worked for Christopher Gibbs, the sixties pioneer of Morocco who had a house in the Urika valley outside Marrakesh. After about an hour of searching, we found Moulay, who invited us home to have lunch. We sat on the floor as his wife prepared *poulet citron* (chicken in lemon) – one of Issie's favourite dishes. That night we went for dinner in the Souk. In a small candlelit room lounging on beds with jugglers and castrato musicians, we felt as if we were watching entertainment from 300 years before.

The next day we drove up to Christopher's house in the Urika valley. It was set in the side of a hill, with great views and was the same pink colour as the hillside. Moulay was happy in Christopher's house – he was free to enjoy himself. We soon smelt kiff burning. The next day I met the bird scarer, whose only job was to scare the birds from damaging Christopher's plants. Moulay ruefully told us that the poor bird scarer had seven daughters. He had tried to have a son and then given up.

We returned to Marrakesh a few days later. Issie had someone else to look up in Morocco – the actor John Malkovich, who was shooting Bernado Bertolucci's film of Paul Bowles's *The Sheltering Sky*. John invited us to watch him on set the next day. We had missed by a day, he told us, the scene in which a Berber prostitute bears her enormous breasts to him. John was charming. At one time, he had studied materials, and Issie and he chatted away about the amazing array of dressmaking materials available in Morocco.

When we got home, preparations for Christmas, which we would spend at Hilles, were in full swing. We went up to Inverness to celebrate New Year at Beaufort Castle with the widowed Lavinia, who Simon Fraser and Virginia had invited to join them.

Issie wore priest's robes at the New Year dinner. One guest, the Catholic writer Paul Johnson, was furious at this sacrilege and complained to Simon.

'But, Paul,' Simon said, 'they are Protestant robes – not Catholic ones.'

Thus one decade ended and another began with clothes and controversy.

# CHAPTER
# THIRTY-FIVE

## *London Babes*

After we got back from our honeymoon, but before Christmas, Issie was summoned to Vogue House for a meeting. She returned to Elizabeth Street white-faced.

'Det, guess what? I have just been fired by *Tatler*,' she told me dumbly.

Issie said that she had cried and fiddled with some material as the news was delivered.

Looking now at Issie's pages in 1989, I can have some sympathy with the decision. Issie appeared to be concentrating on her life at Hilles. Almost every shoot was set there. She was married and *Tatler* may have thought that Issie was on to a new life.

In fact, Issie had no intention of living in the country full time. After wiping her tears away, Issie calmly walked out of the *Tatler* office and caught the lift up to the fifth floor of Vogue House, where the offices of British *Vogue* were located. She went and spoke directly to the editor of *Vogue*, Liz Tilberis, with whom she had no previous relationship, and told her what had happened.

The next day she received a handwritten note from Liz on her personal stationery. The postcard said, in blue ink, 'I can find a job for you at *Vogue*.'

# LONDON BABES

Issie was given a job at *Vogue* as a contributing editor. It was the fulfilment of a dream she had had since she was 18, when she had visited a friend who worked there on reception.

After New Year at Beaufort, Issie and I returned to London to work – Issie to *Vogue* and I to the Bar, where I had started the previous October my second six-month pupillage in a criminal chambers. I started to appear in court, attending to remands in custody, making bail applications and defending in small criminal trials.

Issie's first-published photograph in *Vogue* appeared in the April issue in 1990. It was a portrait of the Irish singer Sinead O'Connor with close-cropped hair, wearing a metal bra commissioned by Issie from Slim Barrett. It is a piercing portrait. Sinead, like Isabella, was not afraid to wear armour. Wearing uncomfortable clothes, hats and shoes to achieve an elegant, striking and shockingly beautiful visual look was a trademark of Isabella. It inspired her and those who admire beauty, while bewildering and sometimes offending those who think it is ridiculous to want to look different.

The next story Issie did was with Karl Lagerfeld in Paris, 'Ich bin ein Englander', to coincide with Lagerfeld's photographic exhibition at Hamilton's gallery in London. Lagerfeld, Issie wearily told me, did his photography during the night – he was designing during the day. The clothes were by John Galliano and the hats by Philip Treacy, who, at the tender age of 22, was now producing all the hats for the Chanel shows.

In one photograph is my brother Amaury in a top hat, black cape and black eye make-up. He had come to Paris because he was obsessed with a girl who lived there. He fell foul of the fiendishly complex parking arrangements in French cities, and his car was towed away. Almost a year later, Issie finally managed to arrange for a friend to drive it back to England.

For the next four years at British *Vogue* in the early 1990s, Issie was predominantly assigned the task of styling portraits of the artists, designers, divas and literary stars whom *Vogue* featured on their pages. *Vogue* had the pick of the best photographers in the land, from Lord Snowdon, the Eton- and Cambridge-educated former husband of Princess Margaret, to David Bailey, the brilliant, foul-mouthed East End boy from Leytonstone.

The most famous portrait she did in this period was in the March 1992 issue of *Vogue*. It showed Damien Hirst in a Perspex fish tank, a homage to Damien's seminal *The Physical Impossibility of Death in the Mind of Someone Living*, a 14-foot (4.3 m) tiger shark immersed in formaldehyde, which became the iconic work of British art in the 1990s.

Features editor Eve MacSweeny recalls:

It was Issie's brilliant idea for Snowdon to photograph Damien in a fish tank, in honour of the shark. I remember Snowdon complaining like crazy having to do a photograph of this dirty long-haired artist.

Also on the Hirst photoshoot, assisting Issie, was her cousin Violet Fraser, the eldest child of her cousin Simon Fraser. She says:

I remember ordering huge plastic containers and lots of plastic lobsters and crabs. It was great fun preparing for the shoot and Issie took a very conceptual approach. I remember running back and forth from Vogue House, fetching props, and Issie was very specific about what she wanted. The shoot was incredible when it was published, breathtaking, and Issie did the most sensational job. It was such fun to work with her, a real inspiration.

Despite the clarity and originality of her vision and the support of first Liz Tilberis and then Alex Shulman, who succeeded to the editorship in 1992 when Liz went to the United States, Issie found it hard to find a role at British *Vogue*. In the four years she spent there, from 1990 to 1994, Issie only did one fashion story, Steven Meisel's 'Anglo-Saxon Attitudes', which became informally known as the 'London Babes' story, and came out in December 1993. It remains to this day the most expensive shoot ever done at British *Vogue*.

Steven Meisel was then and is now one of the top fashion photographers in the world, and getting him to do the shoot for British *Vogue* was an incredible coup for Issie, as he rarely ventures out of the high-paid US market.

Issie had recently acquired a new assistant who worked with her on the project: Plum Sykes, who was then a young graduate, but has gone on to become one of the most famous writers of her generation. (Plum's brother Tom is my co-writer on this book.)

When Plum, who was doing work experience at *Vogue*, asked Issie if she could work for her, Issie replied, 'Why would someone as conservative as you want to work for someone like me?' Issie relented when she discovered that Plum was the cousin of the photographer Christopher Simon Sykes, whom she admired.

Plum's duties were primarily administrative. Because Issie 'could hardly write a note out to herself', she thought Plum, who was organised, was, 'a total genius. She really over-exaggerated my talents,' says Plum.

Issie swiftly made Plum her new right-hand woman:

I'd to get to the office in Hanover Square at 9 a.m. and I would get a phone call at 9.30 saying, 'I have had far too much gin to drink last night, darling, could you come over here and we'll just work from my bed.' And so I would go to Elizabeth Street, which was painted strange colours – like *dark grey,* which at the time was *very* unusual – and she would be in bed in a negligée. And then I would sit by her bed with my notepad and write down everything she wanted me to do and then go out and do it and then come back. So she didn't always go to the office but she was always genuinely busy doing things. It's just she didn't do them in the conventional way, or in a way that necessarily made sense to a corporate entity like Condé Nast.

Once she had got out of bed, Issie would take Plum on her daily rounds, introducing her in just a few weeks to all the biggest names in fashion.

Issie always liked to have someone with her for moral support, so we would go to see Bella Freud at her studio or Hussein Chalayan or Alexander McQueen or Rifat Ozbeck. She would always introduce me by saying, 'This is my assistant Plum. She is so clever. She went to Oxford and she can send faxes really, really fast.'

The brief for 'London Babes' was to find four beautiful aristocratic English girls that would inspire Steven Meisel.

Issie and I interviewed every posh girl in London who was under 25. They would come into the office. Of course we rejected lots and lots of girls, which was quite embarrassing because we'd see them out at parties. Issie was obsessed with 'blue-blooded' girls. She would always talk about 'blue blood, blue blood', as if it was a real thing that actually existed, as if people really did have blue-coloured blood.

One of the girls who made the final cut was Issie's cousin Honor Fraser. So did Bella Freud.

Stella Tennant, who also made it into the shoot, came in wearing a nose ring. Issie suspected that Stella had not bathed recently, and told people, 'She smells disgusting but she looks amazing.' Plum recalls:

> Issie knew Stella was going to be huge. But there was a big argument over her nose ring. Issie loved the nose ring but Alex [Shulman] hated it, and told Issie to tell her on the shoot to take it out. Issie would have thought that taking out the nose ring would be a travesty, because it would be ruining someone's personal style. Stella refused to take it out. It was obviously the right decision because she became known for the nose ring, it made her 'cool'.

The shoot was based out of caravans in East London and it went on for two weeks. At the last minute, Plum herself was promoted from sending faxes and drafted into the shoot as well.

It should have been a triumphal moment for Issie. But when Meisel arrived in London he brought with him Jo McKenna, a tough Glaswegian-born stylist, with whom he has worked over the course of many years. Issie, who had believed it was 'her' shoot, was wrong-footed by this unpleasant surprise. Issie hated Jo's 'keep it simple, jeans and T-shirts' take on fashion. She despised nothing quite so much as the universal modern, comfortable, casual look.

McKenna was pugnacious. Issie told me at home in Elizabeth Street that Jo had asked her if she was going to make the tea on the shoot. Philip Treacy and I urged Issie to fight back. Issie and Jo had a meeting with Alex Shulman the editor of *Vogue* and Issie returned home more cheerful. Alex had stood up for her against Jo. Jo McKenna was, as he insisted, billed as fashion editor on the shoot and Issie was credited as stylist. Issie told me that Jo had been dismissive of the clothes she had chosen, but the final product was generously imbued with the clothes of the young unknown designers that Issie favoured. Bella Freud wore her own clothes.

A few months later, as a direct result of meeting her on the 'London Babes' shoot, Meisel shot Stella Tennant – complete with nose ring

– for the cover of Italian *Vogue* with the supermodel Linda Evangelista. Stella's career went into overdrive and, shortly after that, Karl Lagerfeld replaced the supermodel Claudia Schiffer with Stella as the face of Chanel.

It was rumoured to be a £1 million contract. During the shoot, Issie had told Stella, 'If I make you famous, I want a bottle of my favourite perfume.'

A bottle of Fracas duly arrived.

# CHAPTER THIRTY-SIX

## *The Death of Evelyn*

After an uneventful Christmas at Hilles in 1992 with all our siblings and Helen, Issie and I flew to Sri Lanka.

It was wonderful to leave cold and grey England and arrive in tropical and sunny Sri Lanka a few hours later. Sri Lanka is an extraordinarily beautiful country, with coconut plantations dotted along the coast. As we travelled by train up to my mother's hometown of Kandy, 1500 feet above sea level, we saw rubber plantations, spice gardens and paddy fields worked by ladies in sarees and farmers in sarongs. When we stopped at stations, small boys would run up to the train offering refreshments, which were paid for by dropping coins out of the windows.

After a three-hour journey, we were climbing into the hills of Kandy, encountering buffalo, birds and elephants bathing on our way. It was hot, tropical and magical. Although it was our third visit to Kandy together, Issie darted from one side of the train to the other to look out of the windows like an excited schoolgirl.

On our way from the train station to the house – which my grandparents had built in the 1940s and to which my grandfather had subsequently added an unsightly 30-room extension to profit from the explosion in package holidays in the 1970s – we passed the Temple of

Taprobane Island, a privately owned island off the south coast of Sri Lanka that my grandfather bought for £300 in the early 1960s. It was designed and built in the 1920s by Count de Mauny-Talvande.

Helga's Folly – my mother's hotel in Kandy, Sri Lanka.

**Issie in the tropical gardens of Taprobane Island.**

the Tooth, which houses Lord Buddha's tooth, and is one of the most sacred places of Buddhist pilgrimage. I showed Issie the less holy spot where our neighbour's dog, tied up outside the kitchen, had been eaten by a passing leopard, leaving only its lead behind.

Issie was enchanted by the bustle of Kandy, with its busy streets selling jewellery and handicrafts, and she dubbed it the Sri Lankan New York. We went into town and Issie insisted that I buy some sarongs, which I had never worn before, having been dressed by my half-Scottish grandmother as a little colonial teenager, with pyjamas, shorts, safari suits and topee.

My grandfather's parents, George and Agnes de Silva, had been prominent in the independence movement in Sri Lanka, and had been instrumental in winning universal franchise in 1931 for Sri Lankans, irrespective of race, ethnicity, language or gender. It was an impressive achievement. Mahatma Gandhi had stayed with them shortly thereafter. My grandfather fondly recalled to Gandhi's grandson, Gopal Gandhi, that his job during the visit had been to make sure the goat was milked. And there was a photograph of Nehru, with his daughter Indira, and my handsome grandfather and his sisters at home.

# THE DEATH OF EVELYN

Issie and my grandfather adored each other. He had been a successful criminal barrister in the central province of Kandy, mayor and,
briefly, MP for his hometown. Disgusted by the death penalty, he had
successfully introduced into Parliament a Private Member's Bill abol-
ishing capital punishment in the 1950s. His law did not last long, but it
showed his compassion. In the late 1960s he had been the Sri Lankan
ambassador to France, and in the 1970s had been on the executive
board of Unesco representing the small countries of the world. My
grandfather enjoyed dancing, and, in the evening, after changing for
dinner, Issie and he would gently dance together to crooners from the
1950s. It was in his ambassador's coat that I had met Isabella, and it
was what I wore when I married her.

Issie was a big hit with my Sri Lankan family. My grandfather's elder
brother, Uncle 'Sunny', who never took life too seriously, told Issie that
Dalkeith, the estate of which her grandfather Jock was part of the
owning syndicate, was the only plantation in Sri Lanka which had tea,
rubber and coconut. Issie also got on well with my grandfather's

**My aunt, Anil de Silva, who wrote a
book on the Buddha in French. She
gave Isabella a lot of her clothes.**

**My mother, my stepfather, our good friend Marie Du Petit Thouars, Isabella and me, at my mother's hotel in Sri Lanka.**

sisters: Aunt Anil, who lived between Paris and Cambridge and had written a life of the Buddha in French, and Minette, who had worked for Le Corbusier. Gifts of sarees, jackets and clothes were given by the family to Issie.

Reality came crashing back into this tropical arcadia when we received a telephone call on 5 January, saying that Evelyn had died at the Leighton hospital in Crewe from congestive cardiac failure and a chest infection. Lavinia and Rona had been with him.

Issie wept at the news, but Evelyn's death was not unexpected. He had been getting weaker throughout 1992. He had been unable to get up the stairs at Hilles when he came to stay.

Issie was in shock and needed to return immediately to England. The funeral was to be held a week later, on the 12th.

Part of the reason we had come to Sri Lanka was because I was in a very fragile mental state, having spent the past six months working for a famously fierce and adversarial London lawyer. My self-confidence and self-esteem were shot, and after six months of permanently thinking I was about to be fired, I was bordering on a complete nervous breakdown. I desperately needed to recuperate. I just couldn't face the funeral. I went into Kandy and bought Issie a first-class airline ticket back home instead. My mother complained about this extravagance, but I feared what was coming for Issie, reasoning that the least I could do was to make Issie comfortable on her journey back to England.

Not accompanying Issie to her father's funeral is something I now deeply regret. I should have been there for her, and I am ashamed that I wasn't.

Dave – our odd job man who lived with his wife Daff in a village near Stroud – drove Isabella and Helen the two hours from Gloucestershire to Evelyn's funeral at Broughton church in Staffordshire. Helen had at first laughed and joked, but Isabella was not receptive. As they came close to Broughton, and Helen started to see familiar places from her marriage, she became quiet and subdued.

The grand service sheet stated under the Delves Broughton crests that Evelyn was 12th baronet of Broughton. Rona and Isabella read from the Bible. Aunt Rosie wrote to Issie on 16 January,

> You read the lesson beautifully and clearly. Your Father would
> have been proud of you, as would Detmar had he been able to
> be there.

**Isabella with her father in 1992, a year before he passed away.**

# CHAPTER THIRTY-SEVEN

## *The Great Betrayal*

It was not clear what Isabella and her sisters would receive from Evelyn's will. Previously, Rona had said to me that on Evelyn's death she did not know where she was going to live. The coded inference to me was that Isabella and her sisters and daughters were going to get some substantial property. All Issie had ever been told by Evelyn was that if she contested his will, she would get nothing.

Maybe this warning should have alerted us to the fact that there was mischief afoot.

On 6 February I received a call from Julia at Hilles.

Had we opened the letter from Rona's lawyer Michael Lewis, she wanted to know?

'No,' I replied.

Julia told me, 'Detmar, it is worse than I possibly imagined. We get £5000 and Rona gets everything outright. There is no trust.'

Sickened to the core, we dumbly opened the letter.

It read, 'Under the terms of his Will and codicils, your father has left you a legacy of £5000.'

In that horrible instant, one of the last remaining foundations of Issie's stability was washed away.

Issie had always, I think, quietly assumed that her father would leave her, if not a fortune, then enough money to comfortably get by on for the rest of her life.

But £5000? That was what her grandmother had left to her house-keeper. And all the power was in Rona's hands. They could do nothing and they would get nothing – no painting, no house in Cheshire, nothing.

Evelyn had effectively disinherited his beloved daughters. It was an extraordinary betrayal from beyond the grave.

By way of explanation Lewis had enclosed a copy of a typed 'Letter of Wishes' to Rona, signed by Evelyn, on 6 May 1990. The note, in which Evelyn claimed to have made 'separate provision' for his daughters while he was alive, echoed his warning to Issie in life not to contest the will. He directed Rona to 'vigorously' resist any attempt by his daughters to claim 'a greater share of my estate'.

To try to understand what had happened, Issie and I went to have lunch with an old friend of her father's, Rafe Cavenagh-Mainwaring of Whitmore Hall in Staffordshire. Cavenagh-Mainwaring was Julia's godfather and he and Evelyn had shared some farm equipment. He wrote Isabella a supportive statement on 15 February 1993 about his feelings, which he said we could use, although he said that he himself was too old to get involved in any litigation.

By 18 February, the *Evening Standard* Londoner's Diary had picked up the story. A lead piece, 'Mischief afoot in Evelyn's will', revealed:

Dynastic battles and intrigue look set to continue in the legendary Delves Broughton family, immortalised during the years leading up to the last war with the 'Happy Valley set' days in Kenya and the subsequent film *White Mischief.* For Sir Evelyn Delves Broughton who died aged 77 at the beginning of the year has left his estimated £6m estate to his third wife ... leaving his three daughters with as little as £5000 each. While this has caused great distress amongst his daughters Isabella, Julia, and Lavinia, Sir Evelyn never gave a hint as to why this imbalance should occur.

Rona was quoted as saying, 'As far as I am concerned there is no dispute whatsoever.'

Isabella was utterly betrayed by her father in death. But there was nothing she could do. On 14 July 1993, Michael Lewis sent Isabella a cheque for £5000.

Rona was heartless. At the May Chester race meet she sponsored for three years the Evelyn Delves Broughton Fillies Maiden Stakes.

The annual prize money was £10,000. Isabella never attended.

# CHAPTER
# THIRTY-EIGHT

## *Alexander*

U nlike some fashion editors who stay in their offices and connect to the world of fashion they are supposed to represent in their magazines only via publicists, 'look-books', 'called-in' clothes and other publications, the vicarious approach was not for Issie. As Anna Wintour has observed, Issie had a passion for hitting the streets in her quest to seek out new talent. At *Vogue* she would trek all over London in her quest to find interesting new designers.

'She was like a truffle hound for talent,' recalls Hamish Bowles, now European Editor at Large for American *Vogue*.

In June 1992, she returned home to 67 Elizabeth Street from one of her many missions, enraptured by what she had just seen at the graduation show of a 23-year-old fashion student from Central St Martins College of Art and Design. The show had been in King's Cross and there had been no seats left, so, pocketing her pride, Issie simply sat on the stairs and watched the clothes go past her.

The student's name was Lee Alexander McQueen.

'Det, his clothes move like birds,' she breathlessly told me that evening. 'He can cut material like a God.'

Issie, who was 33 at this stage, knew from that very first moment that here was a fashion genius the likes of which are seen just once in a lifetime. Much as she had pursued Philip Treacy, she started making incessant phone calls to try and track down the new object of her attentions.

Using detective powers that would put a tabloid journalist to shame, Issie swiftly traced McQueen, then 23, to his family home at Biggerstaff Road in Stratford, a tough industrial area of London's East End. The family home backed on to a site for storing building sand and building materials.

Mrs McQueen – we always called her that out of respect, rather than use her first name, Joyce – told Issie that her son had gone off after his show for 'a two week holiday'.

When he returned from his holiday his mother told him, 'There's this mad lady keeps calling that's in love with your clothes.'

McQueen described how the first time she came to see him she was wearing 'collapsed black organza horns on her head. I just thought she was incredibly fab.'

At that first meeting, Issie asked Alexander how much a jacket would cost.

McQueen told her £300.

Issie replied, 'That's a lot for a student', but she ended up buying the whole collection – taking a few items a month, and paying him in instalments.

This was, in fact, Issie's usual modus operandi. She never had enough money to buy outright the clothes, hats or jewellery that she wanted. The only person who was absolutely strict about payment with her was Manolo Blahnik's sister Evangeline – maybe a legacy of that bounced cheque in New York all those years ago.

To get his cash instalments from Issie, McQueen would come round to see her at Vogue House with his clothes in a bin liner.

McQueen's angry impatience contributed to his social discomfort waiting in the slightly fussy reception area at Vogue House. Chubby, with a rough accent and what Issie described as 'teeth like Stonehenge', Alexander deliberately played up the loutish side of his character there.

On his first visit, McQueen told Peter Rolfe at reception to 'hurry up' when he was calling up to Issie. Peter has guarded with equanimity the reception desk at Vogue House for two decades and – much like McQueen – is a man who has never been particularly overawed by the fashion crowd he works amongst every day. He threw McQueen out of the building and into the street.

# ALEXANDER

The next time Alexander came to see Issie at Vogue House, he brought a friend along to talk politely to Peter.

Having gained entry, Issie and McQueen would chat for a while at her desk, then they would pop out to Issie's bank in Hanover Square to see what she could withdraw from her account. It has been widely reported over the years that the collection cost £5000 and that Issie took a year to pay for it, but in truth the arrangement was much more informal than that. I doubt either of them were keeping count.

Issie believed clothes were for wearing and she really wore Alexander's clothes, to parties, to the office and on the bus. She said herself that she wore them 'to death'. But that didn't mean she was necessarily happy when they did die.

Once, at a party, Issie was approached by an enthusiastic girl who knocked a glass of red wine all over Issie's brand new outfit, a white Alexander McQueen number, completely ruining it.

Issie was eerily calm about this sartorial disaster. A few minutes later, the unfortunate girl's handbag exploded into flames. Issie had quietly dropped her lit cigarette into the girl's open bag to extract her revenge.

# CHAPTER
# THIRTY-NINE

## *Elizabeth Street*

A lexander needed a place to work after his graduation in 1992. In the same year, our home at 67 Elizabeth Street had been badly affected by the literal collapse of both next door houses – Nos. 69 and 71 – both of which the Grosvenor estate was extensively refurbishing. The party wall to No. 67, already frail, was badly cracked and I became involved over the next three years in the time-consuming and thankless task of negotiating, on behalf of my mother who owned No. 67, with the insurance company and the Grosvenor estate to try and repair the house.

Legally, because of the damage to the party wall, we had been instructed not to live there. But Philip Treacy still stored some of his hats there, we had some of our possessions there, and Alexander was able to have the basement for free to live and work in along with his then boyfriend Jimmy Jumble. One member of the McQueen family had been a runner for the Kray brothers, and it made Alexander laugh to have infiltrated the estate of the Duke of Westminster, to be in one of the most prestigious, expensive and elegant parts of London. It was, he would chortle, very different from Biggerstaff Road.

Alexander was signing on under his first name Lee McQueen, and to avoid any trouble with the Inland Revenue he was selling his clothes under Alexander, his middle name. Issie insisted that Alexander should become his only name. 'Alexander', she said, sounded more aristocratic, and he was her 'Alexander the Great'.

Many years later I asked Alexander, 'Do you want me to call you Lee – like everyone else does?'

'No,' he said. 'I have always been Alexander to you and Issie.'

We all became very close very quickly. Apart from the genius of his clothes, we found Alexander quite brilliant in his fast, witty and thoughtful conversation. He reminded me of Harold Pinter. They were both East End boys, and just as one had revolutionised the theatre, so the other, Issie believed, was going to revolutionise tailoring.

Issie and Alexander were both expansively and imaginatively foul-mouthed, leading him to describe her as 'a cross between a Billingsgate fish wife and Lucretia Borgia'. Issie, who knew that I found this type of conversation about cocks and fucking uncomfortable and embarrassing, would indulge in it only when I was, so she thought, out of earshot.

Alexander told us a lot about his early life. He was the youngest of six children and had been a strong swimmer at school, representing his school in national competitions. He had left school at 16 with just one qualification – an 'A' grade in his art O level.

Early on in life, he had developed two powerful fascinations that were to stay with him for life: clothes and birds. At one time, the McQueens lived in a tower block in the East End and he became obsessed by the birds of prey hovering around the blocks. It influenced his design and he would often say he would like to have been a bird. Later in our friendship, Issie would arrange for falconers to come up from Gloucester with their Harris Hawks. McQueen was a natural and soon had them flying and landing on his arm. He liked the big leather glove he had to wear to protect himself from their claws.

His start in fashion had been random enough. Reading the newspaper one day, Mrs McQueen saw an advertisement for a tailoring apprenticeship at a Savile Row tailor. McQueen applied and got the job, and ended up training at Andersen Sheppard. He worked on the suits of Prince Charles and inserted in the lining a note reading, 'I am a cunt.' In a similar note dropped into the lining of a suit being made for the famous financier Lord Rothschild, he wrote, 'I am a rich bastard.'

After his apprenticeship in Savile Row, Alexander went to see Wendy Dagworthy, who was head of fashion at Central St Martins, to ask her to help him sell his clothes. Dagworthy told him that she did not sell clothes but that he should do a degree at Central St Martins. The McQueens did not have £3000 for the course fees, but a wonderful aunt lent him the money.

Alexander and his mother adored each other. Silver-haired and with a kind, warm smile, she was immensely proud of her son's work. After practically every show he would come out after the show to acknowledge the rapturous applause and give her a kiss – and another to Issie.

In those days, Alexander had a difficult relationship with his father Ron. Ron was a cabbie, originally Scottish. I met him once at McQueen's show at Borough Market. It must have been a shock for him when he discovered that his youngest son wanted to make clothes for women. The men in the McQueen family, Alexander told us, were 'bricklayers and cabbies' – not gay fashion designers. It must have seemed to Ron that his son came from another planet.

All of us shared darkness in our lives – Issie and I had our suicides and abandonment and Alexander told us he had been sexually abused as a child by some distant family member. He said he knew he was gay from a young age – but he was angered by the abuse he had suffered which, he said, had robbed him of his innocence. Sexually, Alexander told us, he needed to be dominated.

'I like rough sex, Detmar,' he told me.

Some of the sexual activities he got up to upset Issie a great deal. She felt that in a very important way Alexander did not respect himself. Of course the tragedy was that she recognised this lack of self-respect only because the condition plagued her too.

In 1992, British *Vogue* published a feature on Issie and me titled 'Over the Hilles and far away' for the November issue. In July, a crew of 12 came down to Gloucestershire for the shoot. Amongst them was Alexander. He had made the clothes for Issie and for me. Issie wore a pink and black beetle-shaped coat, with one of Philip's hats in black felt with thistle and rose detail. I wore a light pink Regency waistcoat with flower petals in a see-through material, and one of my collarless barrister's shirt with a white ruff, with yet more rose petals in the see-through gauze material.

It was the first time Alexander's work was seen in *Vogue*. He was only three months out of college.

In the photograph of Issie and I in the archway at Hilles, there is a bunch of flowers above our heads hanging from the arch. It was an upside-down Alexander who was, off camera, holding them there.

Alexander came to stay with us regularly at Hilles. Initially he would come on his own but later he would bring boyfriends and his fierce-looking Staffordshire bull terrier dogs Minter and Juice, to whom he was devoted. My sister Selina had her own feisty black Scottish terriers. Looking out of the window one weekend at Hilles I saw, running across the lawn, Minter, chased by Selina's terrier, in turn followed by Alexander, in turn chased by Juice. Alexander was trying to protect his massive 'Staffies' from Selina's tiny Scottie. Once he caught up with Selina's terrier, he planted a great big kick in it with his large black Doc Martin boots. Selina's dog was unperturbed but realised that, for the moment, Minter was off limits.

McQueen felt comfortable at Hilles and admired what we told him about my grandfather's radical political values. My grandfather valued, respected and admired creative and artistic people regardless of their background. Social background was everything in the stiflingly snobbish period before the First World War – but to my grandfather it was unimportant. When he married my aristocratic grandmother at the high altar of St Paul's Cathedral in 1910, he had his workmen sit directly behind his family.

From the date of his graduation in 1992 until he became the designer for Givenchy in 1996, McQueen's business was a financial struggle. But it was unbelievable fun. He would do anything to get a few extra quid. At Elizabeth Street he found some rolls of material belonging to my sister Selina who also designed clothes. Somewhat brazenly, he sold the material. My sister found out and made him pay her back.

'Sorry, Selina,' he grunted as he handed over a few rumpled 20-pound notes. He later gave her a coat he made to make amends, which she still has.

Apart from buying his first collection, Issie supported Alexander financially in other ways, always informally. Alexander was once invited to be interviewed at the ICA. On the podium Alexander told the audience, 'The only reason I am here is because Isabella Blow gave me £10 for the taxi fare.'

Something which I was unaware until researching this book is that Issie also paid off some of his County Court Judgments for non-payment of various bills. She never mentioned this to me. Perhaps she felt that I might have been cross with her. I would not have been, knowing that it was money well spent.

In 1993 it became impractical for Alexander to remain at Elizabeth Street and he moved out to a large first-floor flat on the south side of

Hoxton Square near a nightclub called the Blue Note. Hoxton was run down, boarded up, the light industrial buildings were empty and there were few shops and no restaurants.

To say Hoxton was scruffy would be polite, yet it was a magnet for British creativity at the time. Living there were many of the artists who would later find fame as the YBAs (Young British Artists), including Gary Hume, Sarah Lucas, Mat Collishaw and Tracey Emin. Also in the area was a young curator who would become one of my best friends in the art world, Gregor Muir, author of *Lucky Kunst*, a book about his time with the YBAs in Hoxton. Alexander later moved around the corner to Rivington Street. There was no money for heating and he wore a ski suit while he was designing.

Predictably, this part of Shoreditch swiftly became very fashionable. Alexander guffawed to me that as soon as the local landlords 'saw a few mullet haircuts, the rents tripled'.

Issie was certainly Alexander's most influential cheerleader, but by no means his only one. His brilliance attracted a close-knit bunch of collaborators who worked for him for free.

Some of these other people became de facto rivals for Alexander's attention and, ultimately, patronage. Most prominently, Alexander asked Katy England, a young stylist, to work for him. Issie was irritated because she felt she deserved this job for McQueen, and it painfully reminded her that already, at just 35, she was no longer young in the fashion world.

Issie's 'job' for McQueen was instead to be a walking, talking ambassadress for his clothes and his vision. She wore his clothes and told influential friends like Anna Wintour about him. Later, when McQueen became a star, Issie became defensive about this, bridling at suggestions that all she had done was introduce Alexander to 'rich people'.

That Issie was a deeply significant influence on McQueen is uncontested. McQueen dedicated his fourth show in 1994 to her.

After one early McQueen show, the photographer Mario Testino, one of the leading photographers in the world, asked me: 'Where do all these ideas come from? It is Isabella, isn't it?'

Alexander sometimes described Issie as a 'terminal disease – everything she does rubs off on you'.

Philip Treacy whom Issie had 'discovered' first, sometimes found Issie's championship of McQueen hard to take. He says, 'It was like Issie having two lovers. I was the first one – and now there was a second.'

McQueen's clothes often created a storm in the press, especially his 'bumster' trousers – which showed the crack of a girl's bottom in an erotic way. The bumsters were inspired, McQueen said, by 'builders' bum'. On Issie's slim and elegant figure, they looked incredible.

The press, with one or two honourable exceptions, were generally hostile to McQueen. Particularly offensive to the moral majority was a show called 'Highland Rape' at Hawksmoor's Christchurch, Spitalfields. The theme was the Highland clearances and rape of women, and some journalists snapped their notebooks shut in anger at what they incorrectly interpreted as a mysogynistic show, featuring models with blood tricking down their legs.

I had a small investment in the Highland Rape show, having put £300 on a credit card for McQueen tartan. Issie made full use of this investment to gather in quite a few McQueen tartan clothes.

I asked Alexander whether he hated women apart from his mother and, I assumed, Isabella. He told me he did not. He wanted women to be empowered by his clothes – he wanted them to be strong and elegant.

When McQueen told Issie that he had slept with a girl, Issie was chuffed.

'Your father Ron is going to be pleased to hear this,' she said, her massive cheeky grin plastered across her face, as she picked up the telephone to call Biggerstaff Road with the happy tidings.

Other than 'Highland Rape', McQueen's most dramatic shows were based on dark themes: Dante's Inferno, Bedlam, a show featuring models with prosthetic limbs. But underpinning all the drama was exquisite and highly skilled tailoring. The shows were always staged in fantastic, frequently post-industrial locations – an old bus depot in Victoria or Borough Market before it was developed.

In later years, as the balance of power in their relationship shifted, Alexander's ego grew and he became more demanding, moody, rude and often emotionally cruel to Issie. But between 1992 and 1996, there was much in Alexander's relationship with Issie which was healthy for her. His love for her, his humour and the growing acknowledgement of his talent was important for Issie's seld-esteem and well-being.

I admired McQueen for firmly detaching himself from the dramas that were occurring in Issie's life during this period: her father's death in 1993 and her anger at her disinheritance, and our failure to have children.

'Detmar – I hear you're firing blanks,' was his only comment on the situation.

**Isabella and Alexander McQueen at the edge of the catwalk, 1996.**

# CHAPTER FORTY

## Sydney Street

After 18 months of haggling, our insurance company agreed to repair the party wall at 67 Elizabeth Street. We did not have much money – my earnings at the Bar and Issie's earnings as a freelance stylist were slim – so when we were forced to move out of Elizabeth Street we had to find economical options. We lived for six months with Philip Treacy, who had a flat in West Halkin Street, but by January 1994, we were living rent-free with my maternal uncle Desmond de Silva and his wife Princess Katarina of Yugoslavia, at their home at 28 Sydney Street in Chelsea. Of course, we usually spent the weekends – which could start as early as Thursday and finish as late as Tuesday – at Hilles.

Uncle Desmond is a Queen's Counsel – the rank given to the most senior members of the Bar in England – and was then head of his chambers in the Inner Temple. I had often gone to see him in court and been very impressed by his witty, polished and searching cross-examinations. Aged 12, I had watched him sentencing a villain in Knightsbridge Crown Court, who shouted at him as he was being taken down to prison, 'You're a cunt!'

Uncle Desmond called him back, and then sentenced him, for contempt of court, to a further spell in prison, saying, 'Who is the cunt now?' Cue broad smiles from ushers and others in the court. The villain appealed against the increased sentence but the Court of Appeal upheld it.

My aunt Katarina is a warm and kind woman, with a raucous laugh. She had had a strange life growing up on a small apple farm in Sussex, despite the fact that her grandfather was King Alexander I of Yugoslavia. He had been assassinated in 1934 in Marseilles on a state visit to France by a Croat employed by Mussolini.

We had a small bedroom and bathroom on the ground floor of the house and we lived in London that way for two years. Even though we were away at Hilles at the weekends, it was still quite an achievement that we all lived contentedly together for such a long time.

Sometimes my uncle could be dismissive about Issie's work in fashion and our interest in art. At Hilles once, having been subjected to a tirade of mockery at lunch, Issie stormed off from the table. My uncle soon apologised to Issie. But when Desmond and Katarina were entertaining military and political figures at Sydney Street, we would be asked to keep out of the way. Uncle Desmond was worried that Issie's Philip Treacy hats and outré clothes might shock his conservative guests, and he was not having his nephew spoil any of his stories.

# CHAPTER
# FORTY-ONE

## *Exotic Fruits*

Over the two years we were living with Uncle Desmond and Katarina, we tried three times to have a baby by in vitro fertilisation
(IVF).

When we married, Issie had been excited about becoming a mother,
and before our marriage she told me that she had herself checked out
and believed everything was in order in terms of her fertility. She told
me that she would not think it right to get married if she could not
produce a child.

But I do not know the whole truth to this day. Issie could be
extremely secretive about her interactions with medical professionals.
One of the reasons Issie wanted to have a baby was to produce an heir
for Hilles. A male heir would have gone down well with my mother, and
effectively secured the house for us.

Late one night, after yet another attempt at IVF had failed, Issie told
me about the birth of Titus Groan, Mervyn Peake's creation with violet
eyes, the heir to the 77th Earl and Countess of Groan, who lived at
Gormenghast with its Tower of Flints and Hall of Bright Carvings. After
giving birth, the Countess ordered the nanny to take the baby away,
and said she did not want to see it for the next six years. She preferred
to be with the birds who lived in her hair.

My own childhood had been unusual. My mother had three children by the time she was 21. My father did not like babies, so all of us had been farmed out to neighbours to be raised.

I was sent to Upper Holcombe farmhouse, a mile from Hilles, where Mrs Large, the kindly farmer's wife, looked after me. I loved Mrs Large and her family but it was obviously confusing for a young child to be sent off in this way. My brother Amaury was sent to a great aunt in Hampstead, and Selina was primarily raised by my grandparents in Paris. I was reprieved from this extraordinary existence after a year when I had a nasty bout of pneumonia, and my parents brought me back to Hilles to care for me.

Perhaps because of this traumatic experience of childhood, or perhaps because adult responsibility had been thrust on me at 14, when my father died, I had no great longing to be a father. I told Issie that I had married her because I loved her, and wanted to have fun with her and live my life with her, not because I wanted to have a baby. But Issie did, desperately so.

Issie had been brought up to believe in male primogeniture and still believed in it despite the disastrous emotional legacy of that tradition in her own family and others she knew well. To try and reduce the pressure on her, I told Issie that the sex of a child did not matter. I came up with the names for a child. I chose Andromeda for a girl, because I was fascinated by her story in Greek mythology: she is chained to a rock and rescued by Perseus. If we had a boy, we would call him Plantagenet, as my grandmother's family had Plantagenet blood in their veins. Issie loved the choices.

But nothing happened. After two years, Issie and I had ourselves checked out at the Queen Charlotte Hospital in Goldhawk Road in Hammersmith.

We were fine.

Still nothing happened.

Evelyn's death had triggered in Isabella a hyperactive thyroid condition and we thought that might have something to do with it. Issie went to see a top specialist and even ordered me to stop drinking in our quest to produce a child, but it was all to no avail.

In June 1994, Issie and I consulted Mr Goswamy, a leading expert on IVF, whereby eggs are fertilised outside the body before being implanted back in the womb. Mr Goswamy was the medical director of the Churchill Clinic, situated at 80 Lambeth Road.

On 4 July 1994, Issie, aged 35, started her treatment with a course of injections. Issie liked Mr Goswamy, but I was superstitious and found the photographs of babies on the walls in the Churchill to be dangerously challenging fate. What if it did not work? What horrible effect would that have on Issie?

On 15 July Issie had an operation to deal with her hyperactive thyroid, and then on 13 August we had our first attempt at implanting a fertilised egg. After a few days, we were told it had not worked.

It was an expensive business. In a meeting at Stroud my bank manager asked me what the payments for £3000 were for. When I replied 'IVF', he quickly approved an increase in my overdraft.

The stress of the IVF treatment sometimes caused Issie to behave even more erratically than normal. In October we took the ferry to Ireland for a wedding, and Issie discovered that the boat had a beauty parlour on board. She booked herself a massage and a manipedi. We docked at Rosslare at 8pm, but Issie was still having a great time with her manicurist. She told me she would be another 30 minutes. I was fuming because I had been told that crossing Ireland would take three hours and I was worried the pub we were staying at would now be closed when we arrived. Then, when she finally emerged and we disembarked, Issie insisted that she needed a steak to eat. I cursed her, calling her a 'fuck artist'. She paid no attention to me, calmly ate her steak in the port then came over to the car. But instead of getting into it, she climbed onto the bonnet and started to dance.

'Is this a fuck artist Detmar?' she shouted as she danced, the bemused ferry workers looking on, 'Is this a fuck artist?'

After a few minutes she clambered off the car, got into the driver's seat and furiously drove across Ireland at incredible speed. We got there in an hour and a half.

We ploughed on with the IVF all the next year, but nothing happened.

'We are like a pair of exotic fruits that cannot breed when placed together,' Issie would sigh as each new round of IVF failed.

She tried to put a brave face on it, but the failure to have children hurt immensely. For many years she bought beautiful children's clothes and kept them hidden away in a wardrobe. Many years later, when Plum Sykes had her first child, Issie could not bring herself to meet her friend's child for six months.

After a few years Issie had a contraceptive coil put in. I was very upset. I had always hoped that, like Sarah in the Bible, we may have had a miracle child, but she had clearly given up.

# CHAPTER
# FORTY-TWO

## Highland Tragedy

A s well as the ongoing failure to conceive, a major emotional distur-
bance was wrought in Issie's life at this time by the extraordinary
tragedy that befell the Frasers.

On 15 March 1994, Issie's first cousin Andrew, 42, the youngest son
of Uncle Shimi and Aunt Rosie, was killed in Tanzania by a charging
buffalo. He was, as Issie said, trying to shoot it, but, exhausted after a
long safari, he missed, and the animal killed him.

Issie went up to Scotland with her sisters to the funeral in Eskadale,
the Lovat church in Inverness.

Then, unbelievably, on 26 March, Andrew's brother Simon, 54,
Master of Lovat, dropped dead from his horse in front of Beaufort
Castle from a heart attack, just as the huntsman of the Old Dounie
hunt was whipping in the hounds.

For Issie, to be back at Eskadale to bury her other cousin just two
weeks later was a shattering event. Simon's death subsequently
revealed the massive financial pressure he was under at the time of his
death. His investments – including a huge salmon farm, a water
bottling plant, wineries in Australia, oil-exploration ventures, gambles
on the stock market and Lloyd's Insurance – had all been haemorragh-
ing money. The parallels between him and their mutual grandfather

Jock were all too evident. In the 1960s Simon had inherited an estate that stretched from the east to the west coast of Scotland, but had over the years been selling it off to invest in his business schemes.

More, it was now revealed, needed to be sold. Beaufort Castle, the Fraser family home for 700 years, set proudly above the River Beauly, was sold.

Poor Uncle Shimi could not bear to attend either of his sons' funerals. He was, he told us pathetically when we visited him a few weeks later, a 'broken old bottle'.

Shimi Lovat had described Doddington as the land of milk and honey, and for Issie and I, the Scotland of the Frasers was the same. There had been brilliant conversation, good wine, dressing up for meals, picnics in glens and by the river, shooting and stalking on the hills and fishing in the river. Staying with the Frasers at Beaufort and Filean Aigas had helped heal the hurt Issie felt from the loss of Doddington.

And now it was all gone.

Uncle Shimi never recovered. He died a year later in Aunt Rosie's arms, on the anniversary of Andrew's death.

# CHAPTER
# FORTY-THREE

## *Alexander's Betrayal*

On Saturday 20 January 1996, I set off with Issie and Bryan on the new Eurostar train which left London from Waterloo station, arriving two-and-a-half hours later at the Gare du Nord station in Paris. It was a journey Issie and I would make regularly during the next six years.

Our friend John Galliano had just been appointed designer for Givenchy by Bernard Arnault, who was building up his LVMH luxury goods brand, and we had been invited to his first show. John was thrilled by the new arrangement. Finally, he had the financial security and the back-up to design without endless money worries.

Everywhere on the Métro in Paris there were large images of Isabella from the Steven Meisel shoot in Paris for Italian *Vogue* in 1993. Steven was making money on the image for an advertising campaign. Issie, the model in the photograph and inspiration for it, had received nothing.

We returned to London on the night of Monday 22 January to 52 Elizabeth Street, a flat above a wine shop that we had moved into with Philip and his boyfriend Stefan Bartlett, Issie's former assistant. I sensed that things were starting to hot up for Issie.

Then, on 5 March, Amy Spindler, the fashion writer of the *New York Times,* wrote a story headlined 'In London, Blueblood meets Hot Blood'.

It was about Issie and her two discoveries, Alexander McQueen and Philip Treacy, and described Issie as 'the key' to the McQueen and Treacy shows.

This article in the *New York Times* was an important piece of recognition for Issie. It thrust her back into the American spotlight as well. Back in New York, André Leon Talley spluttered on his coffee as he read of his former protégé's achievements in the paper of record.

Spindler described the venue of Alexander's show at the Hawksmoor-designed Christchurch in Spitalfields in detail, lingering on the detail of a typically macabre McQueen touch – a skeleton seated in the front row.

When Alexander received his ovation at the end of the show, Spindler wrote, he was carrying two bouquets, one of which he gave to his Mum, and one of which he gave to Issie, to whom the show was dedicated.

Alexander would later explain to Hamish Bowles in an interview in American *Vogue* that he had dedicated the show to Issie because it was 'Very Issie – in a way macabre, romantic, theatrical, street-wise, and honest'.

In her piece, Amy Spindler also mentioned the other designers Issie was championing, the most notable of whom was Julien Macdonald. He came from the tough steel town of Merthyr Tydfil in South Wales, where his father worked in the steel foundries and his mother in a light-bulb factory. Issie styled Julien's graduate show at the Royal College of Art, getting Honor to model in it, to the fury of the teaching staff, who wanted the graduates all to use the same models. Honor had to sidestep angry teachers as she went down the catwalk.

A swathe of publicity followed, in both the UK and, importantly for Issie, in American *Vogue* in September. In that interview she told her friend Hamish Bowles:

If you're beautiful, you don't need clothes. If you're ugly like me, you're like a house with no foundations; you need something to build you up.

Issie was riding high, and the rumour mill was crackling with speculation that McQueen would soon be offered a massive deal along the lines of John Galliano's arrangement with Givenchy. As a result, the media pack started going crazy to photograph Alexander. At Philip's Treacy's show, which Issie was styling, I sat in the front row with Alexander and Bryan. As the photographers swarmed around him, Alexander became more and more uncomfortable, telling them to go away.

Bryan told him sanguinely, 'You'll have to get used to this.'

But Alexander never did. 'I'd rather be at home watching *Coronation Street*,' he'd say.

On 27 September, Tanqueray Gin sponsored Alexander's show held in the old bus station in Victoria. Alexander had insisted that I sit in the middle of the front row facing the catwalks, where models splashed through rivers of gin (Issie, who was styling the show, was backstage). On one side of me was Grace Coddington of American *Vogue* and on the other was Suzy Menkes of the *International Herald Tribune* – two of the most important members of the fashion press. It was a spectacular production, but I couldn't help being amused when I looked at the programme and saw that 'Tanqueray' was misspelt.

A few days after this triumph, at the beginning of October, Alexander called Issie. LVMH had been in touch. John Galliano was going to Dior – and they were offering him John's job at Givenchy. He wanted to come down to Hilles to think about it.

Issie called our accountant John Banks, who had been helping me since 1988 to keep Hilles afloat. John and his wife Elaine and their two young sons came over to Hilles for lunch to meet Alexander. Alexander had been hawking in the morning. He was kissing his boyfriend Murray Arthur. John's young sons Garth and James had never seen anything like it before.

Alexander was undecided about taking the job. The money was good but LVMH were not interested in helping him with his own line.

On 8 October, John Banks met up with Alexander at Waterloo station to go to Paris. In the distance, John spied Issie with a porter and a huge pile of hat boxes. Everyone was on edge. During the journey, Issie met up with a friend and, to break the tension, Issie and her friend started swapping clothes.

Alexander was tense, and blamed Issie. 'She is doing my fucking head in,' he told John repeatedly.

At the initial meeting, Alexander did not sign the contract. Issie had borrowed a friend's flat in Paris and she and Alexander went back there to rest before Alexander went back to the meeting, which was subsequently disrupted by a phone call. Could Givenchy send round a locksmith? Issie had locked herself out of the flat.

By the time Issie got to the LVMH offices, a fat three-year contract had been signed.

I had told John to make sure Issie got something. On the train back to London, John broached the subject with Alexander.

'Issie and I are not about money,' was all he would say.

The brutal fact was that after all the help she had given him, Alexander had not given Issie a role at Givenchy.

Then it got worse. It emerged that he was taking Issie's younger rival, Katy England, as his new assistant.

On 14 October the announcement of Alexander's new position was made. The following day found Issie styling the Spice Girls.

Alexander's betrayal of his first and greatest champion was absolute.

# CHAPTER
# FORTY-FOUR

## *Sophie*

Despite her betrayal by Alexander at Givenchy, Isabella gritted her teeth and determined to remain friends with her former protégé. She would continue to be given pride of place in the front row of his shows, and he would still have an open invitation to stay at Hilles. The two did continue to collaborate on various projects over the next few years as well. These collaborations were ad hoc rather than ongoing (and contractual), but it was some consolation to Isabella to retain and be retained by Alexander as a part-time creative conspirator at least.

In a way, Alexander had been right. The relationship between them wasn't about money, it was about ideas, and that they continued to inspire each other was an important feature of both their lives over the next few years.

But the balance of power had definitely shifted, and Alexander could be cruel to Isabella sometimes, and would gloat about his new financial clout.

In January 1997, however, Issie and I, determined to make the best of it, headed over to Paris for Alexander's first couture collection at Givenchy.

Honor Fraser was to be the star. Despite not being on the payroll, Issie had been very involved in the production of the show. I had been sent down to Hilles to arrange for one of her rams to be killed, as the theme of Alexander's first show was loosely based on Jason and the Argonauts and he needed a pair of ram's horns. In Gloucestershire I selected a sheep with very curly headgear for the chop. The next time I saw those horns they were painted gold and being worn by Naomi Campbell.

They looked fantastic, but although Issie put a brave face on, it was hard for either of us to be truly happy at the way things had turned out.

Later that month, Issie's feelings about the debacle with McQueen came out in an interview with Lydia Slater in the *Daily Telegraph*.

There was a birthday on the shoot which Lydia had attended for the piece, and Issie was drunk, 'gulping Bollinger from a workman's mug' according to the writer. As a result, she spoke her mind about the situation.

> The role of a muse is changing. Traditionally, we haven't been paid, but as Bryan Ferry once said to me, one should be paid for ideas as well as the physical manifestation of them. If Alexander uses some of my ideas in his show, and he has, I don't get paid; he does ... I've decided I'm going to be paid from now on too. Before this, my only reward was seeing the people I've discovered taking off, and that drives me nuts, because they leave me behind.

Issie was struggling to make a living. Since leaving *Vogue* at the end of 1994 she had worked as a freelance stylist, organising editorial and advertising shoots, choosing the clothes, looks, accessories and models.

Although work energised Issie – and she had a terrific work ethic – the financial insecurity that was the legacy of her father's disinheritance depressed her. She would often fantasise about being a lady of leisure, amply supported by a rich husband. From time to time, we would meet such women. Once in Istanbul we went to have dinner with some friends who had a house on the Bosphorus. Issie arrived, looking amazing in her Philip Treacy hat, a great dress and Manolo Blahnik high heels and was on fine form. At the dinner there were several very rich women with yachts and private jets. But they looked sad, and bored with their lives. After the dinner Issie said how lucky they were.

'But Issie did you not see? They were fascinated by you – and wanted to be like you!' I said.

'But, Det, they have everything,' Issie replied.

The fashion and advertising industry is fiercely competitive and, as a stylist, Issie found regular jobs tough to come by despite her fame. One photographer who did use her frequently was Lord Snowdon, in his shoots for Aquascutum. Frequently, the location was Hilles. Once, when a few panelled doors were used as a backdrop, Issie had her fee paid directly to a carpenter to remake in oak the garden doors that had begun to fall to pieces. Ever the purist, Issie insisted that the new oak doors should not suffer the indignity of having preservatives painted on to them – insisting that if they were left to 'breathe' they would be able to defend themselves against inclement weather. Issie and I had to physically restrain Dave, who was itching to coat the doors in Cuprinol.

Another campaign Issie got was for a Whirlpool washing machine. Issie put her cousin Honor into the washing machine and spun her around a bit. She was proud of working with our friend Jasper Conran, who had a lucrative contract with Debenhams.

Issie had some successful stylists assisting her during these years: William Baker, who transformed Kylie Minogue; and David Thomas, originally a plumber's assistant from a village in Gloucestershire, who went to Hollywood and found fame working with Angelina Jolie and Mariah Carey. And then there was Stefan Bartlett, who came to Issie from Orlando Campbell's club, Green Street – beloved of Lucien Freud, Damien Hirst, Bryan Ferry and Mick Jagger – who became Philip's boyfriend.

* * * * *

In the weeks after she was dumped by Alexander, Issie discovered Sophie Dahl. Sophie recalls that she had been out to lunch with her mother at a smart restaurant in Elizabeth Street, which descended into a row when her mother insisted she go to secretarial college. Sophie, 18, wanted to go to art school.

In tears, Sophie rushed out of the restaurant and sat down, by chance, upon the steps of our house to smoke a cigarette and gather herself.

It just so happened that at that very moment, Issie pulled up outside Elizabeth Street in a cab. She teetered out of the taxi, laden down with

# SOPHIE

shopping bags and laughing filthily with the driver. Sophie was transfixed. She asked Issie if she needed any help with her shopping bags.
   Issie was impressed by Sophie's offer to help. She later explained:

   I adore good manners. Absolutely love them. So. I said,
   'Actually you could. But what's the matter? You're crying.'

Sophie was size 14 and hardly the classic model shape. But Issie
thought differently:

   I saw this great big blow-up doll with enormous bosoms. I just
   could not believe the size of her bosoms. The voice was gentle.
   The skin – milky white.

When Sophie told her about the fight with her mother over her future,
Issie asked her if she wanted to be a model.
   'Yes, please,' said Sophie.
   And then, recalls Sophie:

   We went and found my mother, and told her I was going to be
   a model. This wasn't at all what she had in mind. But then, it
   was very bizarre, we went back to Issie's and toasted my future
   with champagne. Issie got me dressed up in her clothes and we
   all went out to dinner.

   I was very doubtful of Issie's latest discovery. Sophie did not look
like a model at all. But this did not matter to Issie, who insisted on using
her in her next photoshoot for Italian *Vogue*. Apart from Sophie's
looks, size and personality, all of which Issie adored, Issie shrewdly told
me, 'Sophie's surname gives her good name recognition.' Issie was
banking on the famous Dahl name – Roald Dahl was her grandfather
and the heroine of *The BFG* is named Sophie after her – to help her
turn Sophie into a success.

# CHAPTER
# FORTY-FIVE

## *Freelancing*

Issie may not have been making much money but she did have an important creative breakthrough at this time, challenging the 'heroin chic' look with her own version of gothic styling.

In fact, this was the style of the shoot featuring Honor described by Lydia Slater of the *Daily Telegraph*. Issie was driven to innovate by her fury at what had unfolded with McQueen. She was going to prove that she was not just a woman 'who knew rich people', as those defending Alexander's decision to cut her out of the deal were claiming.

The shoot was for the magazine *The Face*. The photographer was Sean Ellis, a young photographer from Brighton, to whom she had taken a shine. Keen to change Honor's image – Honor had recently done a campaign for Terry's chocolates, which Issie felt was a mistake – Isabella had stained Honor's voluptuous lips with clotted stage blood, matted her hair and painted her face an unhealthy chalk-white.

'Issie and I took on the heroin chic look of photographers David Sims, Corine Day and Juergen Teller (and combined it with) with our modern version of gothic,' says Sean.

It was at about this time that I left the Bar, initially to work for a firm of solicitors in Bristol who specialised in intellectual property. My aim was to assist Issie in trying to gain rewards for her ideas. I had some success when I managed to prove that the story by Isabella and Sean was 'strikingly similar' to a pop video made later that year. We entered into negotiations and I achieved enough compensation for Sean, who as the photographer had the copyright to the images, to buy a new car.

Issie, yet again, got nothing.

# CHAPTER
# FORTY-SIX

## *Theed Street*

On 7 April 1997 we completed the purchase of our new house, 5 Theed Street, which was six minutes walk from Waterloo station. Theed Street is one of three small streets built in brick in the 1820s to house florists and hat makers who worked across Waterloo Bridge in Covent Garden when it was a flower and fruit market. It had accommodated, in other words, characters like the Doolittle family in Bernard Shaw's *Pygmalion*.

The house was tiny with an outside loo and a small garden at the back. We commissioned the firm of Azman Owen – comprising two architects, one Turkish, the other American – to modernise the house, and at the back they built a glass and steel extension to include a bathroom with a fish-tank bath, and a kitchen facing the garden. Issie had her own little dressing room with glass-faced sliding drawers to store her hats. We dug out the basement to make an office and slick storage cupboards for Issie's clothes. Under the Portland stone floor we laid underfloor heating. We borrowed more money to do the work.

Theed Street gradually became a showpiece for our contemporary art collection, which we started to put together from about 1999 through our gallery Modern Art. We had a Noble and Webster electric fountain called *Excessive Sensual Indulgence*; a Jim Lambie blue glitter record deck called *Grafitti*, with safety pins hanging from below; a Simon Periton portrait of the Duchess of Windsor; a Nigel Cooke painting, *Carpet*, which had lots of cigarette butts and chicken bones; and paintings by Simon Bill, Rachel Howard and Clare Woods. On the ground and first floors was an orange and black floor installation by Richard Woods called *Rustic Daisy Pattern.*

Issie's photographs with Sean Ellis were framed by Colin Glen, who was in charge of making Damien Hirst's pill cabinets. They were stunning. Mario Testino told Issie, 'I am not surprised you are short of money. This framing must have cost a fortune.'

Architecturally it was a triumph. The transformation of 5 Theed Street won a prize at the RIBA.

I hated it.

The rooms were too small, I found Lambeth depressing, and apart from some cardboard furniture by Stefan Bartlett's father David, there was nowhere to sit. In 2005 we sold the house for a profit, but I cannot remember it without a shudder of unhappiness.

# CHAPTER
# FORTY-SEVEN

## *Money Worries*

Burned badly by the experience with Alexander, Issie did make commercial progress, in 1997, at least. On 29 April, over lunch, Sarah Doukas and her brother Simon Williams, the directors of Storm model agency, which discovered Kate Moss, came to an arrangement with Issie to pay her a finder's fee and a commission on the models she introduced to them.

Up until then Issie had made nothing from her models apart from the perfume from Stella. Honor had generously sent Issie £5000 to help with the house purchase.

Sophie was one of the first models Issie discovered to be covered by the new arrangement with Storm – but she knew nothing of it till Issie rang her a few years later to complain that she hadn't been making very much money in a particular year.

On 3 May 1997, Alexander came down to Hilles with a BBC film crew. They were very hungover from celebrating Tony Blair's recent election victory. Alexander was filmed hawking, and talking with Issie at Hilles.

When he was asked, 'Are you irritated that people say you owe your success to Issie?'

He replied, 'Yes' – but qualified his reply, by admitting, accurately, that that he 'owed a lot to Issie'.

The question I wanted to ask for the documentary was, 'Now you are rich and successful, why have you not given Issie a role or some financial remuneration?'

But Issie was too terrified of losing McQueen's friendship and patronage to push it. She wanted to try and remain calm and phlegmatic about his betrayal. I was under a strict gagging order not to upset him. As I smoked a cigar in the Long Room he told me nastily, 'I am the tycoon now, Detmar.'

He did not mean it in a jocular way. It was McQueen telling me that he was richer and more powerful than us now, and that we had better be servile to him – or else. Our earlier happy casual friendship was over.

It was particularly unfair to Issie becauae she had only ever encouraged and helped Alexander, yet he now appeared to want to lord it over her and revelled in that. But Alexander was right, he was in the driving seat now, and although many in the fashion world stood up for Issie in private, rare were those who dared to criticise McQueen publicly. One person who did, however, was Issie's friend, and one of Alexander's most prestigious clients, Daphne Guinness. Daphne, to whom Alexander had of course been introduced by Issie, said, 'Everyone gets a contract but Issie just gets clothes. Clothes allowances do not pay the bills.'

Daphne was one of the friends who stood by Issie to the very end, stepping up to the plate and offering both practical and emotional help in the tough times that were ahead of us.

Although Issie was doing fantastic work at *The Face* and, occasionally, Italian *Vogue,* neither of these magazines paid Issie anything. She needed a platform to show her ideas.

At Hilles we thought about what to do. We talked about it to our friends Peter and Patricia Mitchell when they came to visit us one afternoon. I was loosely working with Peter in his solicitors' firm in Bristol and Patricia was a formidable local businesswoman. They were both Oxford graduates.

Then we had a stroke of luck. The *Sunday Times* casually rang Issie for a quote on a fashion-related story. Patricia, who had answered the phone, replied that Issie would not give a quote but that she would like to do a story for newspaper.

A local artist, Georgina Taylor, was shot by Issie for the cover of the *Style* section as a result of this conversation. Jeremy Langmead, the editor of the section, was so impressed that he called Issie and arranged to have lunch with her. At the Blueprint Café at the Design Museum in Butler's Wharf, just across the River Thames from the News International offices at Wapping, Jeremy asked Issie whether she would consider being the Fashion Director of the *Sunday Times*. The money, he apologised, was not much at £40,000 pa.

Issie, with no regular income, did not have to think long.

'Yes,' she replied immediately.

It was, after Anna Wintour in 1984, the second big break of her professional life. I was summoned by Issie from Gloucestershire to have lunch with Jeremy. He was charming. I knew Issie would work well with him.

On 29 May 1997 Issie received a letter outlining her contract from Anthony Bambridge, the managing editor of the *Sunday Times*. Issie had to produce 12 fashion stories and was to have an advisory role in other fashion stories. She was back in business. Alexander told her, 'I hear you have been resurrected, Issie.'

And she had been. But she had not lost her principles.

She gave 10 per cent of her contract to Patricia.

# CHAPTER FORTY-EIGHT

## *The* Sunday Times

Issie, 38, was, of course, delighted with her new appointment as Fashion Director at the *Sunday Times,* and she was particularly gratified to receive congratulations from her mother, Helen. We were trying to mend fences. Helen was coming to stay regularly at Hilles for Easter and Christmas and Issie would use part of her salary to pay the service charge on her mother's flat in Pelham Court for the next three years.

The offices of the *Sunday Times* are in a big fortress-like building in Wapping. They are open plan and uninspiring – her then-assistant Chloe Beeny recalls it as 'an office for vampires' with 'no windows or skylight above. It was hard to tell what time of the day it was or what the weather was like.'

Issie, of course, made life interesting by turning up for work in her usual extraordinary outfits. *Style* editor Jeremy Langmead would later recall,

> When she first started I used to make her go a really long way around to her office, so everyone could see her and I could monitor their reactions. She didn't notice a thing. She [thought she looked] quite normal.

Jeremy was married to the formidable writer India Knight and could handle strong women. Other colleagues I became fond of were Issie's assistant Emine Saner of Turkish origin and Rachel Cooke. After Issie died, Emine wrote Issie's obituary in the *Guardian,* and Rachel interviewed me – the only interview I did – in the *Observer.* I also got to know and admire Colin McDowell, who was a great champion of John Galliano.

When Issie started there in 1997, the reputation of the *Sunday Times* for fashion was so bad that designers refused to lend their clothes for photoshoots.

Issie changed all that singlehandedly.

The first person Issie worked with was Mario Testino, who shot photographs of Honor, which appeared on 27 July 1997. Mario worked for free – a testament to the enormous respect in which he held Issie.

When Issie went off to Paris to for the couture shows in July, she wore a gold Givenchy patent dress, a feathered bird hat, and dragged behind her a massive chain by RCA student Amanda Mansell, which represented the burden of women. She carried the oily chain to a party that night at Karl Lagerfeld's house in Rue de l'Université, soiling the white carpets.

Art-loving Karl was magnificently unperturbed.

Issie's presence at the *Sunday Times* gave it a respect in the fashion industry which it had hitherto not enjoyed. As Jeremy Langmead said in 2001:

> She raised the magazine's profile straightaway. Whenever she goes to a show its 'Oh look, there's Isabella Blow with the *Sunday Times.*'

As well as working at the *Sunday Times*, Issie was working harder than ever at Hilles, and had succeeded in renting out Spoonbed Farm on the estate to Thomas Dane, an art dealer, and Hamish Bowles, European editor at large of American *Vogue*. Issie and I loved having him at Hilles, and Hamish reciprocated. And, of course, as one of the great fashion historians of our time, he was always responsive to Issie's outfits:

> She had to go and have a conference with the estate manager and she'd found this young Japanese designer who'd made her a coat out of what were essentially very, very brightly coloured

bin-liners. They were sack-like receptacles that hung limply from the outfit. She was also wearing very high, Manolo, brocade shoes and a Philip Treacy head piece that was all question marks and curlicues. She felt this was an entirely acceptable ensemble for a business meeting.

She then ran backwards and forwards across the courtyard at Spoonbed and of course when you ran in this coat, these sacks that had hung flaccidly around her filled with air. It was quite incredible and I photographed her trudging across the newly furrowed field to have her interview with the estate manager who was waiting in his tractor, and appeared entirely unfazed by this vision.

Every outfit was a delight in lots of different ways, but there was a fetishistic aspect to some of Issie's clothing. I always saw it as armorial. She herself expressed the notion that hats could be a disguise or a veil, and her clothes were the same. They were very expressive but sometimes they were more about veiling her identity than revealing it. When I went to Hilles and saw the actual armor there – the halberds and the breast plates – I felt that it was very close to the way Issie saw her clothing; as a protection against the world, a protection against the inadequacies, as she perceived them, of her own body and her looks. The clothes were a way of refocusing attention away from those things.

# CHAPTER
# FORTY-NINE

## *Hotel du Cap*

The weekend after the couture shows in Paris, Issie brought down to Hilles one of her discoveries, the designer Julien Macdonald, who was now working with Karl Lagerfeld at Chanel, and thinking about his future options.

I was not doing so well, however. I was very tired and finding it hard to get out of bed. I went to see my GP, who told me I was suffering from exhaustion. The following week, Issie arranged for us to go and stay with Sarah St George, the eldest granddaughter of the original William Hill, the bookmaker. A very generous host, she had bought an old farmhouse outside Saint Remy-de-Provence. We set off by train with Prince and Princess Michael's daughter, Ella Windsor.

Through Sarah we had become great friends with Prince and Princess Michael of Kent, who lived five miles away from Hilles at Nether Lypiatt. The Kents would bring their guests to us for a meal as we would take ours to them, including Alexander McQueen. At Hilles, Prince Michael was fascinated to meet Mr Pearl, a former South African dancer who made corsets for the couture houses in Paris, and, as the Prince would often recall in astonishment, had two of his ribs removed to improve his look in a corset.

# HOTEL DU CAP

Issie was horrified to discover during the trip that I had never been to Cap d'Antibes, and insisted we all go and stay at the Hotel du Cap Eden Roc, one of the most beautiful and elegant hotels in the world, set in 22 acres of pine woods facing the Mediterranean and much favoured by heads of state and film stars.

Issie and I had a bedroom facing the sea. The golden bikinis some of their female model guests wore were incredible, the peach bellinis were amazing – but the price, £600 per night, was the most staggering element of all. Sarah kindly paid.

I still owe her.

Issie is a much stronger swimmer than me, and out in the ocean one day she playfully tried to push me under the sea. I had a massive panic attack, the first of many over the next few days. It was a clear warning that there were things in my life that were very wrong, and that it would take more than a holiday in the South of France to cure me.

On my return I went to see a psychiatrist who told me that I should quit working as a lawyer – which I found uncongenial and uninteresting – and go and work in art, which I had for a long time longed to do.

I asked the psychiatrist how long I would take to get better. He said it would have been six months, but thanks to a new wonder drug called Prozac, recovery would be much quicker. After three weeks I stopped taking Prozac, however. I wanted to feel my emotions, and Prozac made me feel that they were being subdued. I preferred to self-prescribe claret.

In September we went to Scotland to stay with Bryan and Lucy, who had rented the Cawdor family hunting lodge at Drynachan. We stalked stags in the Highlands and tried to forget about our troubles with babies and money at home.

Issie got back to London in time for fashion week and then went on to Paris. Issie had no interest in going to the shows in Milan and New York, which were more corporate. At the *Sunday Times*, for the first time in her life, she was independent and did not have to please advertisers. She could do, Jeremy told her, what she liked – except there were to be no nipples in the *Sunday Times Style* section, please.

After fashion week, in early November, Issie went to Paris to do an advertising campaign for John Galliano, and two weeks later she flew to New York to do a commercial shoot with Naomi Campbell and Christie Turlington.

I took Issie to Sicily for Christmas and New Year. Everything was going so well for Issie, but still throughout the trip Issie complained to me of feeling low and depressed and unable to go on. It was my first serious encounter with her melancholia, and it disturbed me deeply. Manic depression is an extraordinarily difficult illness for both the sufferer and their family to cope with.

I tried my best to keep her spirits up. On the advice of Manolo Blahnik, we stayed in Palermo at the Villa Igiea, an art nouveau villa designed for a family who had made a fortune out of tuna and Marsala wine. It was grand and empty. After exploring Palermo, which the British had bombed, we visited the Greek Doric temple at Segesta – which Issie told me was better than anything she had seen in Greece. We then drove to Taormina to stay at the San Domenico Palace – which was not a palace at all but a former monastery with beautiful gardens. Issie and I loathed it and moved out to a smaller hotel run by a friend of my cousin Simon Blow.

Simon was something of a legend along the Corso Umberto in Taormina. The antique dealer saw my name was Blow when I purchased a chandelier Issie wanted to give Philip Treacy. He asked me if I was a relation of Simon Blow and then invited us to join him for a New Year's Eve party given by someone he claimed was 'the Queen of Scotland'.

Did the 'Queen of Scotland' really live outside Taormina?

Of course not. The Scottish royal was a fake – and on our way back from the party we mercilessly teased the hapless, snobbish antique dealer.

At the party a guest kept looking at Issie and asking, 'I know you – you're Isabella Delves Broughton. You were at Oxford, weren't you?' Issie would not reply, and it dawned on me that this was a part of Issie's mysterious life she simply did not wish to talk about.

# CHAPTER FIFTY

## *Jeremy*

Shortly after New Year, in January 1998, Issie and I returned to London from Sicily. Two weeks later we headed off with Issie's new personal assistant, Tassos Sofrinou, on the Eurostar to Paris for the couture shows.

We were staying at the Hotel Duc de St Simon, a little 3-star hotel with a courtyard and climbing wisteria on the walls in the 7th arrondissement in St Germain des Prés. It was warm, quiet and very discreet.

Issie was constantly being delivered enormous bouquets of flowers from John Galliano, Karl Lagerfeld, Marc Jacobs, Thierry Mugler and other designers with short, affectionate handwritten notes to her.

The show Issie was most excited about was John Galliano's Dior couture show in the Opera Garnier, inspired by the legend of the twentieth-century aesthete and muse the Marchesa Casati. The wealthy daughter of an Italian cotton manufacturer, she astonished Venetian society by parading with a pair of leashed cheetahs and wearing live snakes as jewellery. Issie was often compared with the Marchesa – particularly her style and extravagance.

Later that month, we read in Suzy Menkes's column in the *International Herald Tribune* that the house of Nina Ricci had been sold to the Puig family from Barcelona, who were skilled perfumers and owned the Paco Rabanne brand. They now needed, Suzy wrote, a new designer for Nina Ricci.

Issie was straight on the telephone to her assistant Emine at the *Sunday Times,* and ordered her to set up a meeting between the Puigs and Jeremy Scott, a young American designer in his early 20s, whom she had recently discovered.

Scott had grown up on a livestock farm on the Prairies, not far from Kansas City in Missouri. He had the gone to the Pratt Institute in Brooklyn, New York to study fashion and had learnt French at the same time. In 1997, he had set up in Paris, gaining a reputation as an enfant terrible with his gold teeth brace, baggy pants, shaven hairstyles, piercing eyes and big mouth.

He was, in other words, just Issie's kind of project.

It is testament to Issie's influence at the time that, although he was not ultimately hired by Nina Ricci, Mariano Puig made an appointment to see Issie the next day at 9 a.m. When we arrived at the Nina Ricci office, I could tell that the takeover of Nina Ricci had been a hostile one: the sellers had even taken the door handles and light fittings when they had left the previous day.

# CHAPTER FIFTY-ONE

## *Modern Art*

B ack in London, in February, Issie was on the cover of *Time Out* magazine for the London ready-to-wear collections, under the heading 'Wild Things'. Her face was on *Time Out* billboards all around London.

In early March we went to a dinner at the new Nobu restaurant in the newly built Metropolitan Hotel off Park Lane to celebrate the ending of a fashion shoot Issie had just done with David LaChapelle for the *Sunday Times* in a cold and dank abandoned lunatic asylum near Heathrow airport.

In one picture, Sophie Dahl lies in a red bath in a red room with her face and middle section covered in spaghetti, leaving only her bosoms and legs exposed. Devon Aoki is standing over her in a skimpy white dress with her long hair covering her exposed breasts and holding an enormous fork and spoon.

In accordance with The *Sunday Times*'s 'no nipples' rule, the models preserved their modesty with artfully positioned hands and cherries.

During our dinner, we were asked if we would like to come downstairs to the Met Bar to meet Madonna.

David did not know Madonna, and Issie thought he should. So after dinner, Issie and her entourage of about 20 went down to the Met Bar to meet Madonna and her entourage of about 10, who were sitting in a booth near the bar.

Throughout dinner I had been talking to Stuart Shave, a handsome and ambitious 23-year-old who had assisted Issie on the shoot. He had brought a neon sign reading 'Forever' by two unknown artists Tim Noble and Sue Webster, which Issie had loved. We sat at the bar, fore-going the opportunity to squish in next to Madonna, and Stuart told me more about his life.

He had done a fine art course in Nottingham and then worked for several contemporary art galleries. He wanted to set up on his own – and so did I. I had actually been thinking for the past year how to go about it. I had been inspired by the success of Jay Jopling, who had come to stay at Hilles a few months earlier. His tiny White Cube gallery in Duke Street, around the corner from Christies, was the hottest gallery in London, representing Damien Hirst and most of the YBAs.

I knew I needed someone like Stuart and on impulse I told Stuart, 'I will open the gallery with you. What shall we call it? Blow and Shave?'

Stuart thought for a moment. 'My mother always tells me she does not understand modern art. Let's call the gallery Modern Art.'

It was perfect.

We made our first sale in May.

Issie was doing an advertising campaign for Wolfgang Joop with Sean Ellis, and she called Stuart to come and meet Wolfgang, who collects art. From some transparencies that Stuart showed Wolfgang of Tim and Sue's work, and another Scottish artist called Kenny Hunter, Wolfgang bought – for £60,000 – three of Tim and Sue's works and four of Kenny's sculptures. It took him all of 10 minutes.

On 15 May, Wolfgang flew Issie and me to Berlin to stay in Potsdam where he lived. Issie was in celebratory mood. She had earned £25,000 from the campaign and now we had Wolfgang supporting Modern Art.

# CHAPTER
# FIFTY-TWO

## *Swarovski*

The wind was in our sails. On 3 June, six months after meeting Helmut and Dana Swarovski, Issie signed a one-year consultancy contract with D. Swarovski and Co at £40,000 per annum.

We were rich.

Issie worked with Swarovski for the next six years, transforming them from a brand best known for glass animals into the purveyors of choice for luxury crystals in the world of high fashion.

Issie had the vision to see the massive potential of repositioning the crystal business. Helmut Swarovski had been charmed when Isabella rhapsodised about the company's glamorous time in the 1940s and 1950s, when Dior and Schiaparelli had made annual trips to Austria to incorporate crystals into their designs. That was the glamour she aimed to recapture.

Isabella went to a meeting with Swarovski wearing a magnificent lobster hat designed by her French friend Erik Halley – descended, she claimed, from the comet. It was encrusted with crystals, and she used it to demonstrate in a practical way her aesthetic vision of the company's potential for glamour and high fashion. The Swarovski executives, though, thought that it would be a mistake to hire such a person. But Issie had an ally. I had earlier had lunch at Nobu with

Helmut's beautiful blonde daughter, Nadja. She had worked in New York and wanted to change the company's direction but did not have the contacts. As Isabella, in her typically high-handed and funny way, said:

> The point was, they didn't know anybody. They're out in Toblerone country. They were sponsoring the wrong events and the wrong people. I told them what to do and they did it.'

It was Nadja who persuaded her father to take Issie on.

Issie would later persuade Swarovski to sponsor Alexander McQueen for his own label, as well as more outré designers like Julien Macdonald, who would replace McQueen at Givenchy in 2001, and Jeremy.

**Isabella in the front row of Julien Macdonald's fashion show at Queen's Gate tent, London, February 1998, wearing one of her infamous lobster hats, made by Erik Halley.**

# SWAROVSKI

Issie's six-year collaboration with Swarovski was a vindication of Issie's commercial acumen. She was always going to be, as she admitted herself, a loose cannon, but with the right team she could produce gold.

With the Swarovski contract signed, Issie and I set off the same day to find a flat in Paris. It had been a dream of mine to live in Paris since I had stayed with my grandparents there as a small boy in the 1960s, and I had worked out that it cost the *Sunday Times* more to pay for Issie to go to the Hotel Duc de Saint Simon for a month every year to cover the two couture shows and two ready-to-wear shows than it would if she had a flat – and McQueen was in Paris.

Alexander was living in a bright and airy apartment in the Marais with a living room, dining room, a bedroom with a huge wardrobe with mirrored sliding doors, a kitchen and a small bathroom. As luck would have it, he was moving to a bigger place, and we got the apartment for 8000 French francs (about £800) per month.

On our return to London, I negotiated with the *Sunday Times* and Swarovski to each pay half the rent, and as a result, Issie had a rent-free flat in the centre of Paris for the next five years.

I was quite proud of myself.

While we were in Paris, my mother arrived in England from Sri Lanka for Selina's wedding in Stroud on 12 June. She had not been at Hilles for 8 years, and, since Issie and I had been together, Issie had used her own energy – and money – to transform Hilles from a desperate, doomed, leaking pile into one of the most exciting country houses in England.

Now, with the return of my mother, we sensed that all we had worked for at Hilles was suddenly threatened. On 25 August, Issie and I got the keys to 1 Rue Tiron and moved in. With Helga back on the scene, we were going to need our Parisian bolthole more than we could have ever imagined.

# CHAPTER
# FIFTY-THREE

## *Russia*

When Isabella was interested in a book she would order several copies – usually half a dozen. She knew she was careless with her possessions and lost books, and she was keen to give copies of whatever she was interested in to those around her.

In July, when we went to Arles to meet David LaChapelle who was having an exhibition there, she was reading one of her many copies John Richardson's biography of Picasso. I was reading *The Age of Reason* by Jean-Paul Sartre. Issie saw it.

She said, 'Det, it is a very depressing book about abortion.'

I quietly threw it away and read another book.

We travelled on to Menerbes, where we inspected the ruins of the Marquis de Sade's Château de Lacoste, and bought a souvenir T-shirt for Alexander, who was, predictably, a big fan of the Marquis.

We returned from Menerbes to Paris for the couture shows, but had to rush back home for the funeral of my 91-year-old godmother Maureen. She was a Guinness, incredibly rich and the niece of Walter Moyne – the lover of Issie's grandmother Vera.

Just the previous year, godmother Maureen's granddaughters, Evgenia and Ivana, who were good friends of Issie's, arranged a white tie, decorations and tiara ball at Claridge's to celebrate Maureen's 90th birthday. The dance was great fun. I spied the Queen Mother in her tiara chatting happily away with Maureen.

Issie adored Claridge's, and the hotel was protective of Isabella as well. In 2005 when the writer A.A. Gill interviewed Isabella for her MAC lipstick campaign, the doorman told him as he left, 'Be kind to Isabella in your article.'

* * * * *

On 1 September, Issie flew from Paris to St Petersburg to see what was going on in fashion in the new Russia following the collapse of Communist rule. She also wanted to support the launch of Russian *Vogue*, edited by her friend Aliona Doletskaya.

Issie loved St Petersburg and the Hermitage Museum – and sent me a postcard of the Peacock Clock in the collection, designed by the Englishman James Cox and bought in 1780 by Prince Potemkin. It was brought to St Petersburg in pieces and reassembled in 1792. When the clock strikes, the gilded peacock comes to life: it spreads its tail, turns and bows to the spectator.

For her journey on the train to Moscow from St Petersburg, she selected a huge black disc hat and some extraordinary psychedelic furs by Tristan Webber. By the time she arrived in Moscow, however, a big financial and political crisis had broken out. The rouble had lost two-thirds of its value in a few days and President Yeltsin was helpless to do anything. Civil unrest was in the air. Issie took refuge in the flat of the *Daily Telegraph* correspondent. When she called me, she remarked that the main problem was that she could not get any cigarettes.

In the end, Emine got Issie back safely to England – and her Benson & Hedges cigarettes.

# CHAPTER FIFTY-FOUR

## 'WOW'

On Isabella's 40th birthday – 19 November – we opened Modern Art gallery, on the ground floor of 73 Redchurch Street, a narrow, former sweatshop off Bethnal Green Road in the heart of the Bangledeshi immigrant community. We had a Muslim butcher a few doors on one side, where we would buy cigarettes and milk, and a mosque on the other side. Across the street there was nothing much happening apart from a friendly old-fashioned pub called The Owl and the Pussycat. We had found the building in August through a Polish estate agent called Stan – short for Stanislas.

Stuart and I commissioned local architects for the gallery: Will Russell, who would later design all the McQueen stores, and David Adjaye, later a nominee for the Stirling Prize.

The opening was a great success. Stuart, his boyfriend Danilo and I had personally licked and closed 2000 envelopes to artists, collectors, critics, museums and others in the art world for our first exhibition: 'WOW' by Tim Noble and Sue Webster.

Our logo was pink and yellow – inspired by Jamie Read's album cover for the Sex Pistols' *Never Mind the Bollocks*. In the first room of the gallery was a sculpture by Tim and Sue of a pile of rubbish that they had accumulated in six months – two seagulls pecked at a pile of trash that included tin cans, toothpaste tube, used condoms and dead rodents. In darkness the 'sculpture of rubbish' became, with a light fixed on it, a perfect silhouette of the artists. In the second room was a large neon 'WOW' in fluorescent colours, which flashed, in sequence, dark and then bright colours. In the third room was the living room where Stuart and Danilo slept.

After the opening, the artists and about 30 of us went to St. John restaurant to celebrate the opening of the gallery, the exhibition and Issie's birthday. I wore a Victor and Rolf inspired outfit for the opening. Stuart complained it detracted from the art.

Stuart had 49 shares, I had 26 and Issie had 25 which gave us a 51% controlling stake. Stuart and I were the gallery directors.

After Christmas at Hilles with Issie's mother and Simon Blow, we flew to Sri Lanka.

It had been an eventful year. Issie had earned well over a £100,000. I was proud of her. And I had fulfilled my dream of many years to open a contemporary art gallery - in the new, exciting East End.

# CHAPTER
# FIFTY-FIVE

## *Dinner with Elton*

Back in London, at Modern Art, we had received a good review from Waldemar Januszczak in the *Sunday Times,* but we had sold nothing from Tim and Sue's exhibition 'WOW'.

Eventually we had one enquiry from a collector who expressed an interest to commission a small rubbish sculpture for £2500 but refused to pay VAT. Stuart handed me the phone to talk to the hard-nosed collector. It is normal in the contemporary art world to split the commission with the artist fifty-fifty. When an artist becomes success-ful, the gallery's commission is reduced. Tim and Sue, however, refused to accept less than £1500, so Stuart, Issie and I – who had the expense of rent, mail out and entertaining the artists – made £750 from the whole show. Later, the collector sold the work for over £70,000.

Issie was a huge supporter of Tim and Sue, frequently featuring them in her shoots, and she was delighted that they were now getting museum interest and showing in public spaces like the Chisenhale, an old Spitfire factory in the East End, where they showed 'The New Barbarians', depicting themselves as two Neanderthal figures coming out of a white curved void. Tim and Sue had commissioned techni-cians familiar in making waxwork to fabricate the work – and to pay the technicians, Tim and Sue themselves had worked for the artists

Gilbert and George, living on thin air and saving their wages from the duo for the concept.

Bryan had come into the gallery to see 'WOW', which he loved. Alas, Bryan, who loves art, collects only Bloomsbury art from the early twentieth century. During London Fashion Week, Anna Wintour took the time to come across London from Chelsea to the East End, a journey of one hour, to see our second show, by Kenny Hunter.

Eventually we started to sell to supportive friends. Lisa Marie, whom we had last seen when she was working with Malcolm McLaren a decade before, was now in London again, starring in her boyfriend Tim Burton's film *Sleepy Hollow*. She bought several works from the gallery.

We went to meet Tim on the set in Hertfordshire when he was shooting the scene of the decapitated horseman. A shoot inspired by the fantastical Hollywood gothic scene shortly appeared in the *Sunday Times*.

We also sold a piece to Elton John and David Furnish.

I had met David a few months earlier at a dinner to celebrate a book launch by Mario Testino. We had got on very well, drank three bottles of wine and exchanged numbers. The next day David called to invite Issie and I to have dinner with Elton and him at their home in Holland Park. I was working that day as a lawyer and moaned, to David's amusement, about my hangover. Issie arranged a dinner for McQueen to meet Tim Burton at Nobu restaurant and I asked David, a filmmaker himself, 'Would you like to come and have dinner and meet Tim Burton?'

David told me he would be delighted. Could he bring 'his boyfriend'? 'Of course,' I said.

Issie and I arrived late for the dinner at Nobu. Around the table were Tim and Lisa Marie, McQueen and his boyfriend, and David and Elton. At 10.30 p.m., Elton and David left to get an early night. McQueen said, 'Bloody skinflint – running off without paying his share of the bill.'

An hour later, when the bill did come, we were told, 'Sir Elton has paid for you all.' Alexander at least had the good grace to look a little ashamed.

Elton and David were to become good friends, helping Issie where they could. When they started their foundation and announced a ball to raise money for their AIDS charity, Issie and I apologised that because of our precarious finances we were unable to afford the tickets. I gave a tiny contribution to the charity.

Elton was charming: 'Detmar, whatever you give is much appreciated.' He did not seek to mock our impecunious state as some did.

# CHAPTER FIFTY-SIX

## *Economy, Issie-style*

With the gallery not doing well financially, we looked for ways to economise – or, at least, I did. On the train to Gloucestershire, Issie travelled first class while I travelled in economy.

One night in the first-class carriage she came across our friends Leopold and Debonnaire Bismarck, descendants of the famous German Chancellor, who lived in the old police station in Belgravia around the corner from Elizabeth Street.

Issie wanted to join the table with the Bismarcks and another friend to talk, but in the fourth seat was a regular commuter who did not see why he should give up his regular first-class seat to sit elsewhere.

Issie sat in the nearest available seat and started talking away about her 'combine harvester' teeth and how they prevented her from giving oral sex. By the time the train reached the first stop at Reading, the businessman only too happily agreed to move seats.

Issie used the rest of that journey to perform a fashion show, recalls Debonnaire Bismarck:

She opened her trunk and pulled out a pair of Manolos that had been specially made for her for a shoot in Germany, out came various hats and finally she wanted to explain to everyone the brilliance of McQueen, which she did by taking off two of the layers of black lace and gold zipped tops (she was wearing) and using the aisles of the carriage as a catwalk she paraded up and down. By the end of the journey, she had won over the entire business world of Gloucester and wasn't even trying to.

I wrote in my diary at this time that we seemed to be living at an exhaustive pace. It was fun but it was enervating, and I was finding it hard to cope with Issie's complete inability to separate her work and private life.

The truth is, we were starting to grow apart.

I now had a busy life in the art world, working in our gallery stand in art fairs and attending artists' exhibitions abroad, and Issie had her 'family' – predominantly gay men working in fashion with a hetero-sexual photographer or two (plus girlfriend) thrown in.

As 1999 wore on, Issie began, more determinedly, to organise her life without prioritising our marriage.

As a result I started going on strictly platonic dates with women who made me laugh and had time to spend with me over meals and at the cinema or theatre and events other than fashion ones.

Issie herself was keen for me to see attractive girls. In 2000, when I went to New York to take part in the Armory art fair, where Modern Art had a stand, she contacted Plum Sykes who was now living in New York to find me some girls with 'good bosoms' to meet up with. Plum suggested the Garnett sisters – Bay and Daisy had 'excellent bosoms', she assured Issie.

# CHAPTER FIFTY-SEVEN

## *Helen's Last Visit*

Helen came to stay with us for Christmas in 1999. It had just been made public in the press that Snowdon had an illegitimate daughter by an editor at *Country Life* magazine, a relationship that began when he was a guest editor there. Helen went on and on over meals that Snowdon would be, as a result, taken by the mother through the courts for maintenance and left destitute.

Issie turned angrily on her mother. 'Why do you revel in other people's problems? And why are you so secretive about your own origins? I have never seen a photograph of your parents and you never talk about where you come from!'

Issie was touching on Helen's embarrassment about her grocery origins. Helen could never forgive Issie this. The next day she left early in a taxi back to catch the train for London. Issie was in the garden. She did not say goodbye to her mother.

We never saw her again.

# CHAPTER
# FIFTY-EIGHT

## *New York, via Iceland*

In February of the new milennium, Issie and I flew to Rejkyavik. I was
on my way to New York for the Armory art fair, for which the gallery
had been selected. Although I had been to LA and Las Vegas, I had
never been to New York before. I had been addicted to the TV show
*Kojak* as a child and I was somewhat paranoid that I would be gunned
down as a result. Issie thought that if I went via Iceland, it might calm
me down.

After checking into the Borg, a wonderful 1930s hotel recommended by a friend, we went out to a bar. The first person we saw was
the singer Björk, whom we had met several times with Jeremy Scott. I
knew her from the Sugar Cubes and we would play her music a lot at
Hilles. She was very stylish, often wearing dramatic outfits by Alexander and Scott. Björk was very friendly and, just like Issie, was very
open in telling us about her life. She told us in great detail about her
recent battles with the director Lars von Trier in the film she had just
made with him, *Dancer in the Dark*. Björk said it had been a struggle,
but that the one thing she had not compromised on with the director
was her music.

I was soon drinking the strong Icelandic drink Brennivin – which
means 'black death' and has a delicious liquorice taste. We spent a

wonderful few days in Iceland, eating smoked puffin and taking the waters at the blue lagoon hot springs, which stank of sulphur, while Issie investigated the very expressive Icelandic fashion scene.

During our stay the British Fashion Council awards took place in London. Missing them didn't bother us. We had given up going long ago. Since 1996, Issie had been recognised all over the world as a key to the London fashion scene, but the British Fashion Council opted to give the stylist of the year award to others. Issie heard that the designer Maharishi Hardy Blechman had won the award for 'Street Designer of the Year', and when he had received it he criticised the Council as out of touch and irrelevant. Issie called him to congratulate him and we were soon wearing Maharishi clothes in support of the designer, whose studio was just round the corner from Modern Art in Redchurch Street.

At the end of our sojourn in Iceland, Issie flew back to Paris and I carried on to JFK. In New York, I stayed with Issie's cousin Aeneas, who lived at 260 West Broadway in Tribeca. Aeneas pointed out the Twin Towers, not far downtown.

A friend of mine, the artist Jim Lambie, was also in New York.

After the Twin Towers went down on 9/11, I discovered that Jim had been artist in residence in the North Tower on the 90th floor. A friend told me not to worry, as he never went there.

The Armory fair went well for us. Tim and Sue's neon *Happy* was photographed in the *New York Times*. The invitation for their exhibition 'I LOVE YOU' at Deitch Projects in Soho featured an Issie-styled image of Sophie Dahl, naked apart from Issie's pink flying saucer hat and a pair of stilettos, in front of our sculpture *Excessive Sensual Indulgence*.

In the exhibition was one rubbish sculpture I particularly liked, *Wasted Youth*. It reminded me that my youth had been taken up trying to sort out my mother's and my family's business affairs rather than looking and exploring. Now in my late 30s, I was getting to do what I should have been doing 20 years before and living my dream, and that I had finally had the courage to do so was all down to Issie.

After New York, I came back to Paris. We were spending more and more of our time here. Paris felt like *Les Liaisons Dangereuses*. In the Rue des Blancs Manteaux was a fantastic hamman, where we were given massages in the basement by strong, beautiful Arab women, the air heavy with scented candles and soulful north African music. The little café in the hamman served pasta with foie gras. Ensconced in a thick white dressing gown, I could smoke a cigar and Issie could smoke her B&H while we both had a manicure.

It was heaven.

Even in Paris I noted that Issie was restless. She started to work hard to improve her French in order to join an intellectual salon. The stuffy salons looked down their nose at Issie, however: fashion was not brainy enough for them. I told Issie not to worry as Sarah St George had been to one – and no one said anything. It was their loss. She gave up on the idea.

Getting taxis in Paris is notoriously difficult, but it was made easy for us when the designer Tom Ford gave Issie his *bonne numéro* – a VIP taxi pass – to quote when ordering a cab. With this, a taxi would arrive speedily, most of the time.

# CHAPTER FIFTY-NINE

## *Economy, Issie-style (II)*

Although Issie was by now earning good money – around £125,000 a year, plus expenses – she was continually out, spending every penny she earned. And at the *Sunday Times* there were beginning to be complaints about her expense claims.

Emine remembers Issie's attempts to cut back:

> When her expenses became too inflated, she agreed to use the Underground instead of taxis, and found that she enjoyed it. I would meet her at the station to show her the back route to the office – it was a daily worry that the sight of her, in stilettos, furs, perhaps her one-legged trouser suit and hat, would cause a road accident on the main dual carriageway.

In 2000, Issie's step-sister Louise married one of the richest men in Britain, the heir to the Dukedom of Bedford. The wedding brought out Issie's competitive streak. She went to S.J. Phillips, the jeweller specialising in antique settings in Bond Street, to get some diamonds. She found a Georgian diamond necklace she particularly liked. S.J. Phillips often lent Issie jewellery, knowing that Issie frequently used their designs in photoshoots and would tell everyone in London that 'S.J.' was the place to go for antique jewellery.

But, in the store, another woman going to Louise's wedding asked Issie, 'Isabella, are you buying that or borrowing it?'

Issie, her pride piqued, told her she was buying it.

It was £60,000. 'S.J.' agreed to let Issie pay in instalments. She paid off just £25,000 of it before she gave up the fight and returned it. The money she had paid was written off.

On 19 October 2000 Issie wrote, in her typically imperious fashion, to Lloyd's Bank in Stroud: she demanded an increase in her overdraft limit on the grounds that she was off to LA where she would be meeting 'Hollywood stars such as Tim Burton and Brad Pitt'.

Despite her problems in Russia in 1998, Issie was keen to continue her exploits in emerging economies around the world, and in 2000 she spent a month in Brazil with the designer Carlos Miele.

I flew out – on a £900 economy ticket – to join her in Salvador, which she was showing to Michael Roberts. Salvador was very beautiful, with amazing colonial Portuguese architecture dating from the sixteenth century, when it had been the capital of Brazil.

With my Sri Lankan heritage I felt very at home in Salvador – many of the food dishes were similar to the ones I enjoyed in Sri Lanka, another former Portuguese colony, and so was the tropical vegetation. Issie had become a friend of Tunga, a leading Brazilian sculptor with an international following. Tunga was charming, and partied hard. I was taken that night to an exhibition sponsored by Tunga of dream homes for poor children. The dream homes were made out of candle wax. It was incredibly moving.

We spent Christmas and New Year in Sri Lanka again. As I sat reading my newspaper in economy, I heard Issie making a commotion in business class. She was saying that she wanted to get off the plane. Flying frequently aggravated Issie's delicate nervous system. The gentle and patient Sri Lankan air hostesses calmed Issie down and persuaded her to take her seat.

# CHAPTER SIXTY

## *Triumph, Disaster and Recovery*

On our return we went down to Hilles to see Issie's sister Lavinia and her three children to give them late Christmas presents. Ever since the tragic death of Duggie, Lavinia had lived with us on the estate, occupying various different houses.

Lavinia and Issie were devoted to each other, and Issie, the elder by more than six years, played the motherly role.

Lavinia was determined to give her children the love and support that had been absent from her childhood. Despite her meagre resources, she fought to educate them privately. Issie, of course, contributed to her nieces' and nephew's education.

On 19 March 2001, a profile came out on Issie in the *New Yorker* magazine. The writer, Larissa MacFarquhar, had spent six months following and observing Issie. It was incredibly prestigious for Issie to be profiled in the *New Yorker*. Issie may have been ignored by the British establishment – there were no honours for her as there were for many of the other designers that she had discovered – but the *New Yorker* more than made up for that.

But at the *Sunday Times* change was in the air. Although Issie's salary had now risen to £60,000 and she was responsible for all the stories, her position seemed more tenuous. The editor was complaining about Issie producing shoots with unwearable clothes, and matters were not helped when, that autumn, Issie attended hardly any shows in London. She was in a very, very depressed and fearful cycle of her manic depression, and increasingly bitter that McQueen – who had now made a multi-million pound deal with Tom Ford at Gucci – had never helped her financially. It was a theme that was to dominate her life for the next years. Friends would urge her, 'Don't be a victim, Issie' – but Issie felt very much that she was.

A few weeks after 9/11 the axe finally fell, and Issie was fired from the *Sunday Times*. The sacking was handled badly. Issie was not told in person and, as she worked in the morning from Theed Street, a courier delivered a letter sacking her because of draconian budgetary cuts. There was the usual polite notice about how future contributions would be welcome, but the *Sunday Times* was over.

Before she even knew about it, the news was leaked on the internet website Fashion Wire Daily: 'Isabella Blow sacked from The *Sunday Times* of London', complete with references to her being a figure of the past from the 1990s. Issie was understandably hurt that a dignified joint press release had not been made.

Her former colleague Rachel Cooke wrote a brilliant piece in the *Guardian* praising Issie's work at the *Sunday Times* which cheered Issie. A colleague at the *Sunday Times* sent her a letter saying that the editor of the newspaper was 'visually blind'.

Within a few days, however, another door opened as Issie won a contract with Du Pont as a consultant for $100,000. She was fighting on.

# CHAPTER SIXTY-ONE

## *The 3 Cs*

In early 2002 Issie called me in a state of high anxiety from Paris. Some French bailiffs had turned up at Rue Tiron to take an inventory. Jeremy Scott had a creditor who had a judgment against his company for 2 million French francs – about £200,000. I, as the manager of his company, was responsible. The company address was registered at our flat. They were going to seize our things.

'How could you be so stupid?' Issie shouted at me. 'You are a lawyer.'

I tried to quietly remind her that I had agreed to be a director of Jeremy's company only because she had insisted upon it.

I called Jeremy. He said that he had money to clear the debt and that everything would be OK.

But I was desperately worried and again sank into a deep depression of my own. I needed to get away to clear my head. I decided to go back to Sri Lanka and rest there to gather my thoughts. On my way to Heathrow airport, on 19 January, Issie received a call from my mother in Sri Lanka. My mother was irritated that I could not bring a suitcase of things for her – and as a result was refusing to provide a room for me at her hotel.

Issie explained to my mother that I could hardly move as I was so depressed, let alone carry a heavy suitcase, and she relented.

# THE 3 CS

When I arrived at Colombo airport, my mother sent a driver and car to collect me. We drove the three-and-a-half hours to Kandy, where my mother had found an ayurvedic herbal masseur for me. In a herbal steam bath, surrounded by lotus flowers, I started to relax. I Fedexed copies of my passport for the court hearing in Paris on 29 January. As Jeremy had promised, everything did work out, thank God, and the angry manufacturer was never heard from again. The next day I returned to London.

On 9 February I flew with Issie to New York. It was to be our only trip together to the Big Apple. Issie had some Swarovski work to do and was helping Philip Treacy with a 16-page shoot of his hats for *Harper's Bazaar*.

Issie had periodic anxiety about flying, and said that she would go to New York City only for the '3 Cs: Cash, the Carlyle and Concorde'.

Well, we did not fly on Concorde, but there was money to be earned, and we did stay at the Carlyle Hotel on 55th Street, where we were upgraded to a suite.

The elegant Carlyle was in transition. The old system of putting notes under the door for telephone messages was being phased out. After two days, the notes stopped and Issie and I saw our bedroom telephone flashing. We had no idea how to retrieve our messages, and nor did anyone else.

Issie went back to London but I stayed on in New York for the Armory art fair, where the gallery again had a stand. Tim and Sue's neon *YE$* appeared in the *New York Times*. One night I went out dancing with Erika Belle, who had danced and worked with Madonna in the 1980s. Erika told me that I danced well for a 'honky'. Another night I met Larissa MacFarquhar at a party, who told me how sorry she was about Issie's firing from the *Sunday Times*.

I returned home in March, and on the 28th we set off for Easter in Scotland to stay with Colin and Isabella Cawdor. While his step-mother lived in the castle, they lived in a small house in a glen, which Colin, a skilled architect, had rebuilt and enlarged. For the journey Issie ordered a picnic from our old cook Valerie Hardie-Stuart to be placed in her antique picnic case. The picnic consisted of garden nectar of beetroot consommé in flasks with no chives, two poached chickens, fish cutlets (deep fried), small new potatoes (minted), asparagus rolls on brown bread, small mutton pies, quail eggs, celery salt, hunt cake, Cox's apples, tangerines, water, red wine, brandy and a dozen goblets.

It was pure Isabella – and the most extravagant picnic I have ever consumed in my life. But once again it was hard to avoid the suspiscion that Issie was using exhibition and show to hide and gloss over the deeper problems in her life.

In May, the extent of Issie's illness was finally revealed to me when I flew to Austria for Nadja Swarovski's wedding. Issie was flying from Paris.

I waited and waited for Issie to arrive. Eventually she called me from the airport in Paris – to say that she had been sitting in the business lounge speaking on the telephone and had missed the first flight, but she was booked on another flight. She called me a few hours later – she had missed the second flight as well.

She made it in the end – a day late but, of course, she looked amazing for the wedding. I was relieved, and of course it made for a good story, but the reality was it was a symptom of her increasingly bipolar state. I tried to be sympathetic but it was hard. Life with Issie was becoming more and more exasperating.

# CHAPTER
# SIXTY-TWO

## *When Philip Met Isabella*

Ever since she had been fired from the *Sunday Times,* Issie had been searching for a new project. She finally found it when Alice Rawsthorn, the director of the Design Museum, proposed an exhibition of Isabella's hats by Philip.

The resulting exhibition, 'When Philip Met Isabella', became a world-wide hit.

There was masses of work to do and Issie threw herself into the task with gusto. Issie and Philip chose 20 of Issie's best hats by Philip, which were to be shown on plinths in clear perspex boxes with Swarovski crystals scattered on the bottoms of the boxes, in a blackened room with spot lighting. It was old Hollywood glamour, reminiscent of the silent movies of Rudolph Valentino.

There were also photographs of Issie in Philip's hats by many photographers, including Richard Burbridge, Mario Testino, Donald Macpherson, Helmut Newton, Nick Knight, Juergen Teller (whom she had once tried to seduce at *Tatler*) Ellen von Unwerth and Karl Lagerfeld.

Issie wanted the exhibition to reflect her interest and love of art. She commissioned Tim and Sue to make a rubbish sculpture of her. They had a raven and a rat – and all they needed from Issie was a pair of

Manolo Blahnik shoes so that when the light shone on the sculpture in the dark it created a perfect silhouette of Issie wearing one of Philip's hats. The sculpture now stands in the National Portrait Gallery.

Philip approached Assouline, a newly opened French publishing house who specialise in luxury books. They agreed to publish an accompanying book *When Philip Met Isabella.*

There was a massive row between Philip and Issie over the acknowl-edgements at the back of the book. Philip did not see why Issie wanted to credit so many people. I had lunch with Philip at Kensington Place to try and smooth things over, but he was angry. Artistic emotions were running high. I tried to explain that as far as I could see Issie had paid for everything, and that although he had found a publisher, he should indulge Issie on this. In the end, Philip relented. Issie and Philip credited 24 people in Philip's studio plus Philip's notoriously aggres-sive Jack Russell Mr Pig, 18 fashion photographers, eight artists, three for drawings and illustrations, and 110 others, including Anna Wintour, our chef Loic Bonbonny, and Dave and Daphne Dale from Gloucestershire.

The museum paid all of the costs of research, installation, produc-tion, invigilation and marketing for the exhibition, but Issie's spending on other costs around the project was so extreme that we were forced to remortgage Theed Street for an extra £50,000.

On 4 July 2002, Isabella and Philip's exhibition finally opened at the Design Museum and Issie went into an even higher gear than ever as a cyclone of press, publicity and media attention swirled around her.

Of course, I was absolutely delighted for Issie that the exhibition was such a success, and extremely proud of her. Over 400,000 people would go to see the exhibition as it travelled around the world over the next five years, and it was important for Issie to receive recognition for her outstanding contribution to the world of fashion.

But, as Issie's bipolar depression took over, she became more and more demanding, and more and more difficult to cope with personally. We had a dinner party at Theed Street to celebrate the opening, and Dave and Daff came up from Hilles to cater the event. This was all quite an extravagance given our straitened financial circumstances, but would have been just about manageable had not Issie then lost the run of herself financially altogether. I remember her ordering taxis for Jean-Paul Goude, Grace Jones's ex-husband, who was coming to the dinner at Theed Street.

# WHEN PHILIP MET ISABELLA

I said, 'For God's sake, Issie, Jean-Paul Goude can get his own taxi.'
But Issie wanted to indulge her fantasy that money was no object.
Sadly, it was.
We ended up being sued by Computacabs for £10,000.

# CHAPTER SIXTY-THREE

## *The Battle of Hilles*

I had hoped that once the exhibition was up and running, and the launch was over, there would be a period of calm in our lives, where we could just have a few cosy nights at home together. This was soon revealed as wishful thinking on my part. Issie could never control herself when she was in a manic phase and continued to behave in a way that I found very hard to cope with for the rest of 2002. She would frequently not come home at night, and would not even call to tell me where she was or what she was doing.

Hanging over all this was the fact that my mother was back from Sri Lanka. She had, we both knew, made a decision to install my sister and her husband and their two children at Hilles. Over the summer, Issie and I had stayed in London or Paris, but we had heard that my mother had moved my sister and brother-in-law into Hilles with their children and had been entertaining our Gloucestershire neighbours to win them over to her plan.

For my mother it made perfect sense. Issie and I had no children, my sister two. My mother disliked that fact that we entertained people at Hilles, which she felt abused the house. And as I had confided in my mother, I was struggling financially to keep things together on the estate. My brother-in-law Charles was a successful doctor with a company that sent out, 24 hours a day, doctors to sick people and had contracts with 5-star hotels, airlines and film companies to cover all their medical problems. He was rich as far as my mother was concerned.

To add insult to injury, Charles was, my mother told me, making more money out of my sister's 150-acre farm than I was with 900 acres. But this was not the real issue. Issie and I knew that my mother would have been happy if we'd had a child. As Issie bitterly said, 'If a woman cannot produce a child, she is not fulfilling her biological duty.'

Under much goading from my mother, I angrily said that we would move out and go to Cherry Hill cottage on the estate. But 24 hours later I wrote to my mother saying that I had changed my mind. I realised that with Issie starting to spend nights away from me in London things were coming to a head with her. I was not prepared to lose her and Hilles as well.

I could do nothing about Issie. The situation at Hilles had stirred up all the deep hurt and rejection she felt from her father, mother, step-mother and McQueen. I told her that in our marriage vows we had sworn to support each other in bad as well as good times. 'Issie, I need you to stand by me,' I said, but she was in a deep rage, with no solutions other than to be cruel to me.

In August Issie and I went to stay in St Tropez at Maison du Cap on a clifftop overlooking the beaches of St Tropez. Tim and Sue were also guests.

One morning we woke up to see that Tim had made, floating on the swimming pool, a sculpture out of the children's swimming-pool toys.

As I walked past the swimming pool in a white linen suit and my new white Comme des Garcons shoes, Issie pushed me in the pool. I laughed it off but I knew it reflected her pathological anger not just at me but at the world in general.

In September my sister Selina celebrated her birthday with a dinner at the Groucho Club. Issie wisely refused to come with me to the dinner and she was right not to come. It was a victory celebration of my sister and brother-in-law's move into Hilles. I got drunk and fell down a flight of stairs.

In October I was invited by my mother to come round to my sister and her husband's house in Notting Hill Gate to meet the family lawyer. I was very tense and wore a pillar-box-red shirt to express my anger. They had earlier had lunch together. I knew that my mother wanted to tell me that she was kicking Issie and I out of Hilles – but she bottled out. She could not bring herself to tell me to my face what she knew would break Issie's heart.

The next day my mother left for Sri Lanka and on 17 October I received a letter from the lawyer giving us 12 months' notice to leave Hilles. The lawyer wrote that 'Hilles and its contents belong to your mother and that my instructions come from her'.

There was, however, one bright spot in our lives. Issie got a new job – she was now Fashion Director of *Tatler*.

Issie was delighted to be back in Vogue House.

\* \* \* \* \*

On Friday 25 October, Issie and I, Philip and Stefan, David LaChapelle and about 50 others set off from Stansted on a private charter to go to David Furnish's 40th birthday party in Venice. On the aeroplane, Issie sat with David LaChapelle in the row behind me as I read Jan Morris's *Venice*. For no reason at all, Issie lent forward and snatched from my hands my book and gave it to David.

'Here, David, this is a book you will enjoy.'

I was stunned and furious.

Elton John put us all up at the Gritti Palace Hotel on the Grand Canal, built in 1525 for Doge Andrea Gritti. The birthday celebrations were happening on Saturday night, so we were free for Friday night. Philip had a Venetian friend who spoke good English and acted as a guide to Venice for non-Italian-speaking travellers. The Venetian was going to take us to a place for dinner. He came to the hotel and took us to a restaurant in San Marco, which specialised in steaks for dinner.

When the bill came – it was about £300 – Issie said, 'Detmar will pay.'

The restaurant did not take cards, so I went out to find a cash machine to pay the bill. When I returned, I heard that the Venetian wanted to come to the birthday party.

Issie said, 'Of course – I will arrange it.'

I glared at Issie, and said, 'This is a private birthday party. Do you think Elton and David would like someone they have never met to come to their special seated black-tie dinner at the Cipriani?'

For once, Issie agreed. The birthday was great fun and we returned reasonably happily – even though I never got my book back.

Back in England, things were hotting up in the battle for Hilles. I knew that I had a strong case as a sitting tenant. I had paid for the running costs of Hilles for 16 years, with a nominal contribution from my brother and sister, and my mother had told me, 'Look after Hilles. One day it will be yours.'

As far as I was concerned, she could not now go back on this promise, so I changed the locks. This upset my brother who, although he lived at Edge Farm, still did his laundry at Hilles. My sister was suggesting family therapy and defended her husband, who became a target for family criticism.

Issie was very upset by the prospect of losing everything we had worked for at Hilles.

As Philip Treacy says:

People thought that Isabella was obsessed with fashion – and Isabella was very interested in fashion – but her obsession really was Hilles ... Isabella's week revolved around going to Hilles ... for years and years there was an underlying understanding that the house would be theirs, and then, when Selina started visiting Sri Lanka a lot with Charles, suddenly there came a moment where Selina and Charles were going to move into the house. That really rattled Isabella. She didn't lash out or fight or get tricky about it, she just left. And that was the beginning of the end for Isabella.

# CHAPTER
# SIXTY-FOUR

## *Separation*

Issie returned to Venice, and the following year started an affair with the Venetian we had met there. Although I was very hurt when I discovered the affair, when I was asked about him by a newspaper diarist, I tried to laugh it off and said that Issie was having an affair with a gondolier. Issie gave the Venetian the portrait of Vera given to her by Aunt Rosie to sell.

On 3 December I flew to Miami for the Art Basel Miami Beach art fair. On 9 December I returned, exhausted, to Theed Street at 8 a.m., having flown across the Atlantic overnight after sitting for hours in the gallery stand each day for a week. Issie was furious with me. 'Your taxi will wake the Brazilians I have staying.'

'What Brazilians?' I said.

It turned out that Issie had three random Brazilians staying, who wanted to party hard.

Instead of going to bed to rest, I had a shower and went to the gallery. I was too hurt to stay at home. Over the next three nights, Issie played music loudly all night with the Brazilians. For the first two nights, with my jet lag, it did not matter. But on Friday night I wanted to sleep. I went downstairs and turned the music off at midnight. Issie objected.

# SEPARATION

She growled at me, 'I am getting a model to come round to fuck Daniel [the Brazilian photographer].'

Issie and I had not had sex for four or five months at this stage.

I told Issie, 'There is going to be no model coming round tonight.'

Issie drunkenly came up to my face. I pushed her away. I didn't think I was being forceful but on her high heels she tottered over. The next morning I felt incredibly saddened by what had happened.

I said, 'Issie I am very sorry about last night. Let's try and work things out.'

But Issie replied, 'It's over.'

I went into the gallery, where I was on my own. The bell rang and I opened the door to Princess Rosario of Bulgaria and her husband Prince Kyril.

'How are you?' Rosario asked.

'I am writing my divorce petition,' I gloomily replied.

In January 2003, I sued for divorce.

In my divorce petition I listed my grievances. Among other issues, I complained that Issie spent more time away from matrimonial home than she did at it, that she had 'a serious lack of interest in domestic life' and 'often spent the night with a hat maker'.

I also highlighted the fact that there were no chairs or sofas at Theed Street because she refused to let me buy any furniture because she was still looking for the 'perfect' set. In desperation I had bought some cheap cane chairs and tables but Issie threw these into the garden. As a result, we were still sitting on Stefan's father's cardboard furniture.

I took issue with Isabella's spending habits, pointing out that Isabella had continuously spent more than she earned. Whenever I asked her to spend less money, Isabella, I wrote in the petition, had reported that 'she had a reputation to maintain'.

Issie's list of financial misdemeanours was long. I pointed out that we had reduced her overdraft from £90,000 to £40,000 by re-mortgaging the house in 2002, and that when she had an appointment with the authorities to whom she owed a great deal of tax, she was not there to meet them, leaving me to deal with the situation instead.

Issie, I went on, constantly criticised me for meanness, saying I was a 'millionaire', and I finished my divorce petition by saying, 'I have come to the conclusion that Isabella will not change and I can no longer live with her.'

My lawyer told me it was the funniest divorce petition he had ever read.

That may have been so, but I was deadly serious.

Issie responded to my divorce petition by going to Russia with David LaChapelle for a month.

My friend the YBA historian Gregor Muir told me, 'Take refuge in the art world.' So I moved out of Theed Street – which I really hated now with its stupid cardboard furniture – and got a flat in Shoreditch.

In February, I was invited to the launch of Sophie Dahl's new book at Claridge's. I rang Issie and suggested we go together, but Issie told me that she was not going. Of course, when I arrived, the first people I saw getting out of a cab were Philip and Issie. I asked her to dance at the after party in a nightclub afterwards, and she said no.

Like millions of her fans, I was from then on relegated to following Issie's progress through the fashion magazines. She was working well, I noted, being very creative and her shoots were looking fabulous.

Work was going well for me too. Ironically enough, British *Vogue* actually did a profile of the gallery.

The next time I saw Issie, it was at an opening at the Serpentine. I walked up and said, 'Hi Issie', and then walked on. It may have been childish, but Issie had snubbed me and now I wanted to give her a taste of her own medicine.

In June 2003 came the death of John Bush, the manager at Hilles, who had been holding everything together over the years. I tried to get hold of Issie and was aghast to discover that she was in the Priory, a private mental-health clinic in Roehampton. McQueen had taken her there. Issie was so dramatically gloomy at the Priory that one of the patients called her 'Miserabella'. Another confided, 'I am checking out and going to Claridge's. This place is too expensive.'

When she was discharged, she invited me to dinner at Julia's in Battersea. We had supper, and she asked me to stay the night. Issie and I made love four times that night.

It was not a permanent reconciliation, though. I was still angry at her and she still wasn't prepared to do what I was asking: to calm down and live a more simple life.

In December I was back in Miami for the Art Basel fair. I was having a fairly wild time, staying in Versace's old house, where I met Stephanie Theobald, a writer, who was interviewing Jeff Koons for Harper's Magazine. Stephanie told me that she was lesbian, and had recently had an affair with a fellow lesbian somewhere in middle America. She

made me laugh, which was what I needed, and we started a relationship. Issie and I were quite unusual people and our extra-marital affairs
were no different. I was seeing an avowed lesbian, and Isabella had
meanwhile hooked up with a Venetian 'gondolier'.

Stephanie and I came back from Miami on the same flight and spent
a lot of time together over the next few months. The relationship
steadily became more serious.

# CHAPTER SIXTY-FIVE

## *Reconciliation*

Two weeks before the launch of Stephanie's book *Trix*, about a lesbian road trip across America, I received a phone call from Issie's new psychiatrist, Dr Wolfson.

He asked me to come into his surgery and see him about Isabella.

I went the same day.

His offices were in Harley Street. They were comfortable and homely. He was a tall, fatherly figure with glasses, grey hair and a very reassuring manner. I was very impressed by him.

As soon as I sat down he said, 'From what Issie has told me, I believe you are key to her well-being. Would you consider reconciling with her?'

I was shocked but delighted, and simply replied, 'Of course I will. She has been very cruel to me, but I have always loved Isabella. We are destined to be together.'

Dr Wolfson is not the kind of man to waste any time beating around the bush, and once this was settled, off I went.

It was a clear blue day and the sun was shining as I stepped out onto Harley Street. Almost immediately my phone rang.

It was Issie.

'Are we reconciled?' she asked.

'Yes,' I said.

# CHAPTER SIXTY-SIX

## *Eaton Square*

When we got back together again in May 2004, Issie and I lived with our pug, Alfie, in Virginia Mews, Shoreditch; Issie was finding it increasingly hard to make any decisions so I suggested that we sell Theed Street and make a fresh start. To get to *Tatler* in Hanover Square, Issie – dressed in a Philip Treacy hat, McQueen dress and high heels – would catch the No. 55 bus in Hackney Road, which took her direct to Oxford Circus.

On the outside she still looked fantastic, but she was using her flamboyant clothes to mask her deep depression.

Dr Wolfson told Issie and I that her depression was very, very serious and that it would take a year or so of hard work to get her into a calmer state. I was relieved that he understood the gravity of her depression and the danger to her life. He gave us his mobile number and told Issie and me to call him at any time. Issie would call him every day.

Many people were irritated or confused by her complaints about her lack of money. Nicholas Coleridge recalls a typical meeting with Issie:

Issie asked to see me one evening because she said she needed some advice. I invited her for a drink in my office and we talked about her recent shoots for a while, until she got to the point. She said she felt desperately poor and needed more money. Could she please have a 100 per cent pay rise?

'When did you last get a pay rise?' I asked.

'Two weeks ago,' she replied. She explained that she had many expenses, clothes, paintings to buy, shoes, travel, dinners, it was impossible to live on her salary. She was totally broke, she would soon have to live rough on the streets, she said.

I said I would try to help and would speak to her editor (Geordie Greig), but she shouldn't be too hopeful of a 100 per cent rise. The following morning I happened to walk past her office in Vogue House. Inside were three smart-looking men showing jewellery on her desk. Dozens of pieces were laid out on green baize, emerald rings, necklaces, diamond bracelets, all of them beautiful. I assumed this was a visit from a jewellery advertiser, showing the fashion director their wares. I went in to say hello.

'Nicholas, I can't decide between the drop earrings and the necklace,' said Issie. 'Which do you like?'

I asked if the pieces were for a particular shoot.

'No, they're for *me*,' Issie replied. 'These men are from S.J. Phillips, I am buying myself a treat. I think I will buy the earrings.'

They cost £15,000, I seem to remember.

The fact that Issie couldn't afford 'treats' like these didn't bother her in the slightest. But afford them she could not. The Swarovski consultancy, which had lasted six years and been a great success, had come to an end.

The diamond necklace and earrings were shortly returned at a considerable loss.

In Gloucestershire, our borrowing was over £1 million, which was a heavy pressure, but at least Issie had her job at *Tatler,* and I was finally starting to earn some money from the gallery.

In August we were invited to go to Turkey by Haluk Ackace, a Turkish artist who had lived with Issie when we were separated, at my suggestion, because I knew how much Issie hated to be on her own.

As a thank you, Haluk had rented a house in Bodrum on the sea in the south of Turkey, and had a flat for us to stay in Istanbul. Issie was in a very aggressive and hostile mood when we set off. When we got to Bodrum, Issie found that Haluk's house had no swimming pool and made us all check into a hotel on the sea.

Issie was full of anger towards me. Each night she stayed out and refused to have any meals with me. I decided I would return to London; I was not going to put up with this nonsense.

As I left, Issie was arranging to charter a boat in Bodrum for £8000 to entertain Haluk and two of our friends. It was absurd and reckless. I returned to London exhausted and upset, and then, on my first day back, Stuart dropped a bombshell. After six years together, he wanted to go it alone.

The break was incredibly painful for me because the gallery was the one area of my life that was going well. But we parted as amicably as could be hoped for, and Issie and I sold our shares to Stuart.

I had to start again, and the following year opened a new gallery in London.

When Issie returned, she was in a dreadful state. She had paid £4000 for the boat in Turkey but she did not have the balance – another £4000 – that she apparently owed. She was worried and stressed about it and we went to see Dr Wolfson.

He asked Issie, 'Did you sign anything for the boat?'

Isabella said she had not.

He said, 'Well, leave it at that.'

Dr Wolfson said that Isabella had behaved 'appallingly' to me.

The boat was not the only problem she had to face on her return. At *Tatler* she was in trouble with her editor – just as she had been with André Leon Talley 20 years beforehand at American *Vogue* – because she had not bothered to tell him about her Turkish trip. She received a written warning.

By September, with the fashion shows again upon her, Issie was depressed and felt unable to go on. She was on medication and seeing Dr Wolfson regularly, as well as speaking to him on a daily basis. Her demon of fear of homelessness was rampant, and she was obsessing constantly about becoming a bag lady and ending her days as a tramp.

It made no sense. We had completed the sale of Theed Street for a handsome profit and had bought, with the proceeds and the aid of a loan from a private bank, a 15-year lease on a large and elegant ground floor flat at 25 Eaton Square – the grandest square in London, just a few hundred yards from where we had lived at Elizabeth Street.

Issie did at least throw herself into doing up our new home. She was helped massively by Camilla, with whom all those years ago she had dressed up as a cleaner. When we had finished, it was a breathtaking salon. The living room had three tall sash windows looking out onto the elegant railed square gardens. The entrance hall was hung with Isabella's hats, dangling from Perspex hooks designed by David Bartlett; the wallpaper for the drawing room was silver and sparkled like the glitter make-up Issie often wore; and the entrance hall was a vivid pink. We filled the apartment with my collection of contemporary art, heirlooms from Doddington and a crystal chandelier, which had been in Vera's boudoir at Doddington. Issie acquired a marble

**Issie at Eaton Square in her pheasant hat and McQueen tartan.**

fireplace, a golden palm tree, consul tables and a Gustavian Swedish sofa. After the cardboard furniture at Theed Street, I insisted on something comfortable to sit on and there was a large Sherwood sofa covered in pink. Natasha Garnett described it, in a story in *World of Interiors*, as 'Opulent, grand, modern and above all very very glamorous – just like Isabella herself'.

Above the dining table was a pink neon by Stefan Bruggemann: 'CONCEPTUAL DECORATION'. Some of our neighbours who peered into our living room thought we had turned the flat into a nightclub. Certainly, it was a hive of activity. Issie and I entertained everyone from transvestites from the East End to artists and royals. We would have breakfast with Martin, the building porter.

# CHAPTER SIXTY-SEVEN

## *Shock Treatment*

Given that there clearly seemed to be a significant biological element to Isabella's depression – Issie believed that she had inherited her depression from her feckless grandfather Jock – Dr Wolfson decided to explore the possibilities of the effect of ECT treatment (electroconvulsive therapy).

ECT is a method of inducing a therapeutic seizure on a patient, utilised when it was discovered that victims of depression who suffered fits were often relieved, at least temporarily, of their depression, following a seizure.

On Issie, the effect of ECT was remarkable: it changed her from a state of profound moroseness and suicidal gloom to the old Issie, who was dynamic, spontaneous, positive thinking, charismatic and voluble.

At Christmas 2004, Issie was feeling much better. Lucy Ferry and her two youngest sons, Tara and Merlin, came to stay at Hilles for Christmas. For New Year, Bryan flew us to St Barts. He had rented an amazing house overlooking the sea, rented previously by Puff Daddy and Celine Dion. The island was swarming with millionaires – and contemporary art dealers, some of whom tried to claim earnestly that they were on holiday.

# SHOCK TREATMENT

The biggest attraction was Paul Allen, the co-founder of Microsoft. For New Year's Eve, we were invited onto his enormous boat, the *Octopussy,* which boasted a submarine and two helicopters. On Gouverneur beach we met Graydon Carter, the editor of *Vanity Fair*, who introduced us to his new wife, saying, 'This is Isabella Blow, and her long-suffering husband, Detmar.'

But by January 2005 Issie was talking publicly about her resentments again. She told one interviewer:

> It just seems pointless, sometimes I don't know why I bother. I've helped a lot of people make money, but I never see any of it. I'm very depressed about my situation.

Along with the periodic ECT sessions, she was taking large quantities of different pills.

Isabella and Philip called her pills her 'Marilyn Monroes'. Anxious to find out what effect the drugs might be having on her, he grabbed a bottle once and took one of them.

'It just completely floored me,' he recalls. 'And she was taking quantities of these pills for a period of years.'

Philip tried to divert Issie from dwelling too much on her problems when they were together:

> Isabella talked to everybody about everything and so she got lots of information and lots of advice. She got used to the sympathy aspect after a while. So I'd say, 'Isabella, let's try not to talk about it.' She would ask me about a hundred times a day, 'What am I going to do? What am I going to do?' and I'd say, 'Issie, let's just slow down. Tomorrow you might feel completely different. Isabella was disappointed and fearful of the future ... she'd give you the last penny she had in her purse, but, as she got worse and worse, she became more obsessed with how she could make some money.

Issie would constantly say, 'Wallis Simpson was the most stylish woman ever because she was fabulously rich, and you can't be elegant unless you've got lots of money.'

One source of money was a deal she signed with MAC cosmetics to produce a range of Isabella Blow branded red lipsticks.

At a party, Issie had met Nicola Stephenson, a feisty Lancastrian with her own public relations agency in London, called Mission. Issie explained to Nicola her commercial frustrations and Nicola, a terrific businesswoman, turned her attention to making Issie some money.

They came up with the idea of Issie doing a lipstick for MAC. MAC, Nicola knew, prefer to use endorsements, editorials and public relations rather than expensive advertising campaigns to promote their products. The concept of an Isabella Blow lipstick was pitched to

**Issie's MAC lipstick, produced in collaboration with MAC cosmetics. The packaging features Issie's signature violet ink.**

**Isabella and Alexander at the launch event for Issie's limited edition MAC lipstick.**

Andrew Perera at MAC – and then taken up by Michelle Feeney, who was in charge of Global Communications and endorsed by John Dempsey, head of Estée Lauder (which owns MAC).

I spoke to John Dempsey in researching this book. The reason he chose to do a lipstick with Issie was, he said, because, 'She was one of the most influential and iconic forces of the last 50 years'.

The lipstick was a limited edition of 10,000, a rich bougainvillea red developed by Issie with Terry Barber of MAC, and made with a special shot of violet pearl. It was packaged in a elegant box with an illustration of Issie by Hilary Knight, who illustrated the *Eloise* series. The launch was well attended at my new gallery, where Issie had on the wall Bruggemann's neon 'THIS MUST BE THE PLACE'. Issie was being mischievous and initially sent a 'healer' to represent her – before Nicola dispatched a colleague to Claridge's to bring Issie from the bar where she was holding court, smoking. Alexander came to the event and there is a happy photograph of them together – Issie in a white McQueen dress with a Philip Treacy hat with 'BLOW' spelt out in white feathers. Afterwards, Issie had a dinner at Cipriani's. There was a fixed menu for the dinner. One of the guests wanted chicken which was not on the menu.

'Who ordered this menu?' Issie demanded.

'You, Issie,' came the reply of Michelle Feeney of MAC.

The lipstick sold out in record time and received worldwide press coverage. Issie earned a fat fee. Yet again it was possible to hope she was turning a corner.

# CHAPTER
# SIXTY-EIGHT

## *The First Attempt*

B ut then, in November 2005, frustrated at her inability to beat her debilitating manic depression, and influenced by her friends who had unhelpful emotional reactions to the news that she was having electric shock therapy, Issie abruptly stopped seeing Dr Wolfson. I was dismayed, but it was no use trying to reason with Issie: she was already off on another manic episode.

Issie's sisters Julia and Lavinia, and Lavinia's three children, were at Hilles for Christmas, but Issie refused to come. She was angry with my mother for trying to wrest Hilles away from us and install in our place my sister and her husband. It was, for Issie, a painful reminder of what she believed her father and stepmother had done to her at Doddington.

In January 2006 I arrived in Paris to stay with Issie at the Ritz. Issie was in a bad way. She had started telling everyone, including Mohammed Al Fayed, of her desire to die. I arrived at her suite with Bryan, who was collecting his girlfriend Katie, who had been staying with Issie. There were two French doctors there who she had called from the American Hospital in Paris.

With no Dr Wolfson to call following Issie's break with him, I did my best to keep Issie's spirits up. And Issie came through. I managed to escape for a drink with my friend Harriet Quick and the stylist Charlotte Stockdale. Many people found it strange that I seemed to cope. Internally I was on an emotional rollercoaster – but externally I remained, as far as I could, calm. Issie needed me to be strong.

In March 2006 Issie went to the ready-to-wear shows in Milan and spent much of her time sitting on the laps of her fashion friends – Manolo, André, and anyone else who would listen – telling them in great detail how she was going to throw herself off a bridge. Anna Wintour was particularly concerned about Issie's decline and told Condé Nast they must help Issie. Lucy was also very anxious about Issie, and suggested a clinic in Surrey which had successfully helped a number of her friends.

Julia and I drove down to Surrey to look at the clinic. When I went around it, I was concerned that, given the gravity and seriousness of Issie's depression, they would be unable to deal with her. Later, back at Eaton Square I spoke to a lady from the clinic and told her this. She asked me if I had any other solutions. Apart from Dr Wolfson, to whom Issie no longer went, I had none.

On Issie's return to London from Milan I collected her from Heathrow airport and drove her straight to the clinic. I had spoken to Issie in Milan and she told me that she was happy to go there. She was, she told me, desperate for something to help her get out of her dark depression.

I was very happy that Lucy and Julia, in suggesting this particular clinic, had appeared to take on some of the responsibility for Issie. God knows I had tried my best. If Lucy and others wanted to have a go at helping Issie, I would not stand in their way. And, following Anna's intervention, Condé Nast had agreed to pay for Issie's six-week course at the clinic.

Initially things went well. They told me that Issie was making progress, and I happily reported this back to the kind and sensitive financial director at Condé Nast, who was taking care of the bills. Positively, I told her, 'Issie will be back at work.'

I wanted to believe this. I held on to the hope that if Issie could get stuck into some stimulating and interesting work when she got out, she would pick up the reins and resume her busy life. I was terrified that she would, as my father had done, take to her bed and become brooding, depressed and suicidal.

With things appearing to be going as well as could be hoped for, I flew to New York for the Armory art fair. I had to try and continue with my own life. I had a call while I was there from Issie; things had taken a backwards step. The treatment, as I had feared, was failing. The clinic was mainly focused on treating drug addiction and was, in retrospect, an inappropriate choice for Isabella, who had an extremely compli- cated and dark depression.

The final straw came when I was contacted by staff at the clinic who told me they 'weren't getting anywhere' with Issie.

'What do you mean you're not getting anywhere?' I asked them tersely down the phone. 'That's your job.'

I returned from New York. Issie called me. She was discharging herself three weeks into the six-week course. On Sunday 19 March, I went to collect her. As Issie left the clinic she was affectionately embraced by a young female patient who, she told me, was suffering from an addiction to sugar. It confirmed my fears that this clinic had been the wrong place for Issie to go. I drove Issie back to Eaton Square. She was quiet and sad.

The next night, Monday 20 March, there was a dinner to celebrate her cousin Aeneas's birthday. Aeneas had invited us to join him for dinner in the Electric Cinema in Notting Hill following the showing of a film to raise money for Leonard Peltier, the Native American activist, and the event was being hosted by Vivienne Westwood. I was excited about the film. My father had been a strong supporter of the Native American Indian Movement. He had donated money, and it is a cause I feel passionately about. Issie knew this and approved.

I said to Issie, 'Darling, do you want to go and see this film and then we can go on to Aeneas's birthday afterwards?'

Issie said, 'No darling, I just want to be quietly at home.'

So I thought, fine, I'll go on my own. After the film, at dinner that night, I was just about to eat my steak and chips when I received a call on my mobile from Stefan Bartlett, Philip's boyfriend.

'Detmar, Isabella's in hospital, she's taken an overdose.'

When I got to St Thomas' hospital, I found Issie in the accident and emergency wing surrounded by curtains. She was weak and frail and apologetic. But, most importantly, she was alive.

I found the doctor, Dr Tullock, who had saved her life, and thanked her. She told me that they had pumped her stomach out and that Issie was going to be OK.

Issie's symptoms, the female doctor told me, were typical of bipolar disorder and she said that Issie had been sectioned under the Mental Health Act.

The doctor also told me that Issie was on a massive amount of medication. I was incredibly angry about that because I had been told that the whole point of the clinic in Surrey was that they did not believe in treating patients with drugs.

It was a complete fuck-up as far as I was concerned.

The next day, when I went to see Issie at St Thomas', I recalled that this was the same hospital where my maternal Sri Lankan grandmother had died of cancer in 1982. As my grandmother lay dying after the surgeon discovered that her cancer was terminal, we had visited her every day during the last bleak weeks of her life.

I went outside for some fresh air and called my mother. I explained to her what had happened. As I paced outside the hospital overlooking the Houses of Parliament, fighting my tears and emotions, I told my mother: 'We both married people who want to kill themselves. I am not going to make it easy for Issie.'

My mother understood.

She did not try to tell me that everything was going to be fine.

I appreciated that.

# CHAPTER
# SIXTY-NINE

## *'I always* hated *Tesco'*

After this suicide attempt, Issie went to another private clinic, recommended by St Thomas', Bowden House in Harrow-on-the-Hill, where she was seen by an Australian psychiatrist. He told me, 'We're going to peel her like an onion to get to the heart of her problems.' He was taking her off all the heavy medication the clinic in Surrey had given her.

But Issie was being wild, and she told me that she hated him. About two weeks later at the beginning of April, Issie ordered a taxi on the Condé Nast account to take her the 320km (200 miles) to Cheshire. On the way she went to Broughton Church in Staffordshire and put flowers near her family vault where her father lay. She then got the driver to take her around the park at Doddington, before dropping her off at The Crown in Nantwich, which was close to Nuthurst, her first school.

By checking into The Crown, Issie was consciously trying to copy her grandfather's suicide. Jock had killed himself with morphine after checking into the Adelphi Hotel in Liverpool and asking not to be disturbed.

Issie told me later that she tried to get some vodka to drink with the paracetamol pills she had been stockpiling to improve the chances of the pills killing her. But in Nantwich all the off-licences were closed early on Sunday night before Issie arrived. She swallowed the pills anyway, but after she took them, she called Philip to tell him that she was killing herself. She wouldn't say where she was but she told him about the Condé Nast car and they were able to trace the driver who had picked up a clearly disturbed woman from a hospital and driven her to a pub several hundred miles away in Nantwich via a graveyard.

The manager of The Crown forced his way into Issie's room and called an ambulance. She had her stomach pumped, and was back in Harrow the next day. She was offered an injection to help protect her organs from the damage of the paracetamol pills but declined.

When I went to visit Issie in Harrow I spoke to some of her fellow patients. They told me that Issie had been very clear and open about her suicide plan.

Two weeks after that, in mid-April, Issie came down to Hilles for the weekend. We had Haluk staying, with whom we were very close at that time. On Sunday night, at about 11.30, I went to bed and left Issie and Haluk in the Long Room by the fire, talking. At about 12.30, I came down and Issie wasn't there.

'Haluk, where is Isabella?' I asked.

'She went to bed,' said Haluk.

'Oh God,' I said.

She had taken my car keys from the kitchen and the car was gone. I rang Bowden House and they alerted the police and then there was absolutely nothing we could do. We were just waiting. I was very tense. I tried to think of Issie's life philosophically. Eventually I spoke: 'Issie's had a great life, Haluk. We have to celebrate that.'

Haluk seemed rather shocked by my statement. He did not under-stand that I was trying to prepare myself for the news of Issie's death.

We got the call at about 3 o'clock in the morning. I was elated and relieved to learn that she was alive, and unhurt.

The car, however, was a write-off. She'd driven it straight into the back of a Tesco lorry on the A417 dual carriageway, about 7 miles away from Hilles. She had been taken to a cell in Stroud police station. Haluk wanted to go to the station. I declined. I knew from my childhood only too well the problems of going to police stations to find people. When I was about six, my father had been arrested for drink-driving in London. After my mother and I had waited and waited for him at the police station, we discovered that he had been released hours earlier.

Isabella and Bryan Ferry at Eaton Square. You can see, on her right foot, the scar she had from jumping off the bridge.

No one had bothered to tell us.

I knew that I had to keep strong, which meant, in this case, getting a few hours' sleep.

The next morning I called Stroud police station. She had been taken at 5.30 a.m. by an ambulance to the Harrow clinic. When I visited her, I asked her why she had done it.

'I always *hated* Tesco,' she replied disdainfully. She raved madly about being saved by the car's 'wretched air bag'.

But with Issie in the clinic in Harrow, there was at least a semblance of normal life for me. After three suicide attempts in six weeks, I just wanted Issie to be safe. Friends like Bryan and Katie made the trek to Harrow to see her, and so did my mother. My mother was shocked by Issie's state.

Issie all the while angrily repeatedly her terrifying new mantra, 'I want to die. Let me die.'

I could only hope that after these three failed attempts in such quick succession, Issie might see the futility of failing to kill herself and decide to live. I had to hope.

# CHAPTER SEVENTY

## *The Overpass*

Three weeks later in June 2006, Issie escaped from Bowden House again, this time ostensibly to have tea with a friend in London. On the way back, she got the taxi to drop her on the side of the A4 elevated section in Ealing. She was determined to throw herself to her death. At the last minute, however, she changed her mind. 'I decided I didn't want to jump but it was too late,' she said. She clung on to the side of the flyover.

She fell anyway.

Isabella's tiny feet and ankles were completely smashed by the fall, broken in several places.

An ambulance was called and Issie was taken to the nearby Ealing NHS hospital off the Uxbridge Road.

I was absolutely horrified by what was happening to Issie, but I didn't seem to be able to say – or do – anything to help her. When I saw her, her feet were bandaged up and she was angry and raving about how she had failed to kill herself by not jumping properly in front of an oncoming car.

With some difficulty, I got hold of the surgeon at the hospital. He was very hostile: 'I try and save people – this woman wants to kill herself. She needs psychiatric help.'

I quietly said I was aware of that.

He said, 'I've got better things to do than this.'

He went on to explain that Issie now had two metal bars in her ankles and that she would suffer a stiffness in her feet. She could not wear high heels again, but she would be able to walk.

Up until this time I had been careful to keep Issie's three previous suicide attempts as quiet as I could. I still hoped the old Issie would come back, and that she would be able to resume her busy life again. Another reason for being discreet was that I believed if I told everyone about Issie's attempts it would look as if I was wanting attention and sympathy for myself. As a result many people, some vaguely aware that Issie had made some earlier attempt, thought that this was Issie's first or second attempt at suicide and not her fourth in two months.

Geordie Greig, Issie's editor at *Tatler,* came to visit her. He was very sad. He had been a loyal and understanding editor to Issie and had dealt sensitively with her moods and high-handed behaviour. He told me he was moving Issie from Fashion Director of *Tatler* to Editor at Large. It was a sensitive and generous solution.

Issie's suicide attempt was not the only mental-health problem I had to deal with. On a bus to see Issie with a Lebanese take-away, my phone rang. It was a lady from a clinic my brother had gone to in America to be treated for his own depression.

She said: 'Please can you come out to California for a family conference. It is very important that you are there.'

I replied that much as I wanted to help Amaury, I was now on my way to visit my wife who had just tried to commit suicide for the fourth time in two months by jumping off a bridge, so I wasn't going to be able to make it. The lady persisted in urging me to come. It was like speaking to an automated message. She did not seem to grasp my position at all.

'Look, I am very sorry but I cannot come to California now. My wife is trying to kill herself,' I shouted into my mobile. There were a few glances from other passengers on the bus.

Issie would say that since she could not wear high heels again, there was no point in living, but I knew that this flip comment actually disguised her profound inner anguish about what was happening to her. Yes, of course it was bad that 'Isabella Blow' would never be able to wear high heels again, but the real problem was her crippling manic depression. She felt that she was 'not good enough as a human being to exist'.

# THE OVERPASS

Until her feet were sufficiently healed to walk on, she was pushed around in a wheelchair, which she found humiliating. She regularly asked people who visited her, to get her some heroin, some horse tranquillisers or a gun so that she could finish herself off.

Everybody declined.

# CHAPTER
# SEVENTY-ONE

## *Battles*

W here would Issie go after her feet were healed, and she was discharged from the hospital on Uxbridge Road? She had been sectioned again, and clearly wasn't well enough to come home.

After being treated so unsuccessfully in the private sector, I wondered whether the NHS wasn't worth a shot.

To look at Issie's options, I arranged to meet with Issie's GP and invited Julia and Lucy to attend. They were keen to be involved and wanted Issie well. Dr Gormley said that there was a psychiatrist at the Capio Nightingale, Dr Stephen Pereira, of whom he thought highly. America was mentioned, but Dr Gormley was not an expert on it. And what, I asked, was the NHS mental-health treatment like at the Gordon Hospital, which was almost next door to us, in Victoria.

Dr Gormley told me that drugs were the main form of treatment in the NHS. Julia and Lucy both were understandably reluctant. Dr Gormley warned us that unless Issie cooperated it did not matter where she went. The meeting ended. I was non-committal. I wanted to do some more research of my own.

I contacted Philip Treacy's brother, Oliver, whose judgement I trusted and who administered an NHS mental-health trust in north London, a part of which, bizarrely enough, Issie had actually officially opened in happier times. Oliver told me that the NHS mental-health treatment was far from a waste of time. I asked others whose common sense and intelligence I trusted. The consensus was that in times of crisis, the NHS, with the resources of the state behind it, was not to be underestimated.

Julia and Lucy had their views, but after the fiasco of the Surrey clinic I was not inclined to follow them. Clearly they meant well, but they were not experts on mental health. I was angry about the experience of the two private health clinics. It was time, I felt, for the state to have a go.

Issie was admitted, under the Mental Health Act, to the Gordon Hospital in Victoria in June 2006.

It was like a prison. It was grim. But it was easy for me to visit, and since Issie was put on suicide watch, I felt that at least she was safe. All I cared about was that she was alive. And, I hoped, it might just shake her.

Unsurprisingly I soon received an angry call from Lucy. 'Detmar, you can't be serious about leaving Issie in this ghastly hospital.'

I was exhausted and angry. One part of me wanted to shout at Lucy: 'What the hell do you know about mental health? What the hell was that clinic in Surrey you suggested about?'

But the other part of me appreciated Lucy's deep love for Issie, so I kept calm and agreed with Lucy that we should have a meeting with Julia.

A meeting was arranged in the morning at Matthew Mellon's flat in Eaton Place a block away from Eaton Square. I did not know Matthew – but I knew that Issie and he were very fond of each other, and, although Issie denied it to me, I guessed that they had some sort of affair when we were separated. The press had been on to it, but Issie had put them off with strenuous denials.

At the meeting Matthew Mellon was very supportive and respectful of me. He said that he'd been sent to a state place and it 'sure as hell' had 'shook' him.

He was firm with Lucy and Julia, telling them, 'Detmar is Isabella's husband and you're disrespecting him. You've got your own views but I'm with Detmar.'

At the Gordon I attended a meeting with Issie and the Gordon psychiatrist. At the meeting the psychiatrist asked Issie what was behind the hats and clothes she wore? Who was she? He extracted the word 'hope' from Issie, and ended the meeting with, 'Let's hold on to "hope".' But when I tried to speak to him after the meeting he walked straight passed me without replying.

I felt very alone.

I arranged a meeting with the psychiatrist Dr Stephen Pereira recommended by Issie's GP. I had invited Lucy to come, Julia could not make it. When Lucy came into the waiting room of his office she did not acknowledge my greeting. We sat in tense silence. We both spoke to Dr Pereira separately, who said afterwards that it sounded as if we were talking about two different people. This feeling was not unfamiliar – everybody always seemed to have a different view of Issie.

Lucy and I left without speaking to each other. When I returned home, I angrily deleted Lucy's number from my mobile phone. What was the point if we weren't going to speak anyway?

Issie gave me a copy of Ted Hughes's book of poetry, *Birthday Letters*, which deal with his relationship with his wife Sylvia Plath, who committed suicide. The poems focus in part on how he was blamed for his wife's suicide by people who knew absolutely nothing of their relationship.

The feeling is well known to me.

The fact is, we were all being driven completely insane by the situation. As anyone who has experienced the mental breakdown of a family member can attest, you do at times find yourself saying the unsayable and thinking the unthinkable.

Yes, I lost my patience on many occasions, but all I remember saying to Issie, over and over again, is, 'I am not going to make it easy for you to die, Issie, I am not going to make it easy for you to die.'

One visitor to the Gordon was her cousin Kim Fraser. He recalls:

On arrival I was told to take the lift to the second floor and wait outside the door until I was let in. The door eventually opened after being unlocked from the inside and there was Issie with her nurse/jailor. She was dressed in a towelling dressing gown and woolly slippers and, as far as I could make out, nothing else. Issie threw her arms around my neck and gave me a huge hug.

We walked back along a long corridor with a polished linoleum floor and blank white walls, with a naked bulb overhead. On the way we passed the occasional inmate, all of whom, on seeing Issie brightened up and greeted us warmly.

Issie threw a warm circle of light around her even amongst these poor semi-demented inmates.

We talked for a long time about family, cousins, friends and shared memories. She told me about wanting to end her life and of how she had tried and only succeeded in smashing her ankles. She cried at times and laughed at others.

In July 2006, with no improvement in Issie's mental condition, Issie transferred to a private clinic, the Capio Nightingale, where she was treated by Dr Stephen Pereira, the same psychiatrist who would later treat Alexander McQueen. They put Issie on a suicide watch. Issie's private health insurance policy – paid for by her stepmother – agreed to pay.

She was much happier at the private clinic, where she had a nice sunny bedroom. The staff were friendly and sympathetic and Issie liked Dr Stephen Pereira. It was more like a private home. I was able to take her whitebait from the fish and chip shop next door. Rupert Everett came to visit daily. Although I had been adamant on trying the NHS route, I was very happy that she was happier here.

Anna Wintour visited and took her a bottle of her favourite Fracas perfume as a bedside gift. Issie was very touched by Anna's thoughtful gesture. Says Anna:

There is something incredibly depressing about arriving at a hospital empty-handed. It makes the visit devoid of any hope or joy. That's why I took her the perfume. There was a romanticism to it; a whiff of the life she'd once had.

Anna was shocked by Issie's mental condition. Issie fantasised in great detail to Anna about her eventual suicide:

She related in great and exacting detail how everything would play out when she died. She would return to Eaton Square, surround herself with peonies, and drink Cristal. Except, while she described the scene, it seemed as if she'd overlooked the fact that she wouldn't be around to witness it. She laughed about it, while also being utterly serious about it. And because Issie was so rational about it, you went along with it. I felt like I was talking to a totally rational person – until I left her.

Anna came away fearing the worst. 'There was a saddening inevitability about what was to going to happen. She'd decided to embark on the journey, and she had every intention of taking it.'

Issie told me later that when she saw Anna she was 'raging' and had on her 'wild beast' look. I knew exactly what Issie meant, having experienced it myself many times over the years.

Dr Pereira started treating Issie with drugs, therapy … and electric shocks. Everybody had attacked me when Issie was having electric shocks with Dr Wolfson, as if it was the worst thing in the world, but now here we were, back to square one. Issie had now smashed her legs and feet up, we'd all gone through hell and we were back to electric shocks again because that was the only thing that seemed to keep Issie going.

I couldn't help but wish that Issie's friends had taken the time to have Dr Wolfson explain to them how electric shock therapy works in the first place.

Of course, the Capio Nightingale was expensive and the next thing was that Issie's insurance policy started to run out. Alexander McQueen and other friends paid for much of her treatment at Capio Nightingale.

# CHAPTER
# SEVENTY-TWO

## *India*

In August 2006, Issie was feeling better and was discharged from the Capio Nightingale clinic and decided to go straight to India from the hospital without any convalescent period. Dr Pereira said that she needed aftercare – therapy, drugs, electric shock treatment – and she needed to stick to this to have any chance of making a long-term recovery.

But nothing I or the doctors said could change her mind. Issie just flew off to India on her own. There was no way I was going to go with her. I just couldn't get sucked any further into Issie's insanity, and, anyway, I had to work.

In the event, she came back home from the trip to India without incident. In fact, she seemed completely fired up by the experience and was suddenly into all things Eastern. She wanted to do Islamic furniture, she wanted to do a Lotus handbag; she was even discussing the possibility of doing a fashion show on Al-Jazeera. So that's Issie, and that's manic depression: one moment she was planning to kill herself, the next she was planning a new show on TV.

But, as Dr Wolfson had originally said, once again she was cavalier with her medication and neglected the electric shock treatment. She felt she didn't need anything because she was firing on all cylinders.

**Isabella at Eaton Square, planning her trip to India.**

In October, Issie returned to India with Rupert Everett and her assistant Kentaro. They went to Mumbai on a trip sponsored by Dulux paint, where they sat at a fashion show that featured models in saris in all the colours of Dulux paint. Issie was hoping to get a consultancy with Dulux, but soon realised that this was not going to happen. After a few minutes Issie walked out of the show, taking Rupert with her.

**Isabella in India.**

In Mumbai, Rupert and Issie ran across a platform to be in time to catch a train. Rupert was pleased to see how mobile Issie was. Issie sat on a bench and threw a crumpled tissue on the ground, which she told Rupert represented how she felt. Rupert told her, 'Issie, you can still run.'

Issie replied, 'That was acting.'

# CHAPTER
# SEVENTY-THREE

## *Cancer*

At Hilles that Christmas I had Julia and Lavinia and her children staying, but Issie decided she didn't want to be in Gloucestershire. Fortuitously, Issie got a job in Goa, working for a hotel.

I was filled with foreboding, and, on New Year's Day, I got the news that she had taken yet another overdose on the beach in Goa. The fact I had been expecting something like that didn't make it any easier to deal with.

I felt sick to the bottom of my stomach with fear.

Because it was New Year's Day, there was no way I could get a flight to India – but truthfully I wouldn't have gone anyway. Of course I was incredibly concerned by all that was unfolding, but I had been driven to the brink already by Issie's suicide attempts. I would be no use to her if I had a mental breakdown as well. Thank God Issie pulled herself together and was able to get back home.

There was a little bit of treatment with Dr Pereira again in early 2007, but I was saddened by the sense that the doctors had given up on Issie. With mental health, whether the problem is alcoholism, depression or addiction, all treatment ultimately comes back to the patient's willingness to sort themselves out. That was something my father would never do, and Issie wouldn't cooperate either. The biggest regret I have is that maybe some more coercive treatment in America would have done something for Issie. But I think it would have had to have happened a lot earlier on.

In February 2007, Issie flew to Kuwait to complete an assignment she was working on for Sheik Majed of Kuwait, shooting a catalogue for his new line of clothes. She'd been working on the project for several months, and had spent thousands of pounds of her own money on it. Then, the day before the shoot, the Sheik switched the photographer from the two young photographers Issie had chosen to a Portuguese photographer who had shot commercial campaigns for Condé Nast.

Issie was furious and asked me, 'Det, what the hell ever came out of Portugal apart from sardines?'

Issie was enormously offended. Her response was to take another overdose – of lorazepam, venlafaxine and olanzapine. It was her sixth suicide attempt in less than two years.

In the hospital in Kuwait, whilst undergoing treatment and tests following this attempt, a grim discovery was made. A 'large abdominal mass' was discovered. All the indications were that poor Issie, on top of everything else, had ovarian cancer.

On 24 February 2007, the day after she got back from Kuwait, at a quarter past nine in the morning, Issie presented herself at Stroud General Hospital Accident and Emergency Department. She was accompanied by Lavinia's old boyfriend Julian, who lives at Hilles. Her notes record that she was feeling 'awful and suicidal and crazy'. She requested a repeat prescription for her medication. The doctor noted that Issie felt 'More supported being with her husband and [Julian]'.

She was referred to the Stroud Crisis Team, which saw her twice a day from then on.

Dr Ian Pennell, consultant psychiatrist for the Stroud Crisis Team, reported after his visit to Hilles on 28 February that, despite the fact that her 'background mood' was depressed, Issie was 'able to access a jovial and sociable exterior when in company'. He added:

She described a recurring idea that she would in the end kill herself, an idea which had possibly been with her since early childhood and she described a recurrent persistent thought that she wished to be dead but had no energy to do anything about it. She had a number of depressive symptoms including thoughts of unworthiness, of being a failure, lacking in motivation and drive.

On 1 March she was seen by her GP in connection with a 'suspicious cyst' and referred for ultrasound investigation at Stroud General Hospital. The scan showed that there was an 'irregular, 15cm [6in] mass present'. Issie was advised she might have to have a hysterectomy.

'She feels that she would be unable to accept this under any circumstances,' the gynaecologist wrote. Issie specifically noted she did not want me or Lavinia to know about her diagnosis or treatment options.

On 10 March Issie saw Dr Pereira for an ECT session.

It did no good. On 16 March, Issie and I were in London. Bryan was doing a concert at the Royal Albert Hall. I was in Eaton Square, waiting for Issie to arrive to go to the concert together. Issie's mobile telephone was switched off, a bad sign.

As I waited and worried where Issie was, I received a telephone call from Haluk at Bryan's concert – Issie had called him to say that she had been 'apprehended' and was in police custody at Croydon railway station.

I set off from Victoria to collect Issie in Croydon. I guessed what Issie was up to: she was planning to end her life like Tolstoy's Anna Karenina by jumping in front of a train. At Croydon, the police told me that they had been called by several train drivers, who had seen Issie hanging around a lonely part of Redhill station and were concerned that she was a potential suicide.

I took Issie back to Eaton Square. I was both in a rage and in despair. I asked Issie why she had called Haluk and not me, her husband, from the police station.

'Because I have caused you enough trouble already,' she replied meekly.

# CHAPTER
# SEVENTY-FOUR

## *St Joan*

L avinia had arranged for Issie to have an operation to remove her 'irregular mass' in a private hospital in Gloucester. That would take place in almost a month's time. After the train experience, I wanted Issie out of London and in the countryside at Hilles with her sister Lavinia, and her nieces and nephew. If Issie was going to succeed in killing herself – and I had begun to accept that eventually she would – it would not be under a train in Redhill station.

Issie, being Issie, kept busy. She contacted our land agent, Richard Skeates, saying she wanted to rent a farm building at the Chadwick home, Lypiatt Park, to design wallpaper and ceramics. She started riding again. She went to a local farm beneath Hilles and went over three jumps in his all-weather ring, and then, fired with enthusiasm, rang her assistant Ali Chiu in London and told her to take a McQueen jacket to Kilgour's in Savile Row – along with some images of the nine-teenth century Austrian Empress Sisi in her hunting outfit – and ask them to make her a proper riding coat and outfit.

Issie contacted another neighbour, Jayne, Lady Porchester, who is an expert on horses, to find her a suitable pony. Jayne found a white show pony for £15,000. Issie went into one of her classic sulks when I told her we couldn't afford to buy it.

She played tennis with her 14-year-old niece Harriet, whom she thrashed. Physically, she appeared to be doing well.

Although Issie had missed Bryan's concert at the Royal Albert Hall, he invited Issie to see him in Oxford. She looked great, in a tiny midriff jacket that showed her bosoms to full advantage. Although she was upset about not wearing high heels, she danced in the aisle to Bryan's music.

On 14 April, surgery was performed on Issie. The large mass was removed, as were her ovaries. The sample was sent for analysis.

Alexander McQueen had come to Hilles while Issie was waiting to have the operation, bringing two female friends and Juice and Minter. Issie had gone to a lot of trouble to arrange delicious food for him: beetroot sorbet, a lemon and anchovy mousse, poached wild sea trout with saffron mash and salsa verde.

Alexander looked haggard and exhausted and asked the cook if he had 'some simple cheddar cheese'. Issie had arranged for Alexander to go to various beautiful houses but he did not want to leave his bedroom. McQueen was unsettled by Issie's nervous, unconfident state and Issie was upset by Alexander's failure to appreciate the effort she had gone to make his weekend enjoyable. It was the last time she saw him.

A happier lunch took place on Sunday 22 April at Hilles. We had invited Ghaukhar Ashkenazi, a young and beautiful new friend from Kazakhstan. Issie was fascinated by Ghaukhar, who ran a mining company in Kazakhstan and had told Issie about hunting wolves there.

Issie took Ghaukhar in her new Bentley car down the muddy track to look at Edge Farm, which Amaury had agreed could be sold – and which Issie thought might appeal to Ghaukhar.

After seeing Edge Farm – Ghaukar was unimpressed by the rundown building – our convoy headed for tea at Stanway with Jamie and Amanda Neidpath. A tame parrot flew overhead in the ballroom at Stanway while we ate. It was a wonderful day.

Issie's sample results came back on 25 April, showing that the mass had indeed been cancerous and confirming that Issie had ovarian cancer. The recovery rate is 94 per cent with a hysterectomy, but Issie, who was too old to have children by now anyway, just could not agree to a hysterectomy. The only other option was chemotherapy.

Her mental state was in freefall. The day before she had received the formal cancer diagnosis, she had been 'informally admitted' to Wooton Lawn, the mental-health unit of the Gloucestershire Royal, after attempting to jump out of a moving car being driven by Lavinia. Matters were not improved when an in-patient managed to commit suicide the following night.

On 29 April, after spending the night at Wooton Lawn, Issie travelled to London with Lavinia to take part in a shoot of British fashion icons for *Vanity Fair*. She hadn't wanted to do it at first, saying, 'I don't want to get involved in any of this, Detmar. I just want to die. Will you kill me?'

No, Issie, I said, I would not.

Of course, Issie perked up the moment she got into her chauffeur-driven Condé Nast car. Back on set again, life was the way it should be: clean, glossy, with plenty of assistants and pure white backgrounds illuminated by the brilliant glare of a dozen photographers' lamps.

Issie was dressed as Joan of Arc.

She was happy, Lavinia reported, back in her element, but death was still not far from her mind.

'A funeral done really well,' she was heard to remark to one of her co-icons, 'is just like a good wedding.'

# CHAPTER SEVENTY-FIVE

## *Issie's Farewell*

The picture is a wonderful portrait. But I realise now that Issie was preparing herself, readying herself for her final act. She must have seen this as her last performance. She was to be sacrificed like St Joan. She was bidding a cruel world farewell.

I had spent the last years of our marriage trying to keep Issie alive, but Issie was always trying to die, always planning the grand exit.

After the photoshoot, Issie took the chauffeur-driven town car back to Wooton Lawn. Then she took a taxi from there to the farm shop in Thornbury, which is quite some distance away. That was where she bought the poison.

The next day she wrote a letter of wishes to her accountant, making some bequests and changes to the will that she had made in December 2002, when we were separating, which had left her estate to her two sisters. She made bequests in this letter of wishes to her godchildren, her sisters, her nieces and nephew, Philip Treacy, Stefan Bartlett, myself and three girlfriends, including Lucy. There were hats for Matthew Mellon and Haluk. There was no mention of Alexander McQueen.

On Friday evening I was exhausted. I had been working at the gallery, and I did not get back to our London flat in Eaton Square until late.

# ISSIE'S FAREWELL

It was a bank holiday weekend, and I decided that, rather than try to catch the busy Friday train down to Gloucestershire, I would go to Rebecca Fraser's 50th birthday party that evening. Philip and Stefan were coming down to Hilles the next day and could give me a lift.

Issie was so ill that I hadn't RSVP'd to anything over the previous few months, but I knew Rebecca wouldn't mind if I showed up.

The first person I saw was Emma Roper-Curzon, at whose wedding I had first set eyes on Issie 18 years previously. Then I talked to Alex Shulman, who asked how Issie was. I was upbeat, because I was always trying to protect Issie and promote her work. I told Alex about Issie in Kuwait doing a photoshoot for the Sheik, and said that she was designing a Lotus handbag in India and furniture and wallpaper from her studio in Gloucestershire. She was even thinking of working on a new fashion programme for Al-Jazeera.

But then, during our conversation, I suddenly crumbled. I said to Alex, 'Issie has tried to commit suicide again.'

Alex replied, 'I'm very, very sorry, Detmar.'

I stayed only briefly at the party after that before coming home to Eaton Square with a renewed sense of anxiety and despair.

The following morning, while waiting for Philip and Stefan to collect me, I received that horrific telephone call from Lavinia.

\* \* \* \* \*

When we found her at the hospital, Issie was propped up in bed, looking sallow, and wearing a thin white nightgown. She was on a drip, and looked and sounded weak.

She said, 'Hi Det.'

I was distraught and in shock, so I let Philip approach her first. Philip was talking to Issie when two nurses came in. They worked in Accident and Emergency and were young, cheerful and professional.

Issie told them that she worked in fashion – hoping, I think, that they may know who she was. I was touched by Issie's vanity; they worked in the Gloucestershire Health Service and I doubted whether they were keen readers of *Vogue* or *Harper's Bazaar*. But it turned out that one of the nurses had seen *The Devil Wears Prada* on DVD the night before. Issie told her, 'I worked for the editor.'

The nurse said, 'What – Meryl Streep?'

Issie replied, 'No, the real person, she's called Anna Wintour.'

Issie brightened up then, smiling and seeming to be on good form, regaling the nurses with her stories of Anna and *American Vogue*, saying, 'I remember running for those steak sandwiches and cappuccinos.'

She was so ill – but she was proud, and wanted them to know that she was somebody.

'Google me!' she ordered them.

Philip and I were then taken to see the doctor on duty. The A & E ward was a busy place. An effort had been made to find us seats and some privacy, but there were no cosy consulting rooms, so we were taken to a room full of medical equipment. The doctor was young, kind and sensitive.

He began, 'I have seen many half-hearted suicide attempts, but this is serious.'

I broke in: 'Doctor, before you go on, my father committed suicide by drinking poison. I do not want you to tell me that Isabella has no hope. So long as she lives I will never give up hope.'

The doctor looked at us gently and then continued, 'Okay, I understand your position Mr Blow, and in that context I will explain to you the situation. Your wife has swallowed poison. We have sent her blood to be analysed in Birmingham to find out the quantity and strength of the poison. We will have the results back tomorrow.'

I managed to persuade myself that this meant that perhaps Issie would survive again, something I desperately wanted to believe.

Eventually Stefan, Philip and I went back to Hilles and had some sort of supper. There were green stains all over our bedsheets, where Issie had vomited up the poison.

The next day I drove to the hospital on my own. I wanted to be alone with Issie.

I had chosen to wear a punk Harris tweed jacket with an old Rhodesian flag on the back of it and an Umbro label on the front; after all, there was no point in being conventionally dressed for Issie. I bought some flowers on the way. She liked white, scented flowers, so I bought a bunch of white lilies and freesias from a garage's rather meagre selection. But when I went into Issie's room, she had deteriorated substantially and I suddenly wished I had bought more flowers, many more, all the flowers in the world, a whole roomful of them. She was fighting for breath and it was plain to see that she was dying.

I sat with her. It was very peaceful, almost odd that for once there was no drama, no telephones ringing. We were together and there was nobody else.

I talked to Issie about the gallery and we gossiped about a friend who had wanted to get married in a gold dress worn by Issie. The friend had thought Issie's dress was designed by McQueen – but Issie told me it was by Giles Deacon.

I wanted to make her laugh, so I told her that Stefan was cooking lunch. It worked, and we both started giggling because although Stefan is a good and enthusiastic cook, he makes a hellish mess of the kitchen. After one Stefan meal, Lavinia and I had washed and cleaned the kitchen solidly for three hours without making much headway into the mountain of mess and dirty pans. He can hardly boil a bowl of rice without leaving about 20 pots strewn about.

Then Issie said she wanted to go to sleep, and I said, 'Well, you go on.'

I was emotionally exhausted. The person I had fallen in love with at a wedding at Salisbury Cathedral all those years ago was leaving me

Her tastes were unorthodox, her style was uncompromising and her expenses were legendary. Even in the world of fashion, which celebrates flamboyance and idolises the outrageous, the stylist, muse and taste-maker Isabella Blow was a true original. Her death this week, aged just 48, has left her friends and colleagues in shock. **Susannah Frankel** salutes a style icon

*Independent*, 9 May 2007.

for ever. The love, the laughter, the magic – I welled up at the thought that it was all about to vanish into memories.

I went for a coffee at the hospital café. I expected Issie to have fallen asleep, but when I returned, she was still awake.

'Det, you should have bought me the white pony I wanted,' she chastised me sleepily.

Tears were now rolling down my cheeks.

'Issie, I would buy you anything darling.'

And then Issie pulled herself up in her bed, looked at me with those haunting eyes and said, 'darling, do you remember when we met, I was a little ray of sunshine?'

I looked at my wife, my eyes brimming with tears, and said, 'Issie, you will always be a ray of sunshine for me.'

She fell back on her pillow, closed her eyes and slept.

I knew then.

I kissed her on the cheek and whispered in her ear, 'Goodbye, Issie. I love you.'

And that was it. I left the hospital and drove home. At 5.30 a.m. the next morning, the hospital called.

My darling wife had gone.

I was terrified that she had died in agony, like my father.

'Were her hands clenched?' I asked

'No, Mr Blow,' the nurse replied. 'Her hands were not clenched.'

I was thankful for that at least. I put down the phone and closed my eyes against the first light of a new dawn that Isabella would never see.

After her tumultuous, extraordinary and inspiring journey, my beloved Isabella was at last at peace.

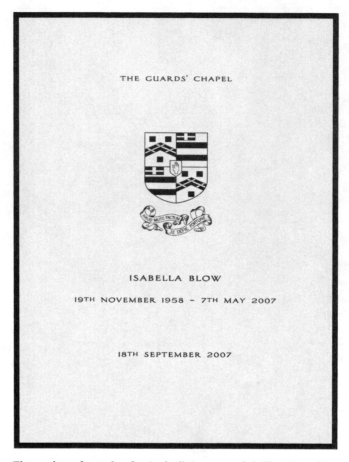

THE GUARDS' CHAPEL

ISABELLA BLOW

19TH NOVEMBER 1958 – 7TH MAY 2007

18TH SEPTEMBER 2007

The order-of-service for Isabella's memorial, The Guards' Chapel, 18 September 2007.

# Sources and
# Acknowledgements

My main source of reference for my life with Isabella has been my diary, which I have kept since 1980.

When I met Isabella in 1988 I asked her how she spelt the shortened, more informal version of her name. She told me 'I-S-S-I-E'. It was, I discovered, how she spelt it in her friend Christie Saunders' leaving book at Heathfield, when she was 16, and the way she asked Larissa MacFarquhar to spell it in her *New Yorker* profile in 2001.

The early life of Isabella was written from what she herself told me about it, interviews with her stepmother, godparents, her sister Lavinia and other members of her family, as well as from the few personal papers and photographs which Isabella gave to me.

Her schooldays at Heathfield were re-created from interviews with many of her school contemporaries who rallied to the school motto, 'The Merit of One is the Honour of All.' In January 2010, I was shown around the school by my first cousin Victoria de Silva, a pupil in her final year of the 6th form, and a goddaughter of Isabella's. I would like to thank the current headmistress, her secretary and members of her staff for all their help and information about the school during Isabella's time.

Her post-Heathfield years were based on interviews from her friends and contemporaries, especially those who were at Oxford

---

during the time Issie spent there, such as Giles Roe, Christine Selby, Christie Saunders and Emily Dashwood.

Much of the information about Issie's married life with first husband Nicholas Taylor comes from her former brother-in-law Sebastian Taylor and other contemporaries.

Issie's time in America could not have been recorded without the generous assistance of Anna Wintour, Andre Leon Talley, Bryan Ferry, Hamish Bowles, Aeneas Mackay, Benjamin Fraser, Colin Cawdor, Natasha Grenfell and Alexander Cohane. Thank you.

For details about Issie's time at *Tatler*, in the mid-to-late 1980s, I thank Michael Roberts, Char Pilcher, Alex Shulman, Emma Soames, Nicholas Coleridge, Juergen Teller, Alastair Thain, Dan Lepard, Mary Killen, Eve MacSweeney, Francis Bentley, Craig Brown, Sarah Hamilton and Kate Bernard.

I would particularly like to thank those members of Isabella's family and my family who have helped and supported me in the creation of this book. I apologise for any intrusive or painful invasion of their privacy, and I hope they consider the end product justifies any distress caused.

Thanks to *The Times* for permission to reprint the account of Johnny's death and the inquest.

Thanks to the *Daily Telegraph* for permission to reprint part of Issie's interview with Lydia Slater.

Thanks to the *Evening Standard* for permission to reprint the item from Londoner's Diary.

Since Issie's death, Julia has done a brilliant job with Issie's estate. The sculpture 'The Head of Isabella Blow' by Tim Noble and Sue Webster is in the collection of the National Portrait Gallery, London. Issie's hats and clothes and other artifacts from the Design Museum exhibition have been acquired in total by Daphne Guinness, who I thank.

I thank Isabella's godmothers the Dowager Marchioness of Cholmondley, Lorna Lady Cooper-Keys, her sister Lavinia Verney, nieces Rosamond Dawes and Harriet Verney, and her nephew Frederick Dawes. Also her stepmother Dowager Lady Delves Broughton and her distant kinsman the writer Philip Delves Broughton.

I thank her cousins the Hon. Kim Fraser, Hon. Violet Fraser, Hon. Aeneas and Mrs Mackay, and Issie's Fraser 'cousins by marriage': Rebecca Fitzgerald, Flora Fraser, Mr and the Hon. Mrs Benjamin Fraser, her godson Thomas Fraser, Orlando Fraser and their inspiring mother Lady Antonia Fraser.

# SOURCES AND ACKNOWLEDGEMENTS

I wish to record my gratitude to the Hon. Mrs Simon Fraser and her late husband Mr Frank Johnson, Hon. Hugh and Mrs Fraser, Lady Charlotte Fraser, who was at Heathfield with Isabella and is the widow of her first cousin Hon. Andrew Fraser, Lord Lovat, the Hon. Mrs Stavros Merjos, and Mr and Mrs Raoul Fraser.

Thank you to my brother Amaury Blow and sister Selina Blow, my uncle Sir Desmond de Silva QC and Princess Katarina of Yugoslavia, my first cousins the Hon. Mrs David Blacker, Lord Rathcavan, Mr and Mrs David Blow, Mr Simon and Miss Catherine Blow, Mr and Mrs Alexander Warre-Cornish.

Thanks to Nicola Stephenson and all at Mission, and to John Dempsey of MAC.

Thank you to my godmothers Lady Mark Fitzalan-Howard and the Countess of Plymouth.

Thanks are due to my mother Mrs Helga Blow Perera who spoke to me at the beginning of this project – telling me to write what I thought, which I have done – and to my stepfather Mr Desmond Perera, whose courtesy and calmness I have appreciated.

Thanks also to Eva Chadwick, a brilliant psychotherapist, who kept me calm and sane, Gregor Muir, Hon. Rosie Pearson, Minnie Scott, Cosmo Fry, Christie Saunders, Teresa, Lady Clarke (née de Chair), Lucy Hodsoll, Sarah St George, Emily Napper (née Dashwood), Camilla Guinness (née Uniacke), Hugh St Clair, Christine Selby, Anthony Murphy, Mr and the Hon. Mrs Robert Murphy, Giles Roe, Mr and Mrs David Fitzherbert, Hugo Guinness, Christopher Brooks, Miranda Brooks, Hon. Geraldine Harmsworth, Geordie Greig, Colin McDowell, Hon. Augusta Ogilvy, Alexandra Heywood (née Sitwell), Sir George Sitwell Bt, Mimi Lady Manton, Lady Hesketh, Hon. Vicki Watson, Mosh Gordon-Cumming, Lady Emma Marion, Lady Laura Campbell, Joan Juliet Buck, Julian Bond, Michael Zilkha, Phil Athill, Antony Price, Mr and Mrs Seng Watson, Tim Willis, Mr and Mrs Suomi La Valle, the Marquess of Cholmondley, Charles Cholmondley, Manolo Blahnik, Piers de Laszlo, Bianca, Lady Eliot, Tracey Emin, Thomas Dane, Gordon Watson, Daisy Garnett, Natasha Garnett, Maureen Paley, Alice Rawsthorn, the Chadwick family, Lord Moyne, Diana Guinness, James Moores, the Very Revd the Dean of Gloucester and Mrs Nick Bury, the late Malcolm McLaren, Jeffrey Deitch, Isaac Ferry and the Ferry brothers, Iain R Webb, Julian Jones, Rory Knight-Brice, Richard James, Andrew at Richard James, Kamel, Haluk Ackace, Alison Jacques, Edward Helmore, Robin Birley, Mr and Mrs Iwan Wirth, Mr and Mrs Simon Lee, Shahriar

Mazandi, Lord and Lady Renwick, Mrs Elizabeth Pollock, Miss Margaret Martin, Shearer the Hon. Lady Brinkman, Simon Ortiz-Patino, Hon. Peregrine and Mrs Moncreiffe, Peter Rolfe, Amanda Eliasch, Charles Eliasch, Katrina Pavlos, the late Katie Baghot, Alice Bamford, Count and Countess Leopold Von Bismarck, Chantal Hanover, Parisa Wright, Mat Collishaw, Jessica Walsh, Mary Fellowes, Anna Harvey, Mr and Mrs Alistair Hutchinson, the Swarovski family, John Galliano, Rifat Ozbek, Mr and Mrs Amir Farman-Farma, the late Rafe Cavenagh-Mainwaring, Larissa MacFarquhar, Vicky Sarge, Emine Saner, Jeremy Langmead, Jane and Louise Wilson, Richard Batty, Liliana Sanguino, David Waddington, Pablo de la Barra, Mark Hix, the late Amy Spindler, Murray Arthur, Trino at McQueen, Mr and Mrs John Banks, Colin Glen, Valerie Hardie-Stewart, Sean Ellis, Corinne Day, Julien Macdonald, Stefan Bruggemann, Joanne Robertson, Francesca, Leon Sr Amour, the Hon. Andrew and Mrs Monson, Aileen Baird, Ali Chiu, Kevin Plotkin, Amy Pritchard, Ana Filgueiras, Jose Rebelo, Anna van Wassenear, Caragh Thuring, Charlotte Stockdale, Katie Grand, Mr and Mrs Carlos Noronha Feio, Carmen Julia, Celia Lyttleton, Charlie Glass, Chloe Beeney, Hon. David Windsor-Clive, Gavin Turk, Deborah Curtis, Deborah Milner, Dimka, Donna Loveday, Mr and Mrs Duncan Ward, Emma Collins, Fiona Yarrow, Giles Deacon, Giovanni, Harriet Quick, Helen Thorpe, C. Hoare and Co., Hugh Devlin, Hugo and Carmen O'Neill, Mr and Mrs Hugo Ritson-Thomas, Ivo Hesmondalgh, James Birch, Jason Warner, Miltos Manetas, Jasper Conran, Jayne Lady Porchester, Hilary Riva, Michelle Feeney, Julia Peyton-Jones, Karla Otto, Kentaro, Kenny Hunter, Lee Manigault, Leon St Amour, Linda Watson, Lisa Marie, Lorcan O'Neill, Magdalene Bush, Tunga, Margot Heller, Mariam, Marie du Petit Thouars, Mario Testino, Marion Tubbing, Mat Collishaw, Matthieu Laurette, Oliver Treacy, Omer Karacan, Alistair Dundas, Sir Mark Palmer, Iris Palmer, Pam Hogg, Tina Rink, Sandrine, Pat Marsh, Pauline Daly, Sadie Coles, Los Supa Elegantes, Jeffrey Deitch, Paul Malpas, Helen Hilard, Stefan Bartlett, P.J. Keeling, Mr and Mrs Toby Rowland, Sasha Blow, Mr and Mrs Raymond Lewis, Richard Skeates, Richard Shepherd, Robert Astley-Sparks, Lorna Bond-Neilsen, Rosson Crow, Rui Brito, Sean and Seng, Sophie Dahl, Tara Palmer-Tomkinson, Stefan Ratibor, Stephen Jones, Stuart Shave, Sue Lewis, Mr and Mrs Hans Seegers, Suzy Menkes, Szylvia, Tim Horton, Sir Tobias Clarke Bt, Mr and Mrs Bobbie Taubmann, Beanie, Umkuimiam, Viscount and Viscountess Windsor.

Tom wishes to thank Sasha, Elinor and Bento Sykes, all the Bunburys, especially Turtle who lived through this with him, Alice and Chris Floyd for lodgings, Lucy and Euan Rellie for support in New York, and his mother Valerie.

A special thank you from Tom to Plum Sykes for her interview, her thousands of introductions, including the original one to Issie, and her incisive edit of the text at a crucial stage.

Tom would also like to thank again all who so generously gave their time to this project, especially Anna Wintour, Hamish Bowles, André Leon Talley, Philip Treacy and Dowager Lady Delves Broughton.

To those who Tom and I have not mentioned, I apologise and thank them for their help.

I was very proud that Issie received obituaries all over the world, from Australia and New Zealand, China, India, and across Europe and America. The ones that I read in Britain gave me great comfort. I thank all the journalists for their tributes.

Thank you to my brilliant agent Jonathan Conway at Mulcahy Conway and to my esteemed editor Carole Tonkinson at HarperCollins. Thanks to Victoria McGeown, Anna Gibson and Arthur Heard at HarperCollins.

Thank you to Carrie Kania at HarperCollins US, and to all at the Condé Nast Library in Vogue House, Hanover Square, London

And a very special thank you to Mara Castilho and Philip Treacy, who urged me to 'keep on writing'.

I started planning this book after Isabella died. I have really enjoyed working with Tom Sykes in the writing of it over the last two years. Tom has brought a much-needed page-turning pace to my prose.

Almost everyone who came into contact with Issie during her life was left with a lasting impression and a story. Blow by Blow is my story. I know Issie would enjoy it.

Issie's Broughton family motto 'Haud Muto Factum' translates as, 'Things are not done by being mute'. And the Blow family's motto is 'True'.

# Picture Credits

p12 © *Country Life* Picture Library
p13 © *Country Life* Picture Library
p15 © *Country Life* Picture Library
p36 © Gillman & Soame
p72 © Richard Young/Rex Features
p82 courtesy of *Tatler* © The Condé Nast Publications Ltd
p83 © Dafydd Jones
p85 Alastair Thain/*Tatler* © The Condé Nast Publications Ltd
p86 Image © Jean Francois Lepage/Text © *Sunday Times*
p90 © Christopher Makos
p98 © courtesy of Lucy Roper-Curzon
p113 © *Telegraph*
p115 © *Bristol Evening Post*
p126 © Kevin Davies
p133 © Julian Broad
p134 © Julian Broad
p149 © Desmond O'Neill Features
p162 © Iain R Webb
p196 © Dafydd Jones
p232 © Debra Hurford Brown/Camera Press

# Index

# INDEX

# INDEX

# INDEX

# INDEX

# INDEX